Gay Signatures

Berg French Studies

General Editor: John E. Flower

ISSN: 1354-3636

John E. Flower and Bernard C. Swift (eds), *François Mauriac: Visions and Reappraisals*

Michael Tilby (ed.), *Beyond the Nouveau Roman: Essays on the Contemporary French Novel*

Colin Nettlebeck, *Forever French: The French Exiles in the United States of America during the Second World War*

Bill Marshall, *Victor Serge: The Uses of Dissent*

Allan Morris, *Collaboration and Resistance Reviews: Writers and the Mode Rétro in Post-Gaullist France*

Malcolm Cook, *Fictional France: Social Reality in the French Novel 1775–1800*

W.D. Halls, *Politics, Society and Christianity in Vichy France*

David H. Walker, *Outrage and Insight: Modern French Writers and the 'Fait Divers'*

H.R. Kedward and Nancy Wood, *The Liberation of France: Image and Event*

David L. Looseley, *The Politics of Fun: Cultural Policy and Debate in Contemporary France*

Nicholas Hewitt, *Literature and the Right in Postwar France: The Story of the 'Hussards'*

Laïla Ibnlfassi and Nicki Hitchcott, *African Francophone Writing: A Critical Introduction*

Alex Hughes and Kate Ince, *French Erotic Fiction: Women's Desiring Writing, 1880–1990*

Jennifer E. Milligan, *The Forgotten Generation: French Women Writers of the Inter-war Period*

Martin Evans, *The Memory of Resistance: French Opposition to the Algerian War*

Gay Signatures

Gay and Lesbian Theory, Fiction and Film in France, 1945–1995

Edited by
Owen Heathcote, Alex Hughes and
James S. Williams

Oxford • New York

First published in 1998 by
Berg
Editorial offices:
150 Cowley Road, Oxford, OX4 1JJ, UK
70 Washington Square South, New York, NY 10012, USA

Berg is the imprint of Oxford International Publishers Ltd.

Library of Congress Cataloging-in-Publication Data

A catalogue record for this book is available from the Library of Congress.

British Library Cataloguing-in-Publication Data

A catalogue record for this book is available from the British Library.

ISBN 1 85973 982 2 (Cloth)
1 85973 987 3 (Paper)

Typeset by JS Typesetting, Wellingborough, Northants.
Printed in the United Kingdom by Biddles Ltd, Guildford and King's Lynn.

Contents

Acknowledgements

The editors would like to thank Kathryn Earle for all her help and support throughout the *Gay Signatures* project, and John Flower for his enthusiastic response to the initial idea. Alex Hughes would like, in addition, to thank the British Academy for providing a grant to pursue work on the volume.

Notes on Contributors

Renate Günther is a Lecturer in French Studies at the University of Sheffield, where she teaches courses on twentieth-century literature, feminism in France and critical theory. Her main research interests relate to the work of Marguerite Duras and French feminist theory and its application to literary criticism. Recent publications include *Marguerite Duras: Le Ravissement de Lol V. Stein and L'Amant* (1993).

Susan Hayward is Professor of French at the University of Exeter. She has written extensively on French cinema and television. She is the author of *French National Cinema* (1993), *Key Concepts in Cinema Studies* (1996), and co-author with Ginette Vincendeau of *French Cinema: Texts and Contexts* (1990).

Owen Heathcote is a Senior Lecturer in French Studies at the University of Bradford. He writes on nineteenth- and twentieth-century French literature, notably on Balzac, Guibert, Duras and Wittig. He is currently working on the relations between violence, gender and representation.

Alex Hughes is a Senior Lecturer at the University of Birmingham. Her research interests relate to twentieth-century French women's and autobiographical writing and gender studies. She has published monographs on the work of Simone de Beauvoir and Violette Leduc, as well as essays and articles on Beauvoir, Leduc, Serge Doubrovsky, women's writing and feminist theory in France.

Bill Marshall is a Senior Lecturer in the School of Modern Languages at the University of Southampton. He is the author of *Victor Serge: The Uses of Dissent* (1992) and *Guy Hocquenghem: Beyond Gay Identity* (1996). He has written widely on French film and media, and is currently working on a book on Quebec National Cinema.

Murray Pratt lectures in French at the University of Warwick, and has written a number of articles on Hervé Guibert in both French and English. Other publications include articles on Roland Barthes and masculinity. Currently, he is preparing a book on discourses of AIDS in France.

Brigitte Rollet is a Lecturer at the University of Portsmouth, where she teaches French literature and cinema. Her research interests lie in the field of film and feminist and gender theory. She has published articles on contemporary French cinema and is currently writing a book on the director Coline Serreau.

James S. Williams is a Lecturer in French at the University of Kent. He has written on Marguerite Duras, Roland Barthes, Jean-Luc Godard and contemporary European cinema, and he is the author of *The Erotics of Passage: Pleasure, Politics, and Form in the Later Work of Marguerite Duras* (1997). He is currently working on a study of Camus's *La Peste*.

Michael Worton is Professor of French at University College London. He has written extensively on twentieth-century French literature and on issues in critical theory. Among his recent publications are *Textuality and Sexuality: Reading Theories and Practices* (edited with Judith Still, 1993) and *Michel Tournier* (1995). He is currently writing a book on representations of masculinity and a book on reading.

Introduction: Reading Gay Signatures

Owen Heathcote, Alex Hughes and James S. Williams

Pierre Bergé: Il n'y a pas de création sans sexualité?
Marguerite Duras: Il n'y a pas de signature.

I

Antecedents

Gay Signatures brings together a series of critical essays written during the mid-1990s that reflect upon some of the ways in which French gay and lesbian identity has been inscribed and read in fictional, theoretical and cinematic texts produced in the post-war period. If it has any precursor, it is *Homosexualities and French Literature: Cultural Contexts/Critical Texts*, an edited collection published in 1979 by Elaine Marks and George Stambolian. For a long time this has been the first – and only – port of call for a growing number of scholars interested in questions of homosexuality in French literature. Yet it is perhaps inevitable that *Homosexualities and French Literature* should now appear out of date, for although it strives to be as comprehensive as possible in terms of the French authors and theorists it covers, the very date of its publication means that many of the key names that may be viewed as emblematic of gay culture in contemporary France – such as Hervé Guibert, Cyril Collard and Dominique Fernandez – are not featured. Before we proceed any further, however, it is important to outline in brief the pioneering achievement of Marks and Stambolian, since this will bring the specific nature of our own project into clearer focus.

Homosexualities and French Literature is divided into two sections. The first – 'Cultural Contexts' – is composed of a series of interviews with leading writers, psychoanalysts and critics; the second – 'Critical Texts' – contains a dozen essays that focus on gay writing since the Enlightenment, addressing the work of (among others) Georges Sand, Arthur Rimbaud,

Marcel Jouhandeau, Jean Cocteau, Jean-Paul Sartre and Michel Tournier. As the first study of its kind, one of the book's recurring points of enquiry was the paradox of Marcel Proust, whose *In Search of Time Past* (1913–1927) offers one of the most powerful meditations on homosexuality, Judaism and the workings of desire. If Proust is recognized as a founding father of modernism and gay writing in France, he is also known in his personal life to have been a self-hating homosexual and Jew. This enigma is explored in various ways by Robert Champigny, Jean-Paul Aron, Roger Kempf, J. E. Rivers and Eric Bentley, for whom Proust cured the 'disease' of homosexual love by writing a masterpiece,[1] in the process giving birth to an anxiety of influence that has haunted all subsequent generations of French gay writers. More generally, by foregrounding the diverse ways in which 'a text produce[s] semiotic connections that can be read as homosexual' and by examining the relations between a literary text and the 'unconscious' sexual text (that of its author, for example),[2] *Homosexualities and French Literature* raises questions that are fundamental to any serious discussion of gay writing in France.

One of the central tenets of Marks's and Stambolian's work is that the 'reality of "homosexualities"'[3] can most readily be advertised by emphasizing difference, diversity and pluralism. It is debatable, however, whether this aim is entirely fulfilled in their volume, or even, in retrospect, fully tenable. In the first instance, although the editors state in a brief introduction that their collection is designed to 'transgress boundaries and [to] present a variety of discourses from the theoretical and scholarly to the personal and polemical', *Homosexualities and French Literature* concerns itself almost exclusively with *literary* models.[4] Secondly, its introductory essay signals that, in producing their edited volume, Marks and Stambolian sought not only to 'reformulate many of the concepts, established and new, of literary criticism',[5] but also to provide a source of material for future critical exchanges, most especially between 'the French, who tend to become involved in theorizing about the Text and Discourse, and Americans, who tend to conceive of literature as the expression of an individual mind'.[6] This latter objective, relying as it does on a highly generalized notion of national difference, seems to conform to precisely the kind of binary opposition that Marks and Stambolian aim to call into question, even while it announces the more sophisticated critical debates about French–American relations in the domain of gay writing, theory and politics which, as Section III of our own introduction will reveal, have recently taken place in the wake of the emergence – in the US and elsewhere – of queer theory.

What is ignored by the majority of essays included in *Homosexualities and French Literature*, with the notable exception of Marks's chapter 'Lesbian Intertextuality', is the 'other' tradition of French and francophone lesbian creativity. This gap is greatly rectified by Christopher Robinson's recent study, *Scandal in the Ink: Male and Female Homosexuality in Twentieth-century French Literature* (1995),[7] which provides a vital historical and social context for close textual readings of both major and lesser-known gay and lesbian literary works. Robinson considers the writings not only of Colette, Violette Leduc, Monique Wittig and Christiane Rochefort, but also of the expatriate Anglo-Americans Renée Vivien and Natalie Barney and the Canadian authors Nicole Brossard and Louky Bersianik. At the same time, he addresses literary phenomena such as the French pederastic tradition and AIDS writing, allowing us to see how far gay male writing has now moved into the French literary mainstream, and emphasizing a key theme of recent gay writing, that of erotic violence, notably in the work of Guibert and Tony Duvert.

Yet if *Scandal in the Ink* offers a very useful overview of twentieth-century French gay and lesbian writing and constitutes a valuable resource for current work in the field, it suffers from a number of significant limitations. First, Robinson largely neglects to address the difficulties attendant upon gay cultural identity in the still homophobic climate of post-war France, a climate in which, at its most extreme, the leader of the *Front National*, Jean-Marie Le Pen, has attempted to ostracize HIV-infected gay men, designating them as '*sidaïques*' (as opposed to the more objective, less disease-ridden equivalent, '*sidéens*').[8] Second, his work is founded on an anti-theoretical bias and willingly subscribes to the notion of a specifically gay identity and selfhood established by Proust in *In Search of Time Past* and Gide in *Corydon* (1924). Not only does Robinson end up conflating issues of sexual and textual practice, but he also declines to engage with new theorizations of sexuality, thereby excluding a wide spectrum of potentially illuminating readings. He ignores the whole question of the relations between authorship, gender, sexuality, identity and the performance of identity, which we could perhaps best describe as constituting a problematics of 'gay signature'. The sexual/textual performance of the gay signature will provide a central connecting focus to the following sections of this Introduction.

Section II of the Introduction will address some of the ways in which the concept of gay signature can be understood. Section III will examine some aspects of the relationship between gay signature and queer theory, a radical new mode of reading sexual/textual phenomena that informs a number of the critical essays in our collection. In Section IV, the literary, political and socio-historical context in which the gay and lesbian signature has been inscribed in post-war France will be explored, as will the post-war French gay and lesbian cultural tradition. In Section V, the contents of the individual essays included in the volume will be summarized, with particular reference to the way in which each foregrounds and reads a gay signature (or signatures). After the chapter summaries, in Section VI we will offer some concluding remarks.

II

Signature

The term 'signature' is most commonly understood as the name, special mark or initials used to authenticate a text or document, or as a distinctive pattern or characteristic by which something can be identified. It can thus be used negatively, as in the homophobic hunt for 'signs' of the 'effeminate'. It also, however, carries the more active, authorial sense of 'signing one's name', or of 'authenticating a document by doing so' (*Oxford English Dictionary*). Referring specifically to artistic practice, Jacques Derrida has identified a further two modalities of signature: first, a set of idiomatic marks that a signer might leave by accident in his work (sometimes called the writer's style), and second, a more general signature, or signature of the signature, whereby the work of writing designates, describes and inscribes itself as an act.[9] We want to insist on this material moment of inscription in order to approach gay aesthetic identity as a process in formation. This will allow us to establish the different discourses at stake in the act of gay and lesbian writing, an act that encompasses both the interior, normally private space of creation, and the exterior space of its public reception. Gay texts and films will thus be examined not as authenticating traces of their creator, but rather as products of a historical, physical and sexually specific process relayed – but never fixed and settled – by the reader and viewer. Such an approach renders effectively irrelevant the weary question of what precisely is gay: the work itself, the person who creates it, or the person who receives it and makes 'sense' of it. In fact, we should perhaps talk less of homosexuality than of 'homotexualities', Owen Heathcote's term for the ongoing constructions and deconstructions of both homosexuality *and* its environments.[10]

It is an unfortunate fact, of course, that after heralding the movement of liberation in the 1970s, the 'gay' instance has all too quickly become, in the eyes of many, a mark of premature mortality and finitude. Indeed, to consider the signature of contemporary gay writing in the current context of AIDS is often to read the final tracings of personal testimony in the form of diaries and memoirs. We want to work directly against any sense of fatalism generated by the AIDS epidemic – a feeling aided and abetted by homophobes looking for the image, or stigmata, of the 'gay death' – by privileging instead the productive aspects of what Brian Patton has termed the crisis of authority provoked by AIDS, a crisis that also affects textual authority. If AIDS represents an 'indelible signature',[11] or, as Derrida puts it (reflecting on the ability of AIDS to replicate the human organism and operate as a simulacrum of a disease), that 'absolutely original and ineffaceable [given] marking our time',[12] the concept of 'gay signature' should instead be understood more as a continually shifting series of configurations and relations, of masculinity and femininity, of textual traces of previous signatures – in short, as a process of gay intertextuality. The example of Guibert is particularly pertinent in this respect, since he claimed to experience writing as a form of 'cure': he transforms AIDS into words, and thus, it is inferred, into a movable object of (inter)textual dissemination.[13]

It would be wrong, however, to see the present collection, with its plural editorial signature and multi-authored composition, as simply advocating plurality. The so-called 'truth' of homosexuality has always been conceived of as plural and general, with homosexual discourse in particular being viewed as (i) a metonymy of the whole, (ii) an *apologia* for its very existence, and (iii) the oppositional pole of a heterosexual discourse considered as unique and singular.[14] Rather than identify a collective gay signature, that impossible Proustian sign of a gay 'species', our collection seeks to explore how individual gay signatures are personally and publicly inscribed and received. If, as is our contention, the gay signature is constantly mobile, then one way in which the process of its inscription can be illuminated is via queer theory, a mode of thinking and reading that destabilizes identities and categories by inverting perceived sexual and gender hierarchies. For this reason, the next section of our Introduction will attempt to do three things. Firstly, to expand briefly upon the nature of queer theory. Secondly, to address the lines of connection between queer theoretical analysis, a 1990s creation of the Anglo-Saxon world, and the notion of gay signature as it has emerged in the modern and contemporary French cultural field. And thirdly, to articulate the various ways in which our collection will elaborate and develop these connections.

III

Queer Approaches

i. Queer reading

What exactly is the meaning of 'queer' and 'queer politics', terms that have, as yet, no currency in French culture, where the gap between the old homophobic, passive term '*pédé*' and the more active, homophilic term '*gai*' (and '*gay*', naturalized French during the 1970s) is still being negotiated? It is important to state from the outset that 'queer' is now used in so many different ways and contexts that it cannot be reduced to one single meaning. However, in a brief yet extremely helpful discussion of the subject, Jo Eadie opposes a minoritizing, and ultimately separatist, version of queer as an exclusive, absolute homosexuality, to a more general, fluid notion of sexual diversity as deviance from a norm recognized as unattainable.[15] He asserts that queerness is always relational, since different spaces generate different forms of outlaw desire.[16] Although 'saturated with the facts of heterosexist power and abuse',[17] the term 'queer' refuses in its polysemic, polysexual 'emptiness' to replicate the policing gestures of current sexually purist positions, whether gay or straight. For Eadie, 'queer' signals that which delights in the pleasures of deviance and challenges the demand for conformity and repression.

'Queer' is a deliberately rebarbative, confrontational political term that defies coherent categorization but embraces sexual resistance and sexual diversity in all their variant forms. But what about queer theory (or 'queory', as it is sometimes referred to)? As we have already intimated, queer theory is an Anglo-American critical phenomenon unassimilable to any one single discipline or cultural, social and political discourse, although its key points of scrutiny are sexual practices and desires that depart from a narrow, prescriptive, heterosexual standard. Inflected by poststructuralist theory and postmodern social theory, queer theory enacts, in the words of Gregory Bredbeck, a 'programme of *pure* critique' that aims at exposing the current system in its entirety as a system (as opposed to gay activist critique, for example, which also strives to change that system by intervening directly within it).[18] At its best, in the work of Judith Butler and Lee Edelman, as well as in the landmark 1991 collection *inside/out: Lesbian Theories/Gay Theories* edited by Diana Fuss, queer critical practice, along with its evolving, materialist self-critique (notably the work of Donald Morton and John Champagne),[19] offers a way of understanding gender less as a function of knowledge than as a perpetually reinvented form of cultural performance.[20]

Indeed, if one common idea is shared by these various theorists, it is that the ideologically constructed binarism of straight versus gay is totally inadequate to deal with the fluid operations of sexuality. While it proposes no solutions, queer theory illuminates as no other critical practice has done hitherto, the complex, polymorphous formations of power and discourse that underscore sexual 'identity'.

ii. Queer/French encounters

If 'queer' and queer theory carry little or no meaning in France itself, how have they affected those Anglo-Saxon scholars working both in French and in gay studies? The most interesting and provocative examples to date of convergences between queer theory and the French gay tradition have been Michael Lucey's examination of Gide's sexuality and politics in *Gide's Bent: Sexuality, Politics, Writing* (1995), and Lawrence Schehr's *Alcibiades at the Door: Gay Discourses in French Literature* (1995) and *The Shock of Men: Homosexual Hermeneutics in French Writing* (1995). Schehr's achievement in particular is twofold. Firstly, in a far more constructive way than Marks and Stambolian, he encourages his readers to reflect upon French/American cultural dynamics as they relate, on the one hand, to a French tradition of considerable discretion, even *pudeur*, on the matter of homosexuality and the very notion of homosexual writing, and, on the other, to the identity politics pursued by the constantly evolving American gay and lesbian movements. In so doing, he emphasizes – and tacitly warns against – the kind of cultural pitfalls that inhere in American-authored critical essays that respond to perceived French coyness by seeking to 'out' French gay writing and writers. An obvious case in point is D. A. Miller's highly politicized 'stripping down' of Roland Barthes in *Bringing out Roland Barthes* (1993).

Secondly, Schehr's analysis of French homosexual literature, while it treads a self-consciously sinuous 'queer' line,[21] not only indicates fully the danger of confusing the Anglo-American and French contexts in the name of theory, but also recognizes the textual specifics of the discreet French tradition. In *Alciabiades at the Door*, which examines the work of René Crevel, Sartre, Gide, Barthes and Guibert, Schehr uses the figure of Alcibiades – the 'real' in Plato's *Symposium* – to argue not for the notion of the sexual/textual closet, as conceived by the queer critic Eve Kosofsky Sedgwick in her stunning analysis of the 'spectacle of the closet' at work in *In Search of Time Past*,[22] but rather for the conjoining of public and private spaces, and of theory and praxis. According to Schehr, this method of enquiry offers a more effective way of elucidating the status of French homosexual aesthetic expression than notions of a repressive hypothesis or general system of control, notions already critiqued by Michel Foucault.[23] He endorses his argument by pointing out that, owing to a number of factors, notably the crucial importance of Proust and Gide to French literature and the fact that France decriminalized sodomy almost two centuries ago, French expressions of what he terms 'homosexual poiesis' have been much freer and far less subject to categorization.[24]

In the same vein, in his introduction to *The Shock of Men*, which explores the ways homosexuality and its inscriptions are used as a means of interpretation and general hermeneutics in the work of Gide, Foucault, Proust, Barthes, Renaud Camus, and Tournier, Schehr takes Sedgwick and David Bergman to task for using indiscriminately the term 'Euro-American', and for thus conflating European and American literary traditions, specifically via their focus on the Anglo-American paradigm of the 'open secret'. For Schehr, what characterizes European discourse is rather a continual playing off of identity with history, a process accompanied by the sad realization that anything approximating the American dream of wholeness an integration is impossible. This interaction between identity and history is an important ingredient of the gay signature, and is addressed to varying degrees by all the contributors in this collection.

iii. Queer and the Project of Gay Signatures

Schehr is surely right to problematize readings of homosexual representation which rely upon a wholesale application of queer concepts to a literary and cultural tradition so different from the one where queer politics and theory have come into being. The dangers of situating exclusively within a culturally 'alien', Anglo-American theoretical matrix a range of French gay artefacts, many of which, like Guibert's *To The Friend Who Did Not Save My Life* (1990) and Hocquenghem's allegorical novel *Eve* (1987), overtly signal the cultural tensions that exist between France and the US, are only too obvious. We feel, however, that it is crucial to advance the debate still further by initiating what Schehr, in his eludication of a general 'homosexual writing subject' that questions inherited systems of dominance, power and semiosis, gestures towards but does not actually attempt himself: namely, a bold exploration of the intersecting play of relations between the French and the Anglo-American literary and theoretical traditions. For this reason, our volume seeks to offer a number of distinctively queer readings of modern and contemporary French gay and lesbian cultural production. This does not mean that we aim to convert a 'backward' cultural tradition to a new progressive, queer Order. Our wish, rather, is to foreground and develop notions of sexual and textual dissidence in French literature, film, and philosophical enquiry.

Paul Julian Smith's work in the field of modern Spanish studies is of particular importance here, because it shows what is possible theoretically within the specifics of a national culture.[25] His 1992 book, *Laws of Desire: Questions of Homosexuality in Spanish Writing and Film 1960–1990*, offers not a history of homosexual identity but a series of readings of recent Spanish texts and films grounded in French, English and American literary and cultural theory. It is acutely sensitive to the contradictions and conflicts in the different authors and film-makers studied, and avoids any simple, reductive presentation of gay or lesbian politics. However, as his discussion of Pedro Almodóvar exemplifies, Smith is not afraid to assess the film-maker's representations of homosexual desire in the context of other European and American forms, and in such a way that draws out not only the uniqueness and radicality of Almodóvar's cinema within the Spanish situation (for example, Almodóvar's legitimation of multiple identities and his critique of the representative aspects of dominant institutions such as the family), but also its limitations in terms of a progressive politics.

The fact that *Gay Signatures* privileges a similarly contestatory, cross-cultural encounter between a broadly 'queer' theoretical model and various manifestations of French gay and lesbian creativity does not mean that we do not share Schehr's awareness of the particularity of the gay literary tradition in France. Indeed, in contrast with the view of one critic, referring to gender identity in France, that homosexuality is a subject that does not respect national boundaries,[26] we believe that a proper understanding of nationally specific, cultural, historical and political factors is crucial for any critical exploration of modern French gay and lesbian cultural production. It is with this in mind that we will now sketch out the historical, social and political context in which French gay and lesbian cultural life has inscribed itself since the Second World War.

IV

Gay Signatures in France: Contexts and Constructions

i. Gay Political History in Post-war France

It is perhaps inevitable that any attempt to chart recent gay history in France focuses on Paris where, in the early decades of the twentieth century, homosexual activities were confined to areas such as Pigalle and Saint-Germain. Even there, homosexuality was essentially clandestine. As Bill Marshall has observed, the end of the war in 1945 was a year zero for homosexual political and cultural identity in France. To cite just one instance of the general social oppression of the immediate post-war period, in 1949 the head of the Paris police banned dancing between men in public places.[27] It was not, in fact, until long after the war, in 1954, that the social gatherings attended by André du Dognon, Roger Peyrefitte, Jacques de Ricaumont and, in particular, André Baudry developed into the first 'homophile' organization, *Arcadie*. With its club, journal, and national membership, Baudry's *Arcadie* played an important role in giving 'homophiles' a focus and sense of community. It was at least in part due to *Arcadie* that the late 1960s and early 1970s saw the opening of a group of homosexual clubs in the rue Sainte-Anne, near the Palais Royal. These clubs, the most famous of which was *Le Sept*, were sufficiently expensive to give homosexuality a certain bourgeois respectability while also encouraging a more commercialized homosexual 'scene'. In the late 1970s, however, the financial exclusiveness of the rue Sainte-Anne encouraged a move to the Marais as the developing centre of homosexual – and increasingly 'gay' – activity.[28] The Marais presently incorporates what may be seen as Paris's gay village, based around the rue Sainte-Croix-de-la-Bretonnerie, with its cafés, bars and well-stocked bookshop, *Les Mots à la Bouche*.

In the meantime, dissatisfaction with the political timidity of *Arcadie*, combined with the growing activism of the French women's movement, prompted the formation in 1971 of the *Le Front homosexuel d'action révolutionnaire* (FHAR), with, as one of its main proponents, Guy Hocquenghem. Although FHAR lasted only until 1974, Hocquenghem's own importance as the perceived representative of the French gay mouvement proved (until his death from an AIDS-related illness in 1988) far more enduring, as did that of the writer Jean-Louis Bory, whose simple declaration in 1975 on French television – 'I say I am homosexual because that is the truth' – had an impact similar to that of Jean-Paul Aron's public statement much later in 1987 that he was suffering from AIDS (the first such acknowledgement by a major intellectual figure in France).[29] The 1970s continued with the first Gay Pride March in 1977, the founding in 1979 of the monthly newspaper-magazine *Gai Pied* and, in Marseilles, of the *Comité d'urgence anti-répression homosexuelle* (CUARH). The decade appeared, therefore, to fulfil the liberating promise of May '68. Homosexual organizations, homosexual visibility and homosexual identity had seemingly come of age.

The Mitterrand years began well. Derestriction in radio permitted the founding in 1981 of *Fréquence Gaie*, and on 27 July 1982 homosexuality finally disappeared from the statute book when the Assemblée Nationale voted to establish an equal age of consent for homosexual and heterosexual acts (a position still to be achieved in Britain). However, the 1980s were also the decade of the gradual – and in France far too gradual – acknowledgement of the devastating national and global significance of AIDS. Political and medical inertia was matched by the almost blanket refusal of gay organizations to confront the reality of AIDS (it was even considered in respected quarters such as *Gai Pied* to be a pure invention of American puritanism). It was not until 1984, after the death of Michel Foucault, that his partner, Daniel Defert, founded the first French AIDS solidarity association, *Aides*. The remainder of the decade was marked by a number of slow and pusillanimous countermoves (for example, the advertising of contraceptives in 1987), by the escalation of AIDS-related deaths, including those of Aron and Hocquenghem (1988), by the scandals surrounding '*le sang contaminé*', and by the founding in 1989 of the French chapter of *Aids Coalition to Unleash Power* (*Act Up*). Unlike the aims of *Aides*, a more socially concerned and not exclusively gay organization, those of *Act Up* were – and remain – aggressively and disruptively political, bringing gay people with AIDS on to the streets rather than allowing them to be further marginalized in hospitals or counselling rooms. As the incidence of AIDS continues to rise (over 36,000 cases were estimated in 1995), *Act Up* encourages the homosexual to assume a homosexual identity: hence its controversial strategy of 'outing'. Yet it also seeks to go beyond identity politics by replacing the term 'gay' with the more fluid and provocative '*pédé*' or '*homo*'.

As Frédéric Martel points out in his major study of gay culture and history since 1968, *Le Rose et le noir: les homosexuels en France depuis 1968* (1986), *Act Up* has imposed itself as one of the most important movements of the 1990s.[30] But the decade has also been characterized by an ongoing debate on the importance of organizations in the moulding and reflection of individual and collective identities. If the aim of homosexuals is 'the right to difference', organizations fighting for official partner status (the '*contrat d'union sociale*' and '*certificat de vie commune*'), or for the right of gay couples to adopt children, may well foster an unwelcome homogeneity. If, however, the aim is 'the right to *in*difference', then the focus of organizations on a distinct and aggrieved minority may be counter-productive.

AIDS, too, has exacerbated the already existing ambivalence towards the collective in France, a country where the tradition of the fraternity of citizenship and its supposedly asexual homosociality alienates many feminists and gay men.[31] On the one hand, the illness is symptomatic of a whole society; on the other, it intensifies individual difference and value. It should be added, moreover, that the extremely mixed reception in France of Martel's book, including scathing attacks by *Fréquence Gaie* and the gay magazine *Têtu*, exemplifies some of these divisions. In an extensive article that aims to catalogue the controversy objectively, Martel argues that those who criticize the book so vehemently, in particular for its exposure of the gay denial of AIDS in France during the early 1980s, used to belong to the former extreme left, which, he claims, in the wake of the collapse of the ideals of May '68, is now trying blindly to remould itself through a form of identity and community politics.[32] According to Martel, what this signifies on a broader level is a battle between two conceptions of democracy: on the one hand, democracy as a juxtaposition of different communities (which the State simply maintains in peaceful co-existence), and, on the other, democracy as the constitution of communal life (the fight for equal rights, etc). For Martel, who inveighs against any separatist moves towards gay militantism (equivalent in his eyes to the discredited, ideological utopias of Marxism and Maoism),[33] it is vital for gays to be able to criticize the gay community past and present, even if, like himself, they are not old enough to have experienced all the events of the post-'68 era. Hitherto, gay writing and film-making has generally concentrated on the individual, albeit in complex and challenging ways, as evidenced by the work of Guibert and Collard. It remains to be seen whether future cultural activity engages more strongly with the tensions between the gay individual, the gay collective, and the (non-gay?) nation, as well as with the different potential meanings of each category.

ii. The Gay Tradition: Gay Cultural Production in Context

Over the fifty-year period under discussion in our volume, an ever more vocal gay community has had its interests and preoccupations increasingly recognized in France. One reason for this is the indisputable cultural importance of early-to-mid-century writers such as Proust, Gide and Genet. Although many in France would hesitate to give these authors the title of 'gay writer', and although some of their representations of homosexuals may now seem regrettably self-oppressive, the significance their work accords to homosexuals as characters and to homosexuality as a theme has helped to put the issue of homosexual identity and the 'gay signature' on the modern French literary, cultural and political agenda. The cultural status of the 'gay signature' has been reinforced by the productivity of a further, hardly less eminent group of French writers who deal, at least intermittently, with gay themes. Like Gide and Genet, these other early/mid-century writers –

Cocteau, Jouhandeau, Julien Green, Henry de Montherlant, Roger Peyrefitte and Michel Tournier – offer examples not only of novels but also of theatre, apologias, journals, diaries and letters, thus revealing gay cultural production to be both prolific and multigeneric, with the gay signature interacting with fiction and life in complex and protean fashion. Positing and problematizing gay identity in formally and politically productive ways, the gay signature in modern French literature has always, in fact, been irrepressible and self-ironizing, construct*ing* but also construct*ed*. Long before gender theorists encouraged readers to approach it formally as such, the French gay signature was already, playfully and painfully, a *performance*.

While the notion of a modern French gay literary tradition may not have been actively promoted in France (the recent example of Pierre Bergé – one of the rare publicly 'out' figures in the French media and industry – proposing a specifically gay network of writers including Genet, Crevel, Louis Aragon and Violette Leduc represents a major exception),[34] nevertheless, the indisputable range and richness of earlier gay writing has stimulated younger writers to explore and question different forms of identity and sexuality, whether in relatively traditional (often first-person) novels or via more unconventional narrative forms. Among those who stand out are Guibert, Hocquenghem, Fernandez, Renaud Camus, Conrad Detrez, Hugo Marsan and Yves Navarre. Some of these writers have received the highest literary accolades in France. After going to Proust in 1919 for *Within a Budding Grove* (*A l'ombre des jeunes filles en fleurs*) and to Tournier in 1970 for *The Erl-King* (*Le Roi des Aulnes*), the *Prix Goncourt* was awarded to Navarre in 1980 (*Le Jardin d'acclimatation*) and to Fernandez in 1982 (*Dans la main de l'ange*), with Hocquenghem's *Ève* obtaining two votes in 1987 (the same as Michel Braudeau's *Mon ami Pierrot* in 1993). The somewhat less establishment – but still highly prestigious – *Prix Renaudot* was awarded to Detrez in 1978 for *L'Herbe à brûler* and to Guillaume Le Touze in 1994 for *Comme ton père*, while the innovation-encouraging *Prix Médicis* went to Tony Duvert's *Paysage de fantaisie* (1973), Fernandez's *Porporino ou les mystères de Naples* (1974) and Jean-Noël Pancrazi's *Les Quartiers d'hiver* (1990).

Cultural 'consecration', to borrow the terminology of Pierre Bourdieu, has therefore been bestowed upon contemporary French writing stamped with a 'gay signature', whether it takes the form of a sober but devastating indictment of the bourgeois family's treatment of its homosexual son (*Le Jardin d'acclimatation*), of a playfully corrosive fantasy of erotic violence (*Paysage de fantaisie*), of an elegy to the passing of a Parisian gay club (*Les Quartiers d'hiver*), or of a tenderly positive renegotiation of family (particularly male-to-male) relationships in a world transformed by AIDS (*Comme ton père*). From the scandalously provocative histories of Fernandez to the 'gender-bending' strategies of Hocquenghem, recent male gay writing has been accredited in ways granted to very few French lesbian writers. Indeed, it could be argued that contemporary male gay writing in France not only forms part of a new canon, but also constitutes its own.

A further reason for this public recognition relates, of course, to the prominence and influence of intellectual figures such as Barthes and Foucault, whose work may also be said to offer, at least in part, a gay signature. Schehr states with much justification that Barthes's writing, while typically 'discreet', 'is the celebration of a homosexual love affair with writing', that is to say, the 'transfigured expression of homosexual love for the text of the other'.[35] A very different connection between discourse and gay desire is charted by Foucault in his three-volume *History of Sexuality* (1976–84). Although the later two volumes of the *History* mark a radical change of direction and focus, what is most familiar is Volume I's emphasis on homosex as the most talked-about taboo of modern times. Foucault's analyses have influenced enormously other critics, who contend that heterosexuality is the other of homosexuality, its *vice versa*, a reversal that ties in with the deconstructive approach of inverting and subverting commonly accepted binary hierarchies.[36]

Through his reported sexual practice of sadomasochism, Foucault has also promoted another, if not reversal, then at least interchangeability, of the apparent opposites of pain and pleasure, a process mirrored in some of the writings of post-'68 gay authors such as Tony Duvert, Hervé Guibert and Éric Jourdan. Through their explicit descriptions of male-to-male erotic violence and its arguably subversive force, these writers key into contemporary debates about gay/lesbian erotica, pornography and sexual abuse. When violence takes place between teenagers, as in Duvert's *Paysage de fantaisie* or Jourdan's *Les Mauvais Anges* (1984), recent French gay writing meshes with both the age-old tradition of pederastic literature[37] and that of the *écrivain maudit* associated with Gilles de Rais, the Marquis de Sade, Octave Mirbeau and Georges Bataille. For these reasons, post-war and especially late twentieth-century French gay cultural production inflects a whole range of debates and agendas relating to the area of sexual politics and the policing of sexualities.

A final reason for viewing the status of French gay cultural production as a discrete and recognized form has to be the number of 1980s/1990s works concerned with AIDS. According to Emily Apter, the title of France's 'premier *sida* novelist' goes to Guibert,[38] known not only for his trilogy of 'AIDS novels' (*To The Friend Who Did Not Save My Life, The Compassion Protocol, Cytomégalovirus)* but also for his television appearances (on literary programmes such as *Apostrophes* and *Ex-Libris*) and the documentary-diary of his own body, *La Pudeur ou l'Impudeur*. Since he was also an accomplished photographer, Guibert's work crosses a number of generic boundaries, as does that of the novelist, diarist, and film-maker Cyril Collard, most famous for his novel and film of the same name, *Savage Nights* (1992) (*Les Nuits fauves*). While a number of novelists have used AIDS to demonstrate the loyalty and devotion of gay couples (a central element in Fernandez's *La Gloire du paria* (1987) and Navarre's *Ce sont amis que vent emporte*) (1991)), the disease provides a more generalized sense of melancholy and transience in the writings of Marsan, Pancrazi and Le Touze. Almost all of these works, however painful or anguished, afford the reader a heightened sense of the value of the lives described within them, with the result that AIDS seems to reaffirm the identity of the individual authors and their experience. Such writing offers a compelling testimony to the mutual inextricability of textuality and sexuality, and to the vibrancy of the gay signature.

iii. Lesbian Cultural Production: Politics/Theory/Creativity

In the chapter from *Homosexualities and French Literature* entitled 'Lesbian Intertextuality', which focuses primarily on the writings of Colette, Leduc and Wittig, Elaine Marks seeks to sketch out the lineaments of a modern, French, lesbian-authored literary tradition, which, she argues, exists alongside, and in reaction to, the literary *mis*representations of lesbianism produced in the last three centuries by a cohort of censorious and/or voyeuristic male French writers.[39] As far as post-war France is concerned – and notwithstanding the enthusiasm Marks brings to her project – it is very difficult indeed for her to argue categorically for the existence of a lesbian creative 'tradition' or 'culture'. It is clearly *not* the case that the post-war French cultural field contains no lesbian writing or film at all, or that France's post-war lesbian authors/film-makers are oblivious of the intertextual links that bind their individual creations to those of their 'foremothers'. However, it remains a fact that, in the fifty-year period following the Second World War, lesbian creativity has not been recognized in France as a specific and valid cultural entity.[40] A number of factors can help us to understand the reasons for this.

First, there is the fact that, throughout the post-war era, lesbianism in France has lacked *political* 'visibility'.[41] During the heady days of the 1970s, when the *Mouvement de libération des femmes* (MLF) took off in the wake of May '68, when French women, straight and gay, were reflecting on, and writing about, sexual politics, desire and the body, and when lesbian groups such as the *Gouines rouges* (Red Dykes) formed within the *MLF* around figures like Monique Wittig and Christine Delphy, it did seem as if lesbian activism might acquire the kind of public political profile that the French gay liberation movement was in the process of assuming.[42] As Janine Mossuz-Lavau explains, however, this did not happen.[43] For one thing, lesbian groups of the 1970s and early 1980s, while they made vital contributions to the sexual debates of the day, helping not only to reshape the feminist agenda but also to revise public perceptions of sexuality, never achieved the visibility of gay rights groups. This, claims Mossuz-Lavau, was because they eschewed the formal organization of – and tended to be more short-lived than – their gay counterparts. Secondly, the lesbian political cause was rendered further invisible in the 1970s by virtue of its imbrication within the politics of the 'broad church' of the MLF, which, according to many, failed to address the specific problem of lesbian oppression.[44] The peculiar absence in France of an autonomous lesbian movement has, in Martel's view, persisted to the present day, the result being that lesbian politics continues to lack visibility in contemporary France.[45]

If, in post-war France, the lesbian political profile has been relatively unprominent and is likely to remain so (in the 'post-feminist' climate of the 1990s, the French women's movement is for the most part quiescent),[46] then so, too, has lesbian theoretical enquiry. There exists no body of work in which the lesbian condition is theorized in an enabling and politically expedient manner. Simone de Beauvoir's existentialist analysis of feminine homosexuality in *The Second Sex* (1949) does connect lesbianism with female independence, if not transcendence, and presents lesbian relationships as facilitating an equality precluded by heterosexual power relations. However, Beauvoir's essay also suggests, more problematically, that lesbian subjectivity incorporates a form of narcissism, involves a potential for inauthenticity and bad faith, and even, on occasion, gives rise to pathological behaviour. The lesbian dimension within the theoretical work of Monique Wittig and Luce Irigaray is stronger and more radical than it is in Beauvoir's *The Second Sex*. Yet as Renate Günther argues in her essay 'Are Lesbians Women?' included in this volume, within the (utopian) sexual universes imagined by both women in their theoretical texts published during the 1970s and early 1980s, insufficient room is accorded to lesbians and lesbianism.

The various forms of lesbian invisibility glossed above have undoubtedly militated against the emergence in post-war France of a distinctive, sizeable body of literary and filmic texts that might be taken to emblematize a distinctive, post-war cultural 'tradition' of lesbian signature. So, too, has the resistance that, even during the 1970s, many lesbian (and non-lesbian) French women authors, including those associated in the Anglo-Saxon world with the creation of a polymorphous, polysemic *écriture féminine*, have mounted against the production of essentializing forms of discourse and the phenomenon of sexual-political (self-)categorization.[47] So, finally, has the thoroughly misogynistic character of what Bourdieu has called France's *champ culturel*, dominated in the post-war period by key 'players' such as the publishing house Gallimard, which, during the 1950s, insisted that accounts of lesbian sex should be excised from Violette Leduc's *Ravages* before it could be published. It is not the case, of course, that lesbian creativity has been entirely stifled in post-war France. The accounts of female love published in the 1960s and 1970s by Leduc, Wittig, and, to a lesser extent, Christiane Rochefort, whether or not they were inspired by the socio-symbolic and sexual revolution of the late 1960s and 1970s,[48] combine to constitute a powerful aesthetic corpus where lesbian eroticism and desire are given a female-authored voice and where gender positions are reworked in an increasingly radical way.[49] Recent additions to this corpus include the writing of Jocelyne François (*Les Amantes* (1978), *Joue-nous "España"* (1980), *Le Sel* (1992)), Mireille Best (*Les Mots de hasard* (1980)) and Hélène de Montferrand (*Les amies d'Héloïse* (1990), *Journal de Suzanne* (1991)); Josiane Balasko's film *French Twist* (1995) (*Gazon Maudit*) (discussed in *Gay Signatures* by Susan Hayward); and, arguably, some of the cinematic work of Diane Kurys (*Coup de foudre* (1983)).[50] Yet, as Elula Perrin points out in her *Coup de gueule pour l'amour des femmes* (1995), the fact that, in the mid-to-late twentieth century, French-authored literary and filmic artefacts attesting to a lesbian sensibility have been in distinctly short supply indicates that, in post-war France, the lesbian creative signature has been largely occluded by a cultural climate that has refused to accommodate it.[51]

V

The Contents of the Volume

In view of the mixed fortunes that have dogged French lesbian and gay cultural production in the post-war period, it should come as no surprise that many of the essays included in this volume bear specifically on questions of social (in)visibility and the critique of fixed identities. Yet the posing of these questions is equally a reflection of the fact that France is currently witnessing a spectacular visibilization of gay male lifestyles and relationships, despite – or perhaps, on one level, partly because of – the disappearance of a whole section of the gay population as a result of AIDS. If one theme unites our collection, it is precisely the issue of whether, on the one hand, gay visibility represents progress, or, on the other, merely a confirmation of the status quo.

We have organized the chapters of *Gay Signatures* generically rather than chronologically, and have divided the volume into two distinct yet related parts. The first, entitled 'Theoretical Positions', comprises four essays devoted to issues of gay and lesbian philosophical enquiry. The second, 'Narrative Articulations', concentrates on post-war gay and lesbian writing and cinema. This is followed by a table of important dates, publications and political events in post-war French gay history. Here is a brief summary of the individual chapters.

Theoretical Positions

I. In his chapter entitled 'Cruising (Through) encounters' Michael Worton draws out the parallels between gay erotics and gay textualities, where desire and its fictions – and fictions and their desires – are explicitly figured as fragmentary, mobile and labyrinthine. Unlike pornography, which tends to seal in the body and evacuate evidence of authorship, the writers considered by Worton use their own self-awareness to unfix both their own identities and their writing. Worton's favoured texts are the 'autofictions' of Guibert and the self-consciously 'cruising' texts of Marsan, Barthes, Camus and Chotard. Such literature, or what Worton, after Ross Chambers, identifies as 'loiterature', offers a positive and creative narcissism, and a fragmentary movement that evokes the prospect of 'serial plenitude'.

II. Engaging with the work of Hocquenghem, Bill Marshall also seeks to retain a sense of homosexual identity while avoiding its fixities and totalizations. He aims to move between and beyond 1970s homosexual identity politics, 1980s gay consumerism and uncontrolled post-modern dispersal. A way out of the impasse, he suggests, is to entertain the notion of the baroque, which combines an emphasis on the visibility of both identity and consumerism with the fluidity of the *flâneur* and the gay cruiser. By identifying the baroque in the work of Hocquenghem and tracing its various manifestations in Leibniz, Baudelaire, Benjamin and Deleuze, Marshall provides the contemporary gay signature with a rich ancestry and a potential new radicalism.

III. Renate Günther's chapter explores the relationship between feminism and lesbianism as developed in the theoretical writings of Monique Wittig and Luce Irigaray. By fully situating the sexual-political positions and allegiances of these theorists, Günther establishes their apparently irreconcilable stances *vis-à-vis* lesbian identity and politics. She concludes, however, that their theories have very similar implications as far as the future of lesbianism is concerned, and that ultimately each writer makes insufficient 'room' for lesbian existence.

IV. In the only chapter to engage with pre-war French writers, James Williams considers the effects of Leo Bersani's spectacular return to the tradition of the gay outlaw during his analysis of Proust, Gide and Genet in *Homos* (1995). Williams argues that Bersani's extreme and dynamic approach to these writers, which comes at the end of a long and devastating critique of queer politics and theory, sets up a textual void in *Homos* designed to antagonize the reader. This radical instance of textual counter-signing, or 'friction', has immediate consequences not only for Bersani's 'ethical-erotic' project, but also for the reader of gay theory in general and its status as a critical and artistic practice.

Narrative Articulations

V. Alex Hughes's chapter addresses the queer dimension of Leduc's autobiographical writing, particularly apparent in *La Bâtarde* (1964), and speculates on the effect this dimension will have on Leduc's future 'commodity value'. The chapter focuses on the proliferation of gender positionalities contained in *La Bâtarde* – a text long categorized simply and reductively as a 'lesbian' opus – and explores the way in which Leduc's first autobiographical volume frames gender not as a core or essence, but rather as a fluid process of mutation. Finally, Hughes investigates the heroine's engagement with drag and cross-dressing and establishes the 'political' aspect of Leduc's textual performance with reference to the work of Judith Butler.

VI. Susan Hayward's essay on Balasko's *French Twist* (1995) investigates what happens to the gay signature when a heterosexual woman film-maker produces a film dealing with the issue of lesbian marginality and also takes the central lesbian role. Hayward uses the tension between Balasko's known heterosexuality and her lesbian role to expose sexuality as performance and masquerade. Hayward is particularly concerned to address the subversive potential of *French Twist* in terms of gender and genre, as well as to assess the sources of its humour. Her argument, like that of Alex Hughes in relation to Leduc's *La Bâtarde*, exploits Judith Butler's analysis of the sexual-political impact of drag and gender parody.

VII. Murray Pratt looks at the representation of Guibert's bodily identity in his AIDS 'autofictions'. Whereas some commentators have criticized these as either self-indulgent or reactionary, Pratt argues that they break the silences around death and AIDS. Guibert's narratives may be as fragile as his own body, yet they are also vitally self-affirmative, a paradox epitomized in Guibert's own ironic self-projection as an AIDS patient escaping from hospital and walking, drip in hand, along a motorway. Such an image, according to Pratt, crystallizes Guibert's recourse to an 'optic of astonishment', or 'spectacle of difference', which both marginalizes and centralizes his own precarious yet defiant body, text and signature.

VIII. Owen Heathcote asks whether hunting narratives signed by gay men confirm or question the tendency in such narratives to naturalize the association of violence and masculinity. Although the novels of Duvert, Guibert and Jourdan do indeed appear to endorse a fascination with the male predator, the predator there is also vulnerable and isolated (Duvert), exaggerated and parodied (Guibert), or else trapped in cycles of repetition and death (Jourdan). By combining this subversion of stereotypical maleness with homoeroticism and homosociality, the novels in question are shown to go beyond a homosexuality defined in terms of heteropatriarchy and favour what Bersani has called 'homoness'.

IX. Brigitte Rollet and James Williams examine the ethical and aesthetic questions raised by Collard's film, *Savage Nights*. They show that the huge swing in public reaction to the film, from initial euphoria to outright attack following Collard's death from AIDS in 1993, reflect directly its powerful blurrings of artistic form, gender and sexuality, fiction and reality, all focused around the omnipresent, physical presence of the film-maker himself. The authors argue that Collard's ultimate failure to transcend boundaries results both from the general ambiguities involved in filming the self, and, more specifically, from the fundamental resistance in France to any concrete notion of a gay film about AIDS.

VI

Concluding Remarks

To bring the contents of this introduction to a temporary conclusion: the fluid title, *Gay Signatures*, reflects not merely the prolific, heterogeneous and contestatory nature of post-war (in particular post-'68) French gay and lesbian cultural production, but also, more profoundly, the necessarily provisional nature of any new framework for discussing the relations between gender, the body, language, sexuality, artistic form, and politics. Rather than attempting to formalize a specifically 'gay' or 'lesbian' style and identity – something which is perhaps as impossible to define as *écriture féminine* – our volume seeks instead to open up different homotextualities. The notion of the gay signature both confirms and questions the concept of a gay identity: confirms it, that is, as a platform from which to challenge stereotypical representations of sexuality, yet also questions it as, at least in part, a product of precisely those stereotypical representations. *Gay signatures* is thus necessarily both contestatory and self-contestatory. In addition, the collection provides the first major occasion to assess the usefulness of new critical approaches like queer theory when applied to the specifics of the French cultural and literary field. Our hope is that, like the evolving genre of gay AIDS writing, which mixes conventional fiction and apparent public document to produce a form of *reportage-vérité*,[52] *Gay Signatures* will contribute towards a fundamental rethinking of the relations between writing and theory, sexuality and identity.

Notes

1. G. Stambolian and E. Marks (eds) (1979), *Homosexualities and French Literature: Cultural Contexts/Critical Texts*, Ithaca and London, p. 138.
2. Ibid., p. 29.
3. Ibid., p. 24.
4. Ibid., p. 30.
5. Ibid., p. 26.
6. Ibid., p. 30.
7. C. Robinson (1995), *Scandal in the Ink: Male and Female Homosexuality in Twentieth-century French Literature*, London.
8. See R. Harvey (1992), 'Sidaïques/Sidéens: French Discourses on AIDS', *Contemporary French Civilisation*, vol. 16, no. 2, pp. 308–35.
9. See Chapter 1, 'Sexual Signatures: Feminism after the Death of the Author', of E. Grosz (1995), *Space, Time, and Perversion* (London and New York), pp. 9–24, for an excellent analysis of Derrida's theory of the signature.
10. O. Heathcote (1994), 'Masochism, sadism and homotextuality: the

examples of Yukio Mishima and Eric Jourdan', *Paragraph*, vol. 17, no. 2, pp. 174–89 (p. 176).

11. See L. R. Schehr (1995), *Alcibiades at the Door: Gay Discourses in French Literature*, Stanford CA, p. 195.
12. Quoted in Harvey, 'Sidaïques/Sidéens', p. 328.
13. See E. Apter (1993), 'Fantom Images: Hervé Guibert and the Writing of "sida" in France', in T. F. Murphy and S. Poirier (eds), *Writing AIDS: Gay Literature, Language and Analysis*, New York, pp. 83–97 (p. 95).
14. See L. R. Schehr (1995), *The Shock of Men: Homosexual Hermeneutics in French Writing*, Stanford CA, p.19.
15. J. Eadie (1994), 'Queer', *Paragraph*, vol. 17, no. 3, pp. 244–51 (p. 246).
16. Ibid., p. 246.
17. Ibid., p. 248.
18. See G. Bredbeck (1995), 'The new queer narrative: intervention and critique', *Textual Practice*, vol. 9, no. 3, pp. 477–502 (pp. 479–80). For a fine and diverse introduction to the broad social and political aims of queer theory, see M. Warner (ed.) (1993), *Fear of a Queer Planet: Cultural Politics and Social Theory*, London and Minneapolis, and S. Seidman (ed.) (1996), *Queer Theory/Sociology*, Oxford.
19. See J. Champagne (1995), *The Ethics of Marginality: A New Approach to Gay Studies*, Minneapolis and London, and D. Morton (1995), 'Birth of the Cyberqueer', *PMLA*, vol. 110, no. 3 (May), pp. 369–82, where Morton argues for a queer theory anchored in Marxist historical materialism, as opposed to the prevailing, ludic, postmodernist version of queer based on the supposed autonomy of desire.
20. This idea was first presented by Judith Butler (1990), in *Gender Trouble: Feminism and the Subversion of Identity*, London and New York.
21. Schehr, *Alcibiades at the Door*, p. 22.
22. See 'Proust and the Spectacle of the Closet', in E. K. Sedgwick (1990), *Epistemology of the Closet*, Berkeley, Los Angeles and London, pp. 213–52.
23. See Schehr, *The Shock of Men*, p. 13.
24. Ibid., p. 21.
25. See P. J. Smith (1992), *Laws of Desire: Questions of Homosexuality in Spanish Writing and Film 1960–1990*, Oxford.
26. See M. Maclean (1987), 'Gender and Identity in Modern France: Normality and Reality', in J. Bridgford (ed.), *France: Image and Identity*, Newcastle-upon-Tyne, pp. 220–32.
27. B. Marshall (1996), *Guy Hocquenghem: Theorizing the Gay Nation*, London, p. 3.

28. See J.-N. Pancrazi (1990), *Les Quartiers d'hiver*, Paris, for a fictionalized account of the decline and closure of one such club.
29. J.-P. Aron (1988), *Mon sida*, Paris (first published in *Le Nouvel Observateur*, 30 Oct. – 5 Nov. 1987).
30. See F. Martel (1996), *Le Rose et le noir: les homosexuels en France depuis 1968*, Paris, p. 353.
31. On the relationship between feminism and universalism, see the 1995 issue of *Differences*, vol. 7, no. 1.
32. F. Martel (1996), 'Un *gay* n'a pas à critiquer la commmunauté *gay*', *Esprit*, no. 226, pp. 197–216 (p. 215).
33. Ibid., p. 211.
34. See Bergé's interview in 1988 with Marguerite Duras, 'Duras est SEXY', *Globe*, no. 30 (July–August), pp. 79–83. Bergé, who runs the gay magazine *Têtu*, is also the managing director of Yves Saint-Laurent.
35. L. Schehr, *The Shock of Men*, p. 84.
36. For different approaches to such reversals, see Sedgwick, *Epistemology of the Closet*; J. Dollimore (1991), *Sexual Dissidence: Augustine to Wilde, Freud to Foucault*, Oxford; and L. Edelman (1994), *Homo-graphesis: Essays in Gay Literary and Cultural Theory*, New York and London.
37. For useful definitions and analysis of French pederastic literature, see Robinson, *Scandal in the Ink*, pp. 144–73. As Robinson points out, French concepts of pederasty and pederastic literature are not exclusively centred on adolescent sexuality and '[a]dolescent sex is not, in a French text, automatically a pederastic theme' (p. 146).
38. See E. Apter (1993), 'Fantom Images: Hervé Guibert and the Writing of "sida" in France', p. 83. For studies of AIDS and French Literature,see J. Lévy and A. Nouss (1994), *Sida-Fiction: Essai d'anthropologie romanesque*, Lyon, and J.-L. Maxence (1995), *Les Écrivains sacrifiés des années sida*, Paris.
39. See Stambolian and Marks, *Homosexualities and French Literature*, pp. 353–77. The kinds of voyeuristic male-authored representations Marks targets are offered in the prose fictions of authors such as Diderot, Balzac, Maupassant and Proust. It is worth noting here that rather more interesting, if still highly problematic, C19/early C20 literary accounts of lesbianism and female polysexuality are contained in the prose writings of Gautier and Rachilde.
40. For a pertinent discussion on this subject, see A. F. Garréta, 'In Light of Invisibility' (1996), in *Same Sex/Different Text? Gay and Lesbian Writing in French*, special issue of *Yale French Studies*, no. 90, pp. 205–13.

41. This phenomenon is noted in the editorial preface to the first volume of the gay and lesbian review *Masques*, which asks its readers to reflect on the reasons why the existence of lesbians remains unknown while that of gays is not. See *Masques*, vol. 1, May 1979, p. 2.
42. See J. Mossuz-Lavau (1991), *Les Lois de l'amour: les politiques de la sexualité en France*, Paris, pp. 245–62.
43. Ibid., p. 280.
44. Various studies address the dissatisfaction with the *MLF* experienced by French lesbians in the 1970s, and signal the tensions and divisions it provoked within the women's movement. See F. Picq (1993), *Les Années Mouvement*, Paris; C. Duchen (1986), *Feminism in France from May '68 to Mitterrand*, London; J. Girard (1981), *Le Mouvement homosexuel en France 1945-1980*, Paris; and volume 1 of *Masques* (1979). Useful also on the relationship between lesbian politics and the feminist *MLF* is Martel's *Le Rose et le noir*.
45. See ibid., p. 57. In a later chapter of *Le Rose et le noir*, Martel does note the existence, in the 1980s, of some lesbian separatist groups, organized under the aegis of the 'Front des lesbiennes radicales' and focused around Monique Wittig. He points out that this phenomenon was short-lived and in fact folded in 1982 (see ibid., pp. 138–40).
46. See E. Perrin (1995), *Coup de gueule pour l'amour des femmes*, Paris, p. 9.
47. See Martel, *Le Rose et le noir*, pp. 174–5. For a compelling account of the way in which Hélène Cixous, a key 'exponent' of *écriture féminine*, seeks in her (recent) fiction precisely to eschew a reifying employment of the identity category/signifier 'lesbianism', see E. Wilson (1996), 'Hélène Cixous: an Erotics of the Feminine', in A. Hughes and K. Ince (eds), *French Erotic Fiction*, Oxford, pp. 121–45.
48. Wittig and Rochefort were active in the women's movement, and their work reflects a shared awareness, partly inspired by the revolutionary climate of post-'68 France, of the complex connections between writing, sexuality and politics. Belonging to an older generation, Leduc's writing is less 'political' in its intent, if not its impact.
49. See, for example, Leduc, *La Bâtarde* (1964); Leduc, *Thérèse et Isabelle* (1966); Rochefort, *Les Stances à Sophie* (1963); Wittig, *L'Opoponax* (1964); Wittig, *Les Guerrillères* (1969); Wittig, *Le Corps lesbien* (1973). All of these texts were published by mainstream publishing houses.
50. For a fine bibliography of recent lesbian writing in French, see S. Robichon and A. F. Garréta (1996), 'Select Bibliography of Works in French Related to Lesbian Issues and Problematics', in *Same Sex/ Different Text? Gay and Lesbian Writing in French*, special issue of *Yale French Studies*, no. 90, pp. 242–52.

51. See Perrin, *Coup de gueule*, pp. 21–6, 34–7. It is worth noting here the existence of *Lesbia*, a fairly 'light' cultural/political lesbian monthly journal that came into being in 1982 and is still going strong in the 1990s.
52. F. Boulant, quoted in Harvey, 'Sidaïques/Sidéens', p. 327.

PART I

Theoretical Positions

– 1 –

Cruising (Through) Encounters*

Michael Worton

Hugo Marsan opens his 1983 study of French homosexual behaviour, *Un homme, un homme* (A Man, a Man), with the defiantly defensive statement that '[a] study of homosexuality continues to be a difficult undertaking. "Homosexuality" is a word whose use and meaning are inevitably compromised'.[1] Recognizing that as a practising and self-proclaiming homosexual, he cannot take an objective or, as he puts it, 'innocent' view of the subject, Marsan chooses to base himself essentially on documentary sources, such as interviews, letters, small ads, etc. On the one hand, this choice of a quasi-scientific approach gives his work some sort of authority, and defines the reader as subservient and wholly (and justifiably) credulous. On the other, the number and the diversity of the sources he cites arouse suspicion in the mind of the reader, who encounters these fragmented texts as fictions, as extracts from an unknown and unknowable novel. Furthermore, Marsan offers as a possible alternative title *Fragments d'un discours sur l'homosexualité masculine* (A Discourse on Male Homosexuality: Fragments), explicitly evoking Roland Barthes's *Fragments d'un discours amoureux* (1977) (*A Lover's Discourse: Fragments* (1990)) as a model and thereby inscribing his own text and its reader in a modern tradition of reading as (bound up in) seduction (1983: 13).

Barthes's work has contributed greatly to the redefinition and, crucially, to the eroticization, of both reading and writing, yet what makes his thinking so important is perhaps still insufficiently understood or accepted. In our Western, post-Socratic and Judaeo-Christian tradition, wholeness is privileged, be it a question of faith, philosophical system or whatever. Furthermore, since Ancient Greece, representations of the body, especially the nude body, have tended to figure it as ideal when *undivided*. As Adrian Stokes puts it, 'the human body so conceived is a promise of sanity' (1967: 4). In other words, our cultural tradition consistently and forcefully promotes

* All references in this chapter adhere to the Harvard system. Details of the texts referred to are contained in the Bibliography to this volume.

the belief that fragmentation and the fragmentary are suspect and dangerous, states to be avoided at all cost. This is particularly true of masculinity, which, as psychologist Stephen Frosh argues, has been enclosed in a form of obligatory closedness in order for patriarchy and the phallic order to be preserved: 'Masculinity has been marked by closure throughout its history, holding things in place, symbolized by the unitary sexuality of the penis' (1994: 144). Moreover, for political as well as for religious reasons, our patriarchal societies maintain marriage as the standard model for long-term relationships, thereby ensuring that fixity is permanently inscribed in social practice(s) and, indeed is promoted as an ideal – an ideal not only of family units but also, by presupposition, of individual identities.

Aware of the weight of this tradition, Barthes nonetheless consistently insists on dissolution, dissemination (and dissimulation) in his thinking. Both as reader and as writer, he privileges the fragment, which for him is not a mark of loss or of non-integrity but is a seductive promise: it functions as the promise of a future encounter, an encounter not with a fixed identity but with an identity whose desirability lies in its essential and eternal mobility. The self-driven, self-willed and, indeed, self-justifying nature of Barthes's eulogizing of the fragment merits close examination and analysis, since it modifies itself as his career advances. However, such a study is not my purpose in this essay; rather, what interests me here is the fact that Marsan should choose as the model for his own book a text that speaks about love and desire both in fragments and in terms of fragmentation. *A Lover's Discourse: Fragments* is a text that performs discursively the non-coherence and especially the non-linearity of the love and desire (of) which it speaks; in other words, it not only presents but also performs its non-belonging to any literary category or genre. It is this generic 'abnormality' that is attractive to Marsan, hence his simultaneous adoption and non-adoption of the Barthesian title whose performativity is as important for a reading of *Un homme, un homme* as its meaning. Although this book appears under the sole name of Marsan, it is in fact made up of two parts, each of them hybrid. The major part of the book consists of Marsan's contribution, playfully entitled 'Le chemin latéral' (The sidelong way), which interweaves his thoughts on homosexuality and its operability in modern French society with a series of excerpts from interviews with gay men, identified only by their first names and their ages. These *témoignages* (pieces of 'evidence') undoubtedly have their own authenticity as discourse; however, as only very partially attributed utterances, they also inescapably function as fiction. The second part of the book, described as a postface and thereby accorded the status of a Derridean supplement, is written by the young philosopher Dominique Auffret and entitled 'Philosophie dans la back-room'. More conventionally structured as an essay, Auffret's text nonetheless bears a title that intertextually evokes Sade's *Philosophy in the Boudoir* (itself a hybrid text);[2] and, furthermore, it ends with a poem. Thus it too privileges subjectivity and inscribes fictionality as a mode not only of discourse but also of meta-discourse.

A fragmentary and 'in-between' book that both is and is not social commentary, collection of short stories, philosophical essay and polemical pamphlet, *Un homme, un homme* explicitly recognizes that in order to comment and to theorize one must fictionalize (p. 145). Moreover, Marsan concludes with the assertion that gay men are other, are radically different from heterosexuals (and, indeed, also from lesbians), and this leads him to call for a complete metamorphosis of social structures.[3] Above all, he demands that the hermetic closure of the heterosexual couple and the family unit be shattered, and proposes that gay men live out their difference by continuing their quest for selfhood in a constant renewal of experiences, both erotic and social (pp. 146–7).

In his speculations on gay desire, Marsan defines homosexuality as centred on pleasure and posits the relationship with the other as being above all a theatricalization, a putting into play and working out of the male body (pp. 68–70). Whilst this subjective position is somewhat narrow, simplistic and unlikely to be shared by all gay men today, Marsan nonetheless highlights – both in his own comments and in the choice he makes of 'interviews' – the notions of quest, fragmentation and repetition that inform much modern theoretical thinking and locate cruising at the centre of homosexual identity as well as homosexual practice. Presenting what is in essence fiction as document, Marsan's book textualizes sex; this being one of its main contributions to debates about gayness and sexual identity. Conversely, gay writers of fiction increasingly sexualize text: they do not only write *about* sex, but they say, speak, show sex simply (if also poetically), and thereby rescue the erotic from the domain of the moral, where it has been previously sectioned.

For gay writers, the move away from writing *about* sex and (their) sexual practices towards a direct saying *of* (homo)sexuality represents a liberation: it means that they are no longer writing 'from outside', writing, as it were, like – and therefore *as* – representatives of heterosexual society. They are consequently able to present gay-specific material without feeling that this needs to be validated by the approval or even the understanding of others. However, and perhaps inevitably in our modern confessional culture, this shift has resulted in an outpouring of self-regarding, proclamatory texts whose value tends to be of a political or documentary nature rather than a literary one. These texts have undoubtedly contributed to the creation of a growing sense of community amongst gay men and have furthered the visibility of a wide variety of gay issues, including that of gay sexuality. Indeed, it is one of the more intriguing, if amusing, paradoxes of our current moralizing culture that soft gay pornography, both verbal and visual, has been incorporated into mainstream culture and advertising and that many gay authors, now recognized explicitly as such, from Gide to Genet and Hervé Guibert, have become part of the canon legitimated by the Academy.

Many gay pornographers see themselves also as serious writers and, like John Preston, for example, choose not only to write in the first person singular but also to insist on the authenticity of the stories they tell.[4] Nonetheless, the problem with pornography *qua* pornography is that it is often repetitive and narcissistic, presupposing – and thereby imposing – a particular, *fixed* object of desire and, indeed, mode of desire, and playing, as Barthes would have it, on desires rather than fantasies. Yet this posited object is not, and, in the pornographic text, cannot be (the representation of) a true love object, a genuine other. Rather, the pornographic text fragments desire and is, in one important sense, deeply destructive, since it shatters the fragile coherence of the desiring subject. As the psychoanalyst Janine Chasseguet-Smirgel forcefully argues: 'There is fragmentation [. . .] in pornography, not the total object. This fragmentation is essentially sadistic' (Baruch and Serrano 1996: 150). Pornography undoubtedly represents desire and sexuality, but it fulfils its functions by being transparent (or, at least, appearing to be): it has no real textuality, and so cannot be the site of textual pleasure – although it may serve as a catalyst for physical pleasure. One may thus understand why Barthes describes it as 'not *sure*': because '[t]he pleasure of representation is not attached to its object' (Barthes 1976: 55).[5]

If the literary can be at least partially defined as that which gives textual pleasure through its seductive opacity, its teasing resistance, then a text that speaks transitively and only transitively, and articulates purely denotationally, must exclude the possibility of reading as a creative and imaginatively subjective activity. This is the risk run by pornographers, even such thoughtful ones as Preston, and by all specifically gay writers: 'gaily' self-referring texts can serve to reinforce certain stereotypes of what gay men are and do and, furthermore, by promoting specificity as difference and thus assuming an oppositional position with regard to heterosexuality, they can render themselves unreadable to others.

If, as Jeanette Winterson asserts, 'Art must resist autobiography if it hopes to cross boundaries of class, culture [. . .] and [. . .] sexuality' (1995: 106), the best way to write the self in such a way that others may read it may thus well be to fictionalize the self and its practices – although without losing the seductive resistance and referential specificity accorded by an autobiographical element in the narration. As not only the nature but the very concept of identity is ever more closely and anxiously scrutinized, and as sexuality is increasingly debated in terms of its construction(s) through language (amongst other sign systems), the question of how fictions both make, and are made by, recognizable individual subjects comes to haunt both writing and reading. In the case of pornography, where what counts is actions (or, idiomatically, but perhaps more accurately, *action*), the signatory of the text, the 'author', is often a mere pseudonym, a virtual absence, no more than a cipher characterizing a particular mode of discourse. The pornographer has no identity, he has no past and no present, being rather part of what I have elsewhere called the Author-as-collective,[6] and as such holds no real interest for the reader. However, in the domain of 'real' or literary fiction, writers have sought to problematize their identity creatively and to make present for the reader (and perhaps also for themselves) their own presence-absence through new modes of writing that blur the boundaries between truth and fiction; between documentary, empirically verifiable fact, and imaginative leaps into invention. This has resulted, for instance, in what have been called the 'autofictions' of Guibert (who rewrites himself and his body in his many novels and quasi-autobiographical texts) and in the complexly pseudonymous early writings of Renaud Camus, who published *Échange*, the second novel of his 'Églogues' series, under the name Denis Duparc and who even 'co-authored' in 1978 the novel *Travers* with Tony Duparc, and then, in 1982, this time using his full name Jean-Renaud Camus, the novel *Été (Travers II)* with Denis Duvert; both Tony Duparc and Denis Duvert being pseudonyms for himself! This splitting of the writing subject results perhaps less from 'the will to abolish the self', as Christopher Robinson suggests (1995: 99), than from a desire to explore (and in a public way) the plurality of the author – both as individual and as position.

In *S/Z*, Barthes suggests that the process of interpretation, of reading, should not be a matter of ascribing meaning to a text but rather of understanding and appreciating 'what plural constitutes it' (1974: 5).[7] If it is now virtually axiomatic that the text is not only ambiguous, but actively polysemic and enticingly protean, and if in the past twenty-five years there has been a shift of cultural attention towards the reader and his/her co-creativity, it is hardly surprising that writers have engaged in a process of re-evaluation and redefinition. Gay writers have been particularly important in this process, precisely because their marginal position in society and in the canon allows them to see, say and do more tangentially, and thus perhaps more radically. Since they have to (dare to) speak the name of their own love, their desires, their sexuality (whereas heterosexuals can assume and live out theirs unquestioningly), and since they are exiled from the norm, gay writers are, paradoxically, particularly 'well-placed' to anatomize heterosexuality and its practices. Furthermore, they live in a world whose systems and structures are, if not inimical to them, at least inappropriate for them, and predicated on a variety of premisses and imperatives that are not theirs or, at least, not dominantly theirs. For instance, while some gay men and women may be, or may want to be, biological parents and/or fulfil parental functions, homosexuality by definition 'means renunciation of paternity or maternity' (Baruch and Serrano 1996: 173).

The reality of the lives of many gay men and women is that they live their difference in private but not in public. This means that their daily lives involve the experience of being both same and other (often simultaneously); they therefore (have to) inscribe difference into their ways of living – and of writing, although preferably without becoming invisible or allowing their difference to be erased. If pornography is aimed at a community or section of a community defined by its sharing of similar desires, literary fiction and, indeed, literary theory can serve as agents of solidarity; but they can do more than reinforce a (sense of) community – they can redefine socio-sexual practices and engender re-evaluations of identity.

However, one of the dangers of writing about gay writing, whether one is gay or not, is that one can all too easily become focused mainly on content. Not only does such a thematically based reading practice run the risk of maintaining in circulation over-simplified stereotypes (for example, the promiscuous homosexual or the lonely homosexual), but it can also serve to perpetuate suspect essentialisms. It can even run the greater risk of colluding with homophobia and reproducing those very repressive power effects that gay writing and reading should seek to dissolve. There is thus a genuine dilemma for the gay reader, who wants to see and 'bring out' gayness in a text, since, as D. A. Miller points out in his *Bringing out Roland Barthes* (1992): 'In a culture that without ever ceasing to proliferate homosexual meaning knows how to confine it to a kind of false unconscious, as well in collectivities as in individuals, there is hardly a procedure for bringing out this meaning that doesn't itself look or feel like just more police entrapment (p. 18).[8] For this reason, one might suggest that the gay writer should in a sense be both inside and outside his community as he writes, simultaneously saying and speaking about, ex-posing subjectively and exposing objectively, bringing (his own) marginality to the centre whilst nonetheless maintaining it as marginality. Although this might seem an over-theoretical programme for writing, in practice it can be achieved through an exploitation of fragmentation and the fusing (or even juxtaposing) of genres in order to create 'hybrid' texts that defy narrow classification.

In the context of the fragment, Barthes's responses as reader, writer and theorist are illuminating, for he repeatedly, albeit in different ways, points to how a fragmentary text can be – and can be perceived as – seductive and generative rather than fractured and so somehow damaged. Speaking as a reader, he has revealed that '. . . what I enjoy in a narrative is not directly its content or even its structure, but rather the abrasions I impose upon the fine surface: I read on, I skip, I look up, I dip in again' (1976: 11–12).[9] Furthermore, as a writer, he has a predilection for the creation of short texts, taking delight in capturing and manipulating many different types of idioms, sentences, quotations, turns of phrase, metaphors, etc. Interestingly, he defines this writerly practice in terms that inscribe the fragmentary in what can best be seen as an erotics of the text: 'When I try to produce this short writing, in fragments, I put myself in the situation of an author who will be cruised by the reader' (1975b: 231).[10] Here he is talking about his own theoretical and critical texts and using the term 'cruising' (*draguer*) as a marker of how he wants to inscribe into the acts of both writing and reading them the pleasure that he locates also in the writing and reading of fictions. In his view, if we read a sentence with pleasure, it is because the words were written in pleasure (although the writer may, of course, also have suffered before and during the writing). But does writing in pleasure guarantee that the reader will experience pleasure? His answer is firm but not uncomplex: 'Not at all. I must seek out this reader (must 'cruise' him) *without knowing where he is*. A site of bliss is then created' (1976: 4).[11]

Like many other modern writers and thinkers, Barthes had doubts about the authenticity of the journal form, and in 1979 he wrote a short text, 'Délibération', in which he mused on his own inability to keep a journal, arguing that the only possible justification for a diary would be its *literary* quality – which he defined in absolute terms (see 1995: 1005). However, soon afterwards, on 24 August 1979, he began to keep an intimate journal, one that charted the various forms his gay desire took over the next three weeks and that he apparently intended for publication. These fragments of an autobiography, entitled 'Soirées de Paris', were published with three other uncollected texts in his last book, the posthumous *Incidents* (1987), which is a testament to his commitment to both the erotic and the fragment. As Robert K. Martin (1993) puts it, his 'great achievement was to have written this text without any story, to have accepted discontinuity as a creative principle' (p. 295).

This belief in, and practice of, an intermingling, even an interdependence, of the erotic and the discontinuous may be found on a theoretical level also in what is probably the last text Barthes wrote: 'One Always Fails in Speaking of What One Loves', an unfinished text, written in March 1980 for a Stendhal conference in Milan and published in *Tel Quel*, where he hymns the 'amorous plural' that is Stendhal's Italy, and, significantly, compares the experience of it to cruising, which he sees as a kind of Stendhalian principle involving an implicit theory of *irregular discontinuity* (see 1989: 298; 1995: 1215). This principle is, in fact, as essentially Barthesian as it is Stendhalian, and informs his conception of friendship as much as it underpins his erotics. For him, friendship was a privileged relationship that was absolutely special and singular in both senses of the term; but, paradoxically, he saw no obstacle to having a multiplicity of such privileged relationships. What he wanted, he claims in his 'autobiographical biography', was a plurality of friends – but a plurality seen and loved one by one, separately but not sequentially or hierarchically (see 1975a: 65; 1977: 67).

In Barthes's thinking and in his discourse, lovers, friends and texts can thus all be cruised. In her recent book, *Sexuality and the Reading Encounter* (1996), Emma Wilson has suggested that in his work terms like 'cruise' (*draguer*) are 'potentially free from gender innuendo', affirming that his thematics of sexuality implicitly denies the distinctions between homosexual and heterosexual desire (pp. 10–11). Whilst recognizing the temptation to de-specify the sexual connotations of Barthes's terminology, I would nonetheless argue that in order to understand what cruising means in Barthes's work, and to understand how useful a model it can be for reading and writing (for straights as well as gays), one must recognize how, in Barthes's thinking, cruising emerges both from his own personal, unhappy lived experience as an unfulfilled lover and from the *doxa* that presents gay love as essentially transitory and multiple.

The term 'cruising' returns time and again in his works, so he was, understandably, asked to define it in 'Twenty Key Words for Roland Barthes' (1975b). His answer reveals how this crucial term for him is itself not stable, but finds its meaning in the very process of being articulated, rather than having a fixed *a priori* meaning:

> In talking about it, perhaps I'll arrive at a definition. [. . .] Cruising is the voyage of desire. The body is in a state of alert, on the lookout for its own desire. Furthermore, cruising implies a temporality that accentuates the notion of the meeting, the 'first time'. As if the first meeting was endowed with an extraordinary privilege: that of being withdrawn from all repetition. [. . .] Cruising is anti-natural, anti-repetition. Cruising is an act that repeats itself, but the content and meaning of this act are absolutely new each time (p. 231; translation modified).[12]

In a 1977 interview centring on *A Lover's Discourse* (1990 [1977]), Barthes contrasted the cruiser with the lover, who does not scatter himself through the world, remaining imprisoned with his image. However, if the lover is 'ascetic', static and imprisoned, the typical cruiser's lot is not necessarily any happier, since he cruises precisely to find *someone* to be in love with, and, in his desperate seeking, must inhabit a world that is frequently unattractive: 'In homosexual milieux, at any rate, where cruising is quite extensive, one can cruise for years at a time, often in an unavoidably sordid fashion, given the kinds of places one must frequent, with in fact the invincible idea that one will find someone with whom to be in love' (1985: 299).[13]

Barthes's concept of cruising is both personal and communal. It is also underpinned by a certain fatality and a certain nostalgia for a lost – or perhaps an imaginary – plenitude and fusion with the other. In this respect, his view of cruising is close to Kristeva's belief that homosexual desire is narcissistic and loveless, because the desiring homosexual does not have a proper (ideal) love object who is truly other. According to her, 'beneath homosexual libido [. . .] the chasm of narcissistic emptiness spreads out' (*Tales of Love* (1987), p. 43).

Kristeva clearly views narcissism negatively, and all too often homosexuality has been described as essentially narcissistic and therefore psychically and socially reprehensible, since the desiring subject seeks only an image of himself. However, terms like narcissism and cruising can always be rethought and recoded, and in *Un homme, un homme*, Hugo Marsan describes the erotic life of a modern Parisian homosexual as one continuous party or *fête*, defining it as 'plural and multiplied narcissism' (1983: 97). This appropriation and rehabilitation of narcissism is, of course, of its time (Marsan was writing in 1983, and therefore before AIDS had become an epidemic in France); but it has value as a marker of how gay men can and must react to the forces and voices of oppression – not by denying any part of their nature that is condemned by society nor by trying to effect a simple reversal of the discourses of power, but by rethinking their being and their behaviour in new and positive ways.

Narcissism is, of course, love of the self, but it is not necessarily negative, as Béla Grunberger has controversially but persuasively argued (in his *Narcissism: Psychoanalytic Essays* (1979) and *New Essays on Narcissism* (1988)). Indeed, there is always narcissism in the psychic life of the individual, since one needs to love oneself and to accord oneself value, even perhaps excessive value, in order to survive both individually and in society. Delusion this may be, but it is also an essential reality – and a form of normality. In his thinking on the pathology of narcissism, the American analyst, Otto

Kernberg, conceives of what he speaks of as 'normal narcissism', stating that from a clinical viewpoint, 'narcissism is the regulation of self-esteem' (Baruch and Serrano 1996: 165). For Kernberg, normal self-esteem includes not only the sense of an integrated self but also 'normal gratifying self-regard, pleasure in one's relationships and activities' (ibid.). Rather than denying the narcissism and the episodicity of their erotic lives, gay men can, and should perhaps, strive to rewrite their self-images, for instance, seeing the multiple encounters of cruising not as a fragmentation and shattering of desire, but (potentially, at least) as serial plenitude, whilst also not fearing to inscribe the absences and gaps of their lives into a practice of discourse and desire.

In many ways, this is what Michel Foucault advises with regard to the (gay) self in a 1981 interview with the journal *Gai Pied* in which he distinguishes between (his own conceptions of) desire and pleasure, and argues that we must invent models and structures of desire that are different from both the traditional heterosexual model of the (permanently together) loving couple and the almost equally traditional homosexual model of the (briefly together) sexual couple: 'What we must endeavour to do, it seems to me, is not so much liberate our desires, but make ourselves infinitely open to pleasures. We must continually escape from those two stock notions of the chance encounter and the loving fusion of two beings.'[14] More recently, Robert K. Martin has creatively rethought the implications of the narcissism in and of homosexuality, starting from the premiss that homosexuality is structured on the (at least potential) absence of the creation of an other who will always be the object and never the subject of desire. This absence, he suggests, can actually be enabling, and can 'offer the possibility of creating a language and politics of mutuality' (1993: 284). Furthermore, this can lead to a liberation from the psychoanalytically centred, 'hydraulic' theory of sexuality that over-privileges sublimation, and so enable the homosexual to develop freely as a subject and 'to see his/her body as a site of pleasure, to refuse sublimation' (p. 291).[15] In other words, mutuality and self-pleasuring can be not only permitted but maintained, and love through identification can be recognized and accepted as another mode of yearning to be complete.

Whereas Barthes's and Foucault's inscriptions of pleasure into debates about sex and text have radically altered the ways in which we theorize (and live) them, the anti-psychoanalytic examination of the construction and functioning of desire in a capitalist society by Deleuze and Guattari has had a major influence on French gay thinking, largely as a result of Guy Hocquenghem's *Homosexual Desire* (1972), which has its theoretical (and much of its metaphorical) base in their *Anti-Oedipus* (1984 [1972]). Deleuze and Guattari insist that desire should not be seen or defined as the lack of some real object of desire; rather, they see desire in 'industrial' terms and individual subjects as desiring machines, which are constantly 'coupling' with each other, plugging into and unplugging from parts of other machines in a universal fragmentation of desire. In *Homosexual Desire*, Hocquenghem seizes on this conceptual and metaphorical system, arguing that the mechanical scattering of the homosexual pick-up machine corresponds to the mode of existence of desire itself. He recognizes that homosexual desire is in essence no different from heterosexual desire, although he is also eager to praise homosexual promiscuity, since, when it is free from guilt, it offers a model of anti-capitalist, revolutionary potential – even though it can be experienced as unhappy and lonely and its mechanical scattering translated as absence and substitution. For Hocquenghem, the key specificity of homosexual desire is that to some extent it reveals the process of the self-production of desire, for which some temporality must be constructed. However, this specificity is of a revelatory rather than an exclusive or exclusionary nature, since it 'is in fact a desire for pleasure whatever the system, and not merely inside or outside the system' (1972: 114). Thus, the everyday cruising that is a defining characteristic of modern Western male homosexuality becomes (perceived as) both personal and public, both banal and political, both trivially experiential and metaphysical.[16]

Once one has accepted that desire is not centred or grounded in the 'self', conceived of as a discrete individual subjectivity, desire may be regarded as a process, a constant flow – or series of eddyings and flowings. As Deleuze says in a recent text: 'There is no subject of desire, any more than there is an object. There is no subject of enunciation. Only the flows are the objectivity of desire itself. Desire is the system of meaningless [*a-signifiants*] signs with which flows of the unconscious are produced in a social field' (Deleuze and Parnet 1996: 96–7).[17] Deleuze's concept of desire as a system of flowing, societally produced signs is philosophically and psycho-socially crucial, if challenging, and may perhaps be creatively linked to his thinking on the labyrinth as a *multifold* (much-folded) series of overlappings, since the labyrinth is, in many ways, the pattern of the cruiser's steps as he walks up and down, around and around, ceaselessly and *aimlessly* in search of a trick – that is to say, in a state of desire.[18]

While Deleuzian theories of desire are sexually specific, they usefully illuminate gay behaviour, and are themselves illuminated by the very real vagaries of it. Cruising is essentially about desire, a mode of desire – and of a desire that in one sense is unfocused. In cruising, it is the act rather than the individual object of desire that is important. This act is necessarily and compulsively repeated, and what is sought is simply an encounter, a fleeting encounter where pleasure may be had (often anonymously), rather than an encounter *with* someone, a meeting with an individual who could have an identity and therefore become an Other. In this respect, cruising is radically different from flirting, which is playful rather than compulsive (and, furthermore, is not necessarily sexual). Also, unlike cruising, flirting has in all its forms a teleology of the Other – and a teleology of genuine coincidence, even if not always of permanent togetherness.[19]

In his consideration of what he calls Barthes's 'utopian eroticism', which is, of course, concerned with text as much as with sex, Kevin Kopelson argues that flirtation is a better figure for it than either cruising or the trick, firstly, because flirtation 'nearly escapes stereotypology', and secondly, because 'flirtation is also fun' – unlike Barthesian cruising, which he views as sad and desolate (1994: 148). Furthermore, he argues that 'relatively few people can identify with a cruisy and tricky utopian eroticism, but nearly everyone – women, men, gays, and straights – could identify with a flirtatious one' (p. 149). Now, a Deleuzian or Hocquenghemian response would be that the nature of desire means that in fact everyone, irrespective of their sexuality, cruises or is, at least, bound up in a mechanics of cruising (although it is undoubtedly true that socio-political forces often tend to repress public expressions of such desire). However, it would seem useful also to recognize and learn from gay cruising as a practice with specificity.

In his gay travel book *Le gay voyage* (1980), Hocquenghem reveals that he has no sense of the uniqueness of cities but only an awareness of their gay quarters: for him, travelling from one city to another means in effect moving about within one vast gay quarter, where stations and airports are merely minor staging posts in his meanderings – which take place especially at night. Describing the urban life of gay men (or 'faggots', as he says, using the reverse discourse of an out-gay man), he writes: '. . . faggots live a great deal at night, and they are constantly walking. Tireless scourers of sleeping cities, they can find their pleasure only after interminable explorations, after sinuous and mysterious comings and goings.'[20] Gay men are defined by their constant cruising, by their deliberate, active and usually mobile search for sexual partners in a public setting. Cruising is a way of bypassing the social convention whereby there has to be a 'proper introduction' or some other mediation by a third party when one is seeking an intimate encounter with a stranger, and it is thus fundamentally anti-social. There is a paradox in cruising: it occurs in a public arena, yet it involves intimate sexual contact, normally banished to the privacy of closed doors and locked rooms. Furthermore, while it revolves around sexual intimacy, it refuses the social theology of the couple, preferring serial or multiple couplings. In this respect, again, it is anti-social: 'Thus homosexual desire exists only in the group, yet at the same time is banished from society' (Hocquenghem 1993: 112).[21]

In cruising, the searcher watches out for potential partners, and for signs of interest from others, while displaying a choice of signs (body language, gesture, clothing, even systematic colour and key codes that may be regarded as a social semiotics) to indicate that he is on the lookout. The colour code of bandanas worn in the back-pocket is one instance of how semiotic codes are inscribed into the activity of cruising, in that this code is highly specific, allocating a different colour to different practices. However, while this code is so complicated and so colour- or shade-specific as to be virtually unworkable, the colours function essentially as markers within a code, as signs that certain practices exist and are shared, desired – and permissible.

One of the essential features of cruising is the complicity that is at the very heart of its ethos and that also informs every moment of its enactment: 'If the object of interest does not recognize that he is an object of interest, then he is, in fact, uninteresting. He is not the object which the sign is hailing' (Creech 1993: 94–5). In other words, while cruising is certainly a mode of mechanical scattering, of non-focused (one might say, *generic*) desire, it also includes – serially – moments of movement towards another. These moments are intense, but their intensity comes not only – indeed, perhaps not principally – from the recognition of the other as other and as the ideal love (or desired) object, but rather from the excited awareness that one is participating in a shared system. Another major difference between heterosexual flirting and gay cruising is that cruising is traditionally more systematic, because the searcher is taking serious risks in his cruising: assault by a straight man who resents the sexual approach, queer bashing, entrapment by plain-clothes police, etc. For this reason, gay cruisers take precautions and master cruising skills in order not just to succeed, but to survive. As a consequence of the development of their skills in covert cruising, the myth has arisen that gay men have a sixth sense and can immediately recognize another gay man. This myth is, alas, fostered by some gay men in the misguided hope that this will strengthen the sense of a gay community, but it is undoubtedly true that cruising men have elaborated a complex code of signals that enables them to be private in public.

Secrecy has long been an integral part of gay life in the modern West, and there is a widespread presumption that every gay person will keep all other gay people's identities secret from the public. This is what Richard D. Mohr calls 'The Secret' in his study of the implications of the outing controversy, and he goes so far as to assert that '. . . [t]he Secret is *the* social convention that most centrally defines the [gay] community' (p. 29). Now, if secrecy serves to combine and to define a potentially disparate and threatened gay community, it is not surprising that literary expressions of gayness have tended also to operate through modes of (more or less veiled) secrecy, whereby covert signals, such as references to other gay writers, texts or icons, etc., are smilingly given to gay readers on the assumption that straight readers will miss them. In this sense, it is true, as James Creech puts it, that 'much of the history of early homosexual literature [. . .] is in all likelihood the history of the wink' (1993: 96). However, the wink that is an intertextual allusion or an in-joke can perhaps serve to create a community of readers who are not so much *essentialized* as gay, but, rather, *constructed* as textual cruisers (and objects of textual cruising).

The paradox of 'The Secret' is, of course, that to maintain gayness as secret is to deny its true social viability as an autonomous and interactive grouping – and to keep gayness largely invisible can lead to presuppositions, even within the gay community, that it is worthless or even reprehensible. We know that in Western society, women have long been accustomed and indeed trained to be objects of male desire and of the male gaze, and to see themselves as such. Defined by men (and in patriarchal terms and contexts), women have been positioned as the Other, and consequently have been deprived of true subjectivity and subject position, with the result that they have been estranged from themselves. Now, while I would certainly not dispute the validity and force of this men/women binarism, it seems to me important also to recognize that gay men are in a state of problematic sameness and alterity with regard to 'men', i.e. the heterosexual men of patriarchy, in that they have been positioned not as *the* Other as women have been, but certainly as *an* Other – and as a dangerous Other within.

It is largely because of gay men's interstitial status that gay literature initially operated through the wink, managing to present and maintain itself as literature by situating its content between secrecy and visibility, and by operating (through) a series of multilayered codes. The recent trend in France towards saying sex directly, towards 'telling it like it is', has resulted in a new genre: the quasi-autobiographical, but non-confessional, cruising journal. In such journals, a directness about sexual acts takes the form of a simplicity of discourse that is nonetheless seductively, if problematically, literary, as the physical meanderings of cruising that are recounted are translated into a textual form that wanders, seeming to lack both narrative purpose and formal consistency. The most celebrated of these is Renaud Camus's *Tricks* (1988),[22] which was 'canonized' by the preface Barthes wrote for it, which not only praises the simplicity of its speaking of homosexuality, but suggests that Camus's discourse initiates an ethic of dialogue (see Barthes 1995: 294; Camus 1988: 17). The apparent simplicity of *Tricks* can, however, lead to misconceptions. Lawrence Schehr, for instance, writes: 'There is no apology, nor is there any titillation. These are simple stories simply told. [. . .] Never disguising its own comfortable amorality, *Tricks* is a text pleased with itself' (1995b: 129–30). This makes it seem smug and self-satisfied; yet the very textual simplicity of *Tricks* is what makes it such a complex and interesting text, for *absence* pervades its textual and philosophical fabric, haunting even the author's attempts at defining either his own purpose or the text's function. He can affirm confidently that his book is *not* a pornographic book, *not* an erotic book, *not* a scientific book, *not* a sociological document; but when he comes to say what it is, he can only say that it '*attempts* to utter sexuality, in this case, homosexuality' (Camus 1996: xi; my emphasis).[23] Furthermore, in a note added to the 1988 edition (but not included in the English translation), he reveals that, for him, *Tricks* articulates only one part of his being-as-author, and that he wanted to publish at the same time as the definitive version another text, *Élégies pour quelques-uns*, which is 'the companion to it [*Tricks*], its crosscheck in some ways, thin since it is thick, discursive since it makes no comment, lyrical since it is impassive, sentimental since it speaks only of bodies and gestures'.[24]

Camus's voice is multiple and self-multiplying, its authorial unity residing in its very fragmentation, duplication and duplicity. He even interrupts his narrations to cast doubt on their accuracy (though not on their cruisy authenticity), as in the note of 29 November 1978 that he inserts parenthetically into the Walter Irving episode of 29 June 1978 in order to explain that his memories are somewhat vague. He thus casts himself as reader as well as writer, and so the reader, who has been cruised by the text and become a trick, will partially forget, just as Walter has been forgotten, and will 'write' his own *récits* in response to being tricked, to being cruised as well as duped. In other words, the reader will enter into a speculation on identity and subjectivity that is not described in *Tricks* but that is undoubtedly performed by it.

Although it is not my purpose here to offer a full taxonomic definition of the cruising journal, I would suggest that it can usefully be seen as pertaining to what Ross Chambers calls 'loiterature': 'Loiterature is a genre which, in opposition to dominant forms of narrative, relies on techniques of digression, interruption, deferral and episodicity [. . .] to make observations of modern life that are unsystematic, even disordered, and are usually oriented toward the everyday, the ordinary and the trivial (what is called "*flâneur* realism")' (1993: 207). For Chambers, loiterature is a mode of marginal(ized) literature in which the writer/narrator is someone who in effect performs the failure of writing 'not for its pathos, but as an oppositional comment on the ambitious pretensions of aesthetic sublimity, and on the blindness, rigidity and exclusionary formalism of disciplined and systematic modes of knowledge' (p. 208). In Camus's *Tricks*, the absence of certainty, the ambivalence of repetition, and the non-focused, diffuse nature of his desire (his tricks by no means all correspond to a particular physical or mental type, although they all do afford him some passing pleasure) are actually what give the book its sense and its meaning. Unlike a pornographic text, *Tricks* cannot be read partially, since no episode is paradigmatic of the others; rather, the book finds its meaning when it is read as a *whole* text, when all forty-five or forty-six episodes are seen as a mobile, interactive and kaleidoscopic unity rather than as a catalogue of 'finished' episodes that signify only serially.[25]

A more recent example of the cruising genre is Loïc Chotard's *Tiers Monde* (1994), which superficially takes the form of a novel (and is defined as such on the cover and title-page), but which is, in fact, closely based on the personal experiences of the author. In a final 'Note' after the end of the main text, Chotard reveals that each of the sequences is based on experiences he shared with the thirty-two named men, who are named – belatedly – as the dedicatees of the novel (p. 247). The real is thus included, albeit paratextually, in the novel, and the reader must rethink his relationship with a text that has cruised him for 245 pages, but is revealed to be written for someone else, for several other named people, both alive and dead.

Tiers Monde tells the story of Gérard, a young man who arrives in Paris and learns nothing except how to cruise successfully. He does not even particularly enjoy his cruising, since he has no real idea of what constitutes pleasure, yet he is driven on (aimlessly) by the fact that his only gift is to make others desire him, and, for him, desire is something that others experience and that he merely spectates upon. The novel repeatedly proclaims its own failure or inadequacy: 'There is no story of Gérard, no complex plot and no *coup de théâtre* either. [. . .] It is simply the life Gérard leads, and there's nothing to say about it, about this succession of scenes, of words, in streets, in bedrooms. But it is the life Gérard leads, with no dramas, full of dramas, what does it matter . . .'.[26]

This novel fascinates me, because it presents an aimless cruiser, a sort of 1980s *flâneur* who is constantly loitering *without* intent in the arcades of Paris; it thereby engages the reader in a speculation on capitalist ideologies as models for reading as well as working and shopping. Furthermore, like Camus's *Tricks*, this is a text that is (and says that it is) forgetful and that substitutes for narrative linearity a kaleidoscopic whirl of almost random camera-shots. The reader is drawn into this labyrinth and coaxed into speculating. For instance, an hour or two after a session with Didier, one of the men he has picked up and with whom he fleetingly and partially lives out sexual fantasies, Gérard cannot remember whether Didier penetrated him or not. Characteristic of the way in which gay desire is figured in the novel as always the affair of an (absent) other, this episode challenges the reader to ask why we want to know what happened. Or do we want to know? And if not, why on earth not? Should a story not hold our interest and excite our curiosity?

In another example of the genre, Édouard Malvande's *Déballage* (Outpouring) (1985), we find again (and again in a reverse discourse) an expression of the worthlessness of the cruising journal as an enterprise, literary or otherwise: 'It is because I know now that faggots have no story, no history, that this book has nothing to tell. Or at least I have given it the appearance of telling nothing at all. No chronology, no thread of continuity, no relationship with contemporary history.'[27] Malvande's many encounters range from the tender and intimate to the violent and distasteful, and yet each episode is written in the same apparently neutral tone, just as Camus and Chotard refrain from changing tone or register even when describing radically different emotions and situations. Although he undermines his text by labelling his narrations as 'all this sad, pathetic rubbish'[28] when he shows some pages to his friends, the journal is legitimated, like the others, not only by the fact that the author lived the experiences he recounts but also by a *text*: in his preface, the writer and thinker Georges Lapassade insists on the poetic quality of the work and points to the generic betweenness of *Déballage*, which is neither poem nor novel nor autobiography (pp. 12–13).

Cruising journals escape – indeed refuse – easy categorization, because they must necessarily be in-between texts: between fiction and fact, between novel and autobiography, between fantasy and social document. They tell the same story time and again, yet it is actually never quite the same story, never quite the same experience (for reader as for cruiser), as one of Malvande's friends notes: 'Damien is amazed that it's always the same old thing and never the same old thing.'[29] Repetition is two-faced: it is positive and negative, denoting both hopeful belief in a quest and impotent failure, since one is unable to escape from a rut that leads nowhere.

The cruising journal is a peculiarly interesting modern genre because it says sex, *homosexual* sex, openly, directly and personally. It ex-poses the workings of pleasure and desire, and it makes the private (go) public, makes the personal (become) communal. However, it is usually inhabited by uncertainty and insecurity, and its directness about sex is expressed in a narration that meanders about in labyrinthine loops, as the text looks for its purpose as well as its reader – who, if s/he reads properly, will be cruised *and* tricked by the text. Barthes sees the trick as a metaphor for many adventures that are not (only) sexual, because it is 'a way of not getting stuck in desire, though without evading it; all in all, a kind of wisdom' (1995: 295).[30] The reader of a cruising journal is both active and passive, cruises the text and is cruised by it: above all, the text reveals through its complex, unfinishable unfoldings that what is important is the *process* of reading, rather than any locatable or inventable goal. We undoubtedly need constantly to redefine ourselves, our identities and our sexualities. We need also constantly to reformulate our reading practices and our place within reading as a practice and as a politics of desire. We need to keep cruising . . .

Notes

1. 'Un reportage sur l'homosexualité reste une gageure. "L'homosexualité" n'est qu'un mot à usage compromis' (Marsan 1983: 13). Unless otherwise indicated, all translations are my own.
2. While Sade's text (1795) is usually described as a philosophical dialogue, it is a sort of guide to being a perfect libertine and is essentially erotological, analysing in detail both sexual practices and emotional passions. Dolmancé, the thirty-year-old who is the main initiator into debauchery of the young Eugénie, is above all a lover of sodomy, as both the active and the passive partner.
3. Auffret makes a similar plea, arguing from a philosophical and psycho-analytical perspective (Marsan 1983: 152).
4. See, for instance, Preston's story 'Authenticity' and his justification of it in *I Once had a Master* (1984: 56–68 and 119); see also Preston's essay 'The Importance of Telling our Stories' (1992).
5. 'Le plaisir de la représentation n'est pas lié à son objet: la pornographie n'est pas *sûre*' (1973: 88).
6. See Worton (1994), 'You know what I mean?'.
7. 'de quel pluriel il est fait' (*S/Z*, p. 11).
8. David Halperin expresses a similar point about the dangers inherent in specifying the gay content of a text in a letter to James Creech (Creech 1993: 183–4).
9. 'Ce que je goûte dans un récit, ce n'est [. . .] pas directement son contenu ni même sa structure, mais plutôt les éraflures que j'impose à la belle enveloppe: je cours, je saute, je lève la tête, je replonge' (1973: 22).

10. 'Quand j'essaie de produire cette écriture courte, par fragments, je me mets dans la situation d'un auteur que le lecteur va draguer' (1995: 333).
11. 'Nullement. Ce lecteur, il faut que je le cherche (que je le "drague"), sans savoir où il est. Un espace de jouissance est alors créé' (1973: 11).
12. 'En en parlant, j'arriverai peut-être à le définir [. . .] La drague, c'est le voyage du désir. C'est le corps qui est en état d'alerte, de recherche par rapport à son propre désir. Et puis, la drague implique une temporalité qui met l'accent sur la rencontre, sur la "première fois". Comme si la première rencontre possédait un privilège inouï: celui d'être retiré de toute répétition [. . .] La drague, c'est l'antinaturel, l'antirépétition. L'acte de draguer est un acte qui se répète, mais son contenu est une primeur absolue' (1995: 333).
13. 'Dans les milieux homosexuels, en tout cas, où la drague est très développée, on peut très bien draguer des années entières, souvent d'une façon inévitablement sordide, par les lieux mêmes que cela oblige à fréquenter, avec en fait l'idée invincible qu'on va trouver de qui être amoureux' (1995: 786).
14. 'Ce à quoi nous devons travailler, me semble-t-il, ce n'est pas tellement à libérer nos désirs, mais à nous rendre nous-mêmes infiniment susceptibles de plaisirs. Il faut et il faut faire échapper aux deux formules toutes faites de la pure rencontre et de la fusion amoureuse des identités' (1994: 165).
15. In *Homosexual Desire*, Hocquenghem had already launched a comprehensive attack on sublimation.
16. 'Le désir homosexuel serait plutôt de l'ordre d'un désir de jouir quel que soit le système, et non simplement dans ou hors du système' (1972: 80).
17. For an analogous argument on the specific level of the homosexual text, see Martin 1993: 293.
18. I have begun the study of how labyrinthine patternings may be seen and used in readings of gay texts in 'Labyrinths of Desire'.
19. In her recent book on Simone de Beauvoir, where she considers how Sartre would seem to confuse flirting with seduction, Toril Moi offers a radically different concept to the one I advance, stating that 'flirtation is not a goal-oriented activity [. . .] flirtation is a game from which one can always escape without danger' (1994: 129). Moi's concept of flirtation is, of course, to be seen in the context of her reading of Sartre, Beauvoir and, more generally, patriarchy, and her notion of its being non-goal-oriented is undoubtedly appealing. However, I would argue that while there may not be a goal in the sense of an object of desire

who is to be 'hooked', there is nonetheless always the desire to engage with an Other, albeit fleetingly, and that this constitutes a very real 'goal' – that of being-present-to-an-Other.

20. '[. . .] les pédés vivent beaucoup la nuit, et marchent sans arrêt. Infatigables arpenteurs des cités endormies, ils ne peuvent prendre leur plaisir qu'au terme d'explorations interminables, de va-et-vient souples et mystérieux' (1980: 10).
21. 'Ainsi le désir homosexuel à la fois n'existe qu'en groupe, et en même temps est interdit de société' (1972: 77).
22. It is highly regrettable that the English translation of *Tricks* is not a translation of the entire definitive version published by P.O.L. in 1988, but omits 21 of Camus's 45 chapters – and also the various liminal notes and prefaces to various editions that Camus includes in the 1988 version. These omissions result in the text's seeming to be more a titillating narration of fleeting sexual encounters than a literary text open to, and indeed demanding of, the active, speculative intervention of the reader.
23. See Camus's 'Note liminaire à la première édition française', where he states: 'Ce livre essaie de dire le sex, en l'occurrence *l'homosexe*' (1988: 19).
24. 'Le livre compagnon de celui-ci, sa contre-épreuve en quelque sorte, mince puisqu'il est épais, discursif puisqu'il ne commente pas, lyrique puisqu'il est impassible, sentimental puisqu'il ne parle que des corps et des gestes' ('Note à la troisième édition française', 1988: 25).
25. Camus problematizes his text even in his division of it into chapters, in that 'Dominique and Alain' figures as a plural chapter in the French version (XXX and XXXI), whereas it is unitized and singularized in the English version (XV).
26. 'Il n'y a pas d'histoire de Gérard, pas d'intrigue ni de coup de théâtre [. . .] C'est la vie de Gérard, et il n'y a rien à en dire, cette succession de scènes, de paroles, dans les rues, dans les chambres. Mais c'est la vie de Gérard, sans histoires, pleine d'histoires, qu'importe . . .' (Chotard 1994: 40–1). For further statements expressing similar dissatisfaction with the novel and the value of writing, see pp. 66–7, p. 75, p. 119).
27. 'C'est parce que je sais maintenant que les pédés n'ont pas d'histoire que ce livre ne raconte rien. Du moins lui ai-je donné toutes les apparences de ne rien raconter du tout. Pas de chronologie, pas de fil continu, pas de rapport avec l'histoire contemporaine' (Malvande 1985, back-page blurb).
28. Malvande 1985: 231. Like many other gay writers, Malvande is here

playing with reader, deprecating his life and work in order to seduce the reader into *re*-reading.

29. 'Damien s'émerveille que ce soit toujours la même chose et jamais la même chose . . .' (Malvande 1985: 232).
30. 'Une façon de ne pas s'empoisser dans le désir, sans cependant l'esquiver: une sagesse, en somme' (Camus 1988: 18).

– 2 –

Reconsidering 'Gay': Hocquenghem, Identity Politics and the Baroque

Bill Marshall

Introduction: Conflicting Concepts of Radicalism?

In the recent first issue of a new British radical intellectual journal called *Soundings*, an article on gay lifestyle and consumerism presented some of the insights and dilemmas surrounding identity politics and contemporary society. Arguing that 'the pink pound' and its attendant hedonism provide a positive visibility within the development of a gay politics, Simon Edge considered 'consumerism not as something antithetical to the achievement of lesbian and gay political gains, but as an integral part of the very process through which these gains are slowly but surely being made,'[1] this despite obvious limitations such as the class- and gender-specific characteristics (alluded to in parentheses) of this delightfully conspicuous consumption.

Edge's piece mirrors the context of *Soundings* itself. Seeking to promote a 'new left' discourse without falling back into the totalizations of the socialist tradition, both the journal and the article settle some accounts, for example, with the 'Trots', take on board the 'rightward' trend or simply transformation of political discourses over the past twenty years, and embrace the new opportunities for pluralism, pleasure and participation, while remaining uncertain about the way ahead. Thus Edge's acceptance of the triumph of consumerism over an older, more puritanical gay militancy contradictorily combines a 1970s-style prioritizing of 'coming out' and identity-assertion with a 1990s 'fun' agenda that is happy to equate that true 'self' with a certain range of lifestyle options and appearances. A similar contradiction lurks behind the apparent paradox he points out: 'Market orientation and depoliticization are what we have come to expect in the post-Thatcher years. What *is* surprising is that the gay cause seems to be doing so well out of it'.[2] The response to which may be: are 'gay' and 'radical' therefore inevitably coterminous?

The work of Guy Hocquenghem (1946–88) is fundamental to these debates. The most prominent member of France's first modern gay political movement, the FHAR (*Front homosexuel d'action révolutionnaire*), founded in 1971, he followed an intellectual and political itinerary that would lead him to reject both the certainties of an early 1970s politics founded on fixed and complete identities, and the consensual, consumerist culture of appearances that characterized the 1980s. Thus, for example, he entitled a 1985 article 'Where is homosexuality at in 1985? Or why I do not want to be a "gay writer"',[3] arguing that, in literature as elsewhere, the 'homosexual' had become a marketing category, and asserting that he himself had no ambitions to celebrate the mediocrity of the status quo, of a 'real' that includes sexual identity as finished and ghettoized.[4] The case of Hocquenghem reminds us not only of the contingency of cultural categories (such as 'gay identity' or 'gay lifestyle') in terms of national traditions, but also of the emergence and development of modernity and post-modernity. The French republican tradition since 1789 has prioritized the relationship between the individual and the State, with a fairly weak civil society mediating the two, whereas the American context, as well as favouring liberal individualism and self-invention, has promoted a politics of ethnic voting blocks and interest groups, the new gay politics of 1969 and after having been made possible by the experience of the black civil rights movement earlier in the decade. The FHAR initially emerged in the early 1970s as a challenging offshoot of the post-68 revolutionary left, and not as a mere promoter of the extension of 'rights'. But the outcome of May 1968 can eventually be tracked forward to the Socialist hegemony in France in the 1980s, with its achievements (for example, the important gain of an equal age of consent in 1982) and its disillusionments (the consensus won for discourses of capitalism, competitiveness, and national security). Always wary of a 'gay Jacobinism'[5] operative within the logic of 1789, Hocquenghem was questioning at an early point in the 1970s, and eventually in terms owing much to Foucault's analysis in the first volume of his *History of Sexuality* (1976), the re-regulation of sex that was emerging.

The rejection of the 'repressive hypothesis' (in which 'sex' and its categories are seen as beyond, rather than as the creation of, historical discourses) made it impossible to see 'gay liberation' as 'a gradual and invincible process founded on the progressive bringing to light of a pre-existing and irrepressible reality'.[6] Liberation, in other words, cannot be conceptualized as a straightforward process of more freedom and less repression, being rather a shifting, two-way street; an operation whereby discourses in which sexual norms are constructed emerge and are replaced. Gay liberation is, moreover, as Hocquenghem points out in *La Dérive homosexuelle* (Homosexual Drift) of 1977, the source of new orthodoxies (new *substances*):

> As I drifted in one direction, trying to connect with the ocean of the unformulated, exploring the scarcely specific margins of homosexualities, Homosexuality, now acknowledged, was moving in the other: organizing, rationalizing, not only appropriated but moreover founding new values and why not new empires. Becoming the herald of new repressions, demanding the punishment of gay-bashing hooligans and the integration of homosexuals into the American army and police. Becoming substance, acquiring a body and a culture.[7]

Additionally, this process represents yet another variation in that epistemology of sex (in the sense of the way the culture grounds its knowledge) associated by Foucault with modernity, when the invention of the 'homosexual' as *species* arrived in the nineteenth century to replace the heterogeneity of *acts* of 'sodomy'.[8] Both Foucault and Hocquenghem are acutely aware of the imbrication of modernity with our categories of thought (and not only with those pertaining to sex), and seek in different ways to surpass the Enlightenment legacy of instrumental reason, totalizing thought, and Cartesian identity.

Beyond Foucault's opposition between same-sex *acts* and a (full) homosexual or gay *identity*, further dilemmas born out of the post-68 era turn on the implications of May 1968 and the sexual political movements that have since evolved: that is, the unfettered commodification of life; the cult of appearances or *le look*; the neutralization of a dissent that would call into question the whole system. The article by Simon Edge, for example, risks validating and even celebrating appearances in the name of visibility. Hocquenghem, so concerned to preserve dissent and a freedom of becoming, while at the same time perturbed to see the fruits of his generation's activity producing a caricature of civilized life, was radically disenchanted with the orthodoxies of contemporary society. From what position, however, is it possible to question contemporary society and offer ways forward? The view of the late Frankfurt School, partly articulated in another 'gay liberation' text, Mario Mieli's *Homosexuality and Liberation* of 1977, relies on notions of an authentic critical consciousness that is repressed and distorted by consumerism, and thus on a form of negative aesthetics that awaits its emergence in a communist future. As a consequence, this view faces contemporary life rather undialectically. As far as theories of 'post-modernism' are concerned, while their emphasis on the undermining of binary oppositions structured by hierarchy and power, for example between high and low culture, or in discourses of race and gender, may productively set free all sorts of local pluralities and pleasures, they often lack a critical negativity and fall into complicity with the given fluidities of consumer capitalism.

I

A Way Out of the Impasse: The Baroque

It is at this juncture that the category of the baroque comes to the aid not only of Hocquenghem, but also of others who have sought to think their way out of these current theoretical impasses. This may seem surprising. Not only does the term as it is commonly received refer to a period and style – the seventeenth and eighteenth centuries – that is safely packed away in the annals of art history, but it is also associated with the Counter-Reformation and absolutism, with gaudy spectacle as part of a propagandist and manipulative mass project. However, this caricatured view provides clues as to the term's contemporary relevance to issues of periodization, crisis, and visibility. The baroque runs counter to the Weberian logic of modern development from the Renaissance through Protestantism, capitalism, the Enlightenment and the Industrial Revolution. Faced with the challenge to theological reason, it represents, as we shall see in Leibniz, a last attempt to deal with divergence, but it does so in a perpetual state of instability and precariousness. Its emphasis, in this context, on spectacle, visibility, and artificiality may have much to say to those in the late twentieth century who, bereft of a grounding in founding principles, seek to understand the phenomena of consumerism and the proliferation of signifiers, as well as explore different ways of looking. In addition, it is clear even from standard art histories that the distinction between the baroque and the classical has profound implications for theories of being and the self. Originally a term used by jewellers in the Iberian peninsula to denote an irregular pearl, 'baroque' means 'imperfect' or 'incomplete':

> Classical compositions are simple and clear, each constituent part retaining its independence; they have a static quality and are enclosed within boundaries. The Baroque artist, in contrast, longs to enter into the multiplicity of phenomena, into the flux of things in their perpetual becoming – his [*sic*] compositions are dynamic and open and tend to expand outside their boundaries; the forms that go to make them are associated in a single organic action and cannot be isolated from each other. The Baroque artist's instinct for escape drives him to prefer 'forms that take flight' to those that are static and dense; his liking for pathos

> leads him to depict sufferings and feelings, life and death at their extremes of violence, while the Classical artist aspires to show the human figure in the full possession of his powers.[9]

The rational tradition since Descartes has stressed precisely 'possession' and 'powers' in the duality between mind and body, between subjects capable of action and objects that are acted upon. The manifestations of that tradition can be traced in numerous discourses predicated on identity, on the distinction between 'the same-as' and 'different-from'.

II

The Baroque and Identity: Deleuze/Leibniz/Hocquenghem

How, then, have modern and contemporary thinkers engaged with the baroque? A first point of reference for any response to this question must be Gilles Deleuze's influential elaboration of baroque thought, *Le Pli: Leibniz et le baroque* (1988) (*The Fold: Leibniz and the Baroque*). This text occupies a logical position within the totality of Deleuze's writing, which is not only associated with a philosophy of becoming rather than being, and with a profound critique of Cartesianism and its Hegelian developments, but has also informed Hocquenghem's conceptions of homosexuality. The latter's seminal *Homosexual Desire*, published in France in 1972, draws heavily on Deleuze and Guattari's *Anti-Oedipus* of the same year, in which desire is seen in terms of production, connections and flows (and not of Oedipal lack) that operate beyond the categories of the personal and the human. One advantage of this is that, since distinction is no longer necessary for 'identity', otherness and difference become sources of pleasure and indeed *jouissance. Homosexual Desire* is therefore not about 'identity' based on object-choice, but about the polymorphousness of desire and homosexuality as a royal road back to it. Deleuze also wrote the preface to Hocquenghem's 1974 collection of essays, *L'Après-mai des faunes*, whose key terms, *volutions* and *transversalisme*, eschew the totalizing linearity of 'revolution' and the solidity of the existential homosexual subject of 1971–2 in favour of perpetual displacement. The central metaphor of spirals that Deleuze here employs ('a very mobile spiral [. . .] At one level he can say yes, yes I am homosexual, at another level no that isn't it, at another it's something else again')[10] is redolent of some of the imagery he will identify in the baroque.

Leibniz – the central focus of Deleuze's *The Fold* – is the anti-Descartes. Whereas Descartes represents a thought characterized by rectilinearity and rectitude, and by points of consciousness, the world described by Leibniz is an infinite labyrinth of souls and matter whose geometry and relations are characterized by curves, bending, folds. All matter and every body however small are porously textured and contain folds within folds, so that any organism is defined by the relationship between its infinite capacity for folding its constituent parts and unfolding them to the appropriate degree of development necessary for the species. Similarly, between soul and body, organic and inorganic matter, and different species, there runs a sinuous and zigzagging fold. The notion of the self in this world is not one of autonomous identity but of a certain collection or concentration of singularities within the infinite, convergent series that is the world. The relationship between self and world, that of the world in the self and the self for the world, is expressed in the famous category of the monad.

The monads are the minimum, local units of the series of the world. They are the requisites of matter, principles of energy and life, perceivers, each with their unique point of view, on which material bodies ultimately depend. Deleuze usefully employs two key metaphors, appropriate to baroque culture, to explicate this. The first is the street in the labyrinth of the city. The point of view of a monad is not of one street and its relationship with other streets, but of the variety of *all* possible connections between any street and any other. The second is that of music. A piece of music is always a certain combination or selection of the twelve basic musical notes: 'As an individual unit each monad includes the whole series; hence it conveys the entire world, but *does not express it* without expressing more clearly a small region of the world, the "subdivision", a borough of the city, a finite sequence'.[11] The monads do not penetrate each other; they contain and express each other in the variations they make on the infinite series. They are the unity of the multiple and the multiple of the one. 'Substance' thus has nothing to do with essence and everything to do with a modality or way of being, in other words with movement and change.

The implications of this for 'identity politics' are profound. In Leibniz, what distinguishes monads, and for example individuals, is predicates, not attributes; actions and events, not essences: 'The predicate is the "execution of travel", an act, a movement, a change, and not the state of travel.'[12] Rather than equilibrium and repose, his system is based on disequilibrium, tension even, most notably in the unity of the infinite world and finite self. As in Deleuze and Guattari's *Anti-Oedipus*, all sorts of possibilities arise with liberation from the finite or finished body (*le moi fini*). Leibniz is the philosopher of the baroque because his strategy for plugging the gap created by the decline of classical and theological thought is to invent principles and let them proliferate to excess, while maintaining that this God-created world is the best and indeed only possible one. He creates not a system as such but an infinite labyrinthine series, a baroque machine – in Deleuze's terms, plastic and malleable – to be distinguished from the instrumental and finally inert quality of the mechanism. The Leibnizian world-view is expressed in baroque architecture (massive domes as infinite universes without a centre, divorce between obscure chapels as absolutely interior monads and the exaggerated language of the façade as infinite exterior of matter, as well as between the vertical and horizontal axes) and in baroque music (the relationship between harmony, that multiplicity relating to a determinable unity, and the infinite lines of individual melody, as well as the preparation and resolution of dissonance).

Deleuze's thought is steeped in Nietzsche, and he is well aware that the modernity of the nineteenth and twentieth centuries brings profound modifications to any reading of Leibniz. In Deleuze's work, in consequence, the question of folds remains central, but new ways of folding come into play. As he puts it, the monad is no longer a closed chapel with imperceptible openings, but a hermetically sealed motor-car hurled along a dark motorway. With the disappearance of transcendence, there is no selection of the 'best' world or limitation of the monad to its own 'region' within it. There are simultaneously many possible worlds: dissonance does not have to be resolved, divergences can be asserted, and the monad cannot 'contain' them all and so spirals away from its own centre, the distinction between inner and outer now lost.

III

The Baroque and Modernity: Benjamin/Baudelaire

In order to understand why the baroque has persisted within modernity, we must turn to Walter Benjamin. This – with its consequences for sexual politics – is the project of Christine Buci-Glucksmann in her *Baroque Reason* of 1984, which takes as its points of departure Benjamin's works on baroque theatre and on Baudelaire. *The Origin of German Tragic Drama*, written in 1923, focuses on the seventeenth-century *Trauerspiel* or 'sorrow theatre'. Unlike the myth and emotional reticence of classical tragedy, this genre took historical subjects in situations of crisis and catastrophe, ostentatiously dramatizing the ceremonies of grief. For the purposes of this analysis, it is necessary to stress the extremely scopic nature of this theatre, and by extension of the wider baroque cultural context; the importance of melancholy, associated with the pervasive sense of political catastrophe, with the collapse of tradition and the emergence of an uncertain and destructive present; and the uses Benjamin makes of the trope of allegory.

The received notion of allegory is of a conventional, one-to-one relationship between an image or figure and a pre-given, abstract meaning. Famously, Goethe had demoted allegory, 'where the particular serves only as an instance or example of the general', in favour of 'the true nature of poetry', that is the grasping of 'the particular in all its vitality', which only then may lead to general significance.[13] For Benjamin – as for Buci-Glucksmann and, as we shall see, Hocquenghem – the priority is reversed, for it is the symbol that is seen as the classical expression of a hierarchical, sacred, immutable world, and allegory as the form *par excellence* of a desanctified, enigmatic universe. Just as Leibniz constructed an allegory of the world, baroque culture places an object, often a fragment or ruin, in a dense, mobile network of associations. More like Egyptian hieroglyphics than Christian apologetics, it renders substances totally significant, totally representative of ulterior meanings.

As an archaeologist of modernity, Benjamin saw this aesthetic persisting in surprising ways in nineteenth-century society, with its accelerating commodification, industrialization and urbanization. In his study of Baudelaire, these transformations are read through the prism of Benjamin's peculiar understanding of history, in terms not of linear rationality and progress but of a Jewish-Messianic time of catastrophe and utopia. The modern world, with its loss of aura, is in catastrophic tumult, creating new cultures and new interiorities that are both consistent with the mechanization and seriality of capitalism, and yet also, crucially, always pregnant with new possibilities, new emancipations, and new poetry. Baudelaire's spleen, source of his poetic inspiration, is like a state of permanent catastrophe, a state outside history that can, through a strategy of shock, allegorize the objects in its midst, a process helped by the notion of *correspondances*.

These objects include swans and dead bodies, but especially, of course, women, in the form of passers-by, lesbians, prostitutes. For Buci-Glucksmann, the baroque in Baudelaire and Benjamin represents indeed an alternative cultural resource to the instrumental reason of patriarchal capitalism. On the one hand, the transformations of the nineteenth century impelled transformations in the status and cultural construction of women, who visibly entered the public sphere of work, exchange value, and also mass spectacle and theatralization (accompanied, Benjamin noted, by utopian and other critiques that sought to link femininity and transgression). To these developments can be added what Buci-Glucksmann sees as a general 'feminization' of nineteenth-century culture. In terms familiar from the arguments of Julia Kristeva's *Revolution in Poetic Language*, this is seen as modernism's loss of faith in modernity, in Cartesian consciousness, Enlightenment rationality, language, and even the masculine/feminine binary. Baudelaire's representation of women is thus seen not as part of a generalized misogyny but, in his vaunting of his own 'femininity', as exemplary of a cultural crisis he found both troubling and fascinating. The passer-by, as in the poem 'A une passante', is thus allegorized, a process presented by Buci-Glucksmann in the following terms: 'The image which has been engraved in the *flâneur*'s body, Baudelaire's 'passing woman' who is merely glimpsed in the haze of big-city intoxication, are just particular cases of what characterizes modernity as such: the cult of images, the secularization/sublimation of fleeting and reproducible bodies.'[14]

The lesbian is also an image of modernity, despite the limitations of Baudelaire's representation, because of the blurring of gender binaries echoed by Baudelaire's own 'feminization'. It is the prostitute who becomes the main allegorical figure, rendering ambivalent the categories of nature (the traditional site of femininity) and culture (the new spectacular, urban, exchange), sundering love and sex, the archaic and the technical, the real and the artificial.

Echoing Nietzsche's question in the *Birth of Tragedy*, when he asked why civilization did not become feminine, Buci-Glucksmann extends her equation of the feminine and the baroque by invoking the paradoxical possibilities afforded by the 'nothingness' to which women in patriarchy have been assigned. In negative theologies such as Taoism (and also Hocquenghem's great interest, Gnosticism), nothingness can be active: 'But on the other hand, Nothing is all. By a kind of heretical-mystical and then baroque conversion, this 'nothing of being' changes into an infinity of ecstatic delight [*jouissance*], a plethora of forms.'[15] The historically defeated figures of Helen of Troy, Dionysos and the characters of the *Trauerspiel* transgressively defy the logic of the polis and the boundary, which is based on rational, identity-based communication. Nothingness suggests a relation to alterity different from the traditions of Descartes and Hegel, in that its logic is not based on identity at all. It returns like the repressed of Western culture in baroque forms and their proliferating play of absence and presence, change, movement, instability, mortality. The baroque thus deals happily with alterity, being at home with paradox, oxymoron ('baroque reason'), and the capacity of allegory to mean *something else* from what is said: 'To make of One Many, of the Same another and Others: such is the alchemy of imagination, that baroque reason of intersubjectivity in which everything is material for sensual pleasure, conversion and inversion, captivation by the phantasm and the Other.'[16]

IV

The Baroque and the City: From the 'Flâneur' to the Gay City Cruise

Where does this leave gay identity politics, especially since the notion of identity itself is being discarded? The answer lies in the contradictions and legacy of the nineteenth century, and also in the (literal and figurative) u-topia of the baroque. In Hocquenghem, there is a fictional *hommage* to Benjamin in the 1977 short story *Oiseau de la nuit* (Night Bird). In a variation on Diderot's *Le Neveu de Rameau* (*Rameau's Nephew*), the married, middle-class and 'heterosexual' narrator, '*Moi*'/'Me', the self integrated into the internalized hegemony of social norms, at some unspecified point of crisis in his life, encounters late at night in a mixed Paris gay café his interlocutor, '*Lui*'/'Him', who challenges and disrupts the norms of vice and virtue, beauty and ugliness, sincerity and authenticity. In part to seduce, in part to initiate a flow of discourse about sexuality and the self, *Lui* plies *Moi* with drink, fills him in on the stories of the various marginals assembled there, and leads him on a sexual *promenade* through the Parisian night, culminating in the cruising grounds of the Tuileries gardens and the banks of the Seine. The two part after their chaste but revealing encounter, but a brief coda places them in the downstairs toilets of another café, with *Lui* making what turns out to be a humiliating pass at *Moi* without at first realizing his identity. *Moi* makes off for his home in the suburbs. Hocquenghem's avoidance of the ghettoized club scene of the rue Sainte-Anne rhymes with the heterogeneous, pre-'gay' ambiance of the café, which *Moi* enters by accident.

Just as in Nietzsche, 'value' is smuggled back into *Oiseau de la nuit* via the aesthetic, and, importantly, this aesthetic is materially and historically grounded in the city, in Paris, and, especially, in the nineteenth-century urban. Helped by alcohol, from the outset *Moi* realizes he is embarking on an aesthetic experience, as the seemingly ordinary café now seems 'rich with a revitalized urban poetry, the natural place of nocturnal extravagance'.[17] Just as for *Lui* the 'real' of pornography is in the unexpected and improbable nature of the encounters, so urban cruising is about shock and surprise: 'the catalytic lightning flash between distant poles',[18] 'the movement that is oblique, underside, surprising, because it eroticizes a situation illicitly withdrawn from its ordinary function'.[19] These encounters operate '*percées* [breaks, gaps, openings] in the social tissue'.[20] The urban landscape is crucial to this process, as the encounters are sought in the *parcours*[21] of Haussmann's

Paris, and consummated amidst that décor – the arcades of the rue de Rivoli, the lamps, the statues of the Tuileries, the *pissoirs*. This provides the setting for the 'miraculous' to surge forth against the 'prosaic'. The aesthetic manifests itself when the con-voluted movements and choreographies of cruising men become a baroque disruption of classical order in the Tuileries, and when the scene becomes allegorized, the men as insects, rats, dogs, birds (nightbirds . . .), spectres, unicorns.[22] *Lui* seems to acknowledge he and his kind belong to a past time, to an ephemeral phenomenon of modernity: 'Perhaps we are the last witnesses of customs that will have lasted just a century or two, from the first street-lamp or first *pissotière* to sex education';[23] 'our damned past is worth all normalized futures'.[24]

The baroque aesthetic and 'reason', claimed by Buci-Glucksmann as the dissident potential within modernity, is illustrated in the experience of that other emerging category of modernity, the 'homosexual', for whom the new urban experience has consistently been lived not simply in a dark, hidden side, but in a wholly intensified manner, and for whom it has survived longer. The homelessness and deterritorialization of capitalist society are redoubled; but territories are staked out. For *Lui* in *Oiseau de la nuit*, the nocturnal urban landscape is a shifting, mobile, kaleidoscopic 'home'. One cannot imagine him anywhere else – not for him the socially segmented world of the twentieth-century suburban highway and the 'home' that *Moi* is returning to at the end in a mixture of panic and reluctance. Ironically, *Moi* resanctifies the cruising homosexuals: 'The vaporous globes of the lamps also formed two arcs, symmetrical haloes'[25] – that '*vaporeux*' so redolent of the gaseous lack of fixity of modern life. (It should be pointed out that the French '*halo*', used here, refers to physical phenomena, while it is '*auréole*', the word used by Baudelaire, that also means a saintly or religious halo. The use of '*halo*' connotes rather the auric.) *Moi* marvels at the way the men having sex in the Tuileries emerge from the centre of the action, like dragonfly larvae mutating from 'vegetable agglomeration' to 'distinguished *flânerie*',[26] Benjamin's term for that leisured and invariably male wandering of the city, poised for new experiences and the unearthing of new treasures. The sexual interplay with figures emerging from the crowd in 'A une passante' (in fact, the poem's term *éclair*, or 'lightning flash', is used in *Lui*'s descriptions of gay cruising)[27] is replayed with greater force for the cruising homosexual because of his marginalized and minoritized position on the boulevards, as well as in those areas colonized by his subculture, the *raison d'être* of which is for strangers in the night to exchange glances and for couplings to form and unform.

V

The Baroque, the Fragmentary and the Dissident: Hocquenghem

As we have seen, social, cultural and political developments in the 1980s meant that these dissident, marginalized spaces of the modern urban world would give way to consumerism, identity and spectacle. The question of how to critique that society without falling into the pitfalls of modernity and post-modernity would however persist. This is the project of Hocquenghem's major theoretical work of the 1980s, the suitably oxymoronic *L'Ame atomique: pour une esthétique de l'ère nucléaire* (1986) (The Atomic Soul), co-written with the philosopher and Fourier specialist René Schérer. The diagnosis of contemporary society to be found here has its roots in the critique of the instrumental rationalism of modernity, and its political and institutional failures. Concurring with Adorno that the post-Auschwitz reality calls into question that totalizing Enlightenment legacy that strives to establish the identity of concept or thought with the thing or the world, the project of Hocquenghem and Schérer's volume is to 'explore other avenues', as 'political reason has now only to keep silent'.[28] In the catastrophe of modernity, the closure of myths – as limiting as those scrutinized by Roland Barthes in *Mythologies* – confines 'individuals without individuality',[29] whose lives are, in fact, 'in bits', in 'a system which works by itself'.[30] Mass culture is not in fact totally rejected, since some audio-visual technology is co-opted to its aesthetics, but its dominant practices certainly are: 'Today, the levelling down caused by the democracy of the vulgar is called mass culture or media information: it is expressed in opinion polls, the quest for individual, ethnic or racial identities, in which banalized 'difference' becomes a homage to the norm.'[31] What is 'bad' in contemporary society is the prosaic, flatness, realism, the concept, determinism, myth, ideology, but also 'personalism': 'A permanent return to personalism is complementary and not antagonistic to the dictatorship of technical imperatives.'[32] Since the 'self' and the 'human' are the creations of modernity and thus supremely ideological, Hocquenghem and Schérer move to short-circuit this process. It is at this point that they move away from the dialectical thought so crucial to Adorno, who recognizes – if the non-identity of the particulars of the world is to be dissonant and negating – the need for fragile, provisional notions of identity and totality. Their strategy is to prioritize 'the world' and our place in it, rather than seek to salvage Enlightenment's original promise of freely interrelating, autonomous, individual consciousnesses.

The oxymoronic 'atomic soul' is most certainly not metaphysical: 'The soul reduced to its metaphysical, humanist form is, like the body confined within its organic form, a reactive abstraction, a limit to overcome.'[33] Hocquenghem and Schérer juxtapose the idea of the soul lost during the advent of modernity – with its connotations of the infinite, the opening out to the universe, the irreducible non-closure of the poetic – with the atom, the fragment, the particle, the bits of which everything is made and by which everything happens, a source of unity. The atom is both material and unrepresentable. The inspiration, boldly, comes from both antiquity and contemporary science. The didactic poem *De Rerum Natura* (*On the Nature of the Universe*) by Lucretius debunks the myths of gods prevailing over our destinies, of a finished cosmos, by invoking a metaphysics of the particle. The universe has no centre. It consists of atoms that move, collide, enter into combinations. They transmit sensory signals, they assemble and disperse. The universe is thus a question of creative, dynamic play, and is indeterminate, open rather than closed, since the swerving movement of the atoms in the void – without which their fall would be simply vertical and formless – is unpredictable. This philosophy was the basis of Epicureanism, built not on instrumentalism and action but on pleasure viewed less in a narrow hedonistic sense than in the inclusive sense of well-being, both sensual and serene. As in the case of Deleuze's *The Fold*, developments in contemporary physics such as chaos theory, randomness as opposed to causal determinism, as well as the shifting and vibrating sub-atomic particles of quantum theory, form the scientific 'grounding' for the discourse of *L'Ame atomique*, even as the work seeks to extend such observations into the realms of art and society.

This emphasis on the overcoming of the boundaries between the self and universe, and the aesthetic priority given to those intermittences between man and machine, nature and artifice, real and illusion, recall features of the baroque, and it is on this central but partial section of Hocquenghem and Schérer's argument that I shall concentrate.[34] The ceilings of the Belvedere palace in Vienna, with their multiplication of points of view, spiralling figures that confuse the boundary between up and down, heaven and earth, present a view of a universe devoid of a centre, an ever dynamic proliferation of affects. The gardens,[35] in particular their attempt to give form to the fluid medium *par excellence*, water, present the play of forces in baroque art, the tension between form and movement, nature and history, mastery and powerlessness, an exaltation of imperial rule and a foretaste of its instability. Hocquenghem and Schérer state: 'The destiny of the baroque, what still contributes to its grandeur for us, is to refuse the path of reconciliation; it is caught in a continual tension between a whirling, empty infinity that is a-cosmic, devoid of meaning and entirely open, and the dense proliferation of images.'[36]

The possibilities this opens for a dissident aesthetics, and even ethics and politics, are extended in the preeminence given to allegory, for its anti-anthropomorphism, the potential for its original intentions to be hijacked (or *détournés*, as in *Oiseau de la nuit*), and its ability to reintroduce the enigmatic or marvellous back into the real, all hint at a utopian world or space that is incommensurate with the status quo:

> Faced with the return to the self, with the falling back on and contraction of identity, allegory widens the field, distends the world, brings in some air, detaching itself, like some animated shadow, from the messages, myths and master-narratives it was supposed to convey. It does not reduce all signs to incoherence and insignificance, but defers meaning in an experience that is always unique and always to be renewed, unpredictable, reiterated, eternally transitory.[37]

Hocquenghem and Schérer trace the history of allegory, linking it to those traditions in the classical and Judaic world that believed in the absence of direct communication with the divine, and thus saw the universe as a book full of meaning, but whose textuality was ultimately unfathomable. These traditions, those of Philo of Alexandria and his highly syncretic blend of Greek and Jewish culture, of the Cabbala and of Gnosticism, suggest an alternative cultural lineage to modernity and the two millennia of Romano-Judaeo-Christian civilization. In addition, they, along with the baroque of early and later modernity, proclaim supremely the values of syncretism and cosmopolitanism. However, the supreme allegorist, the one closest to the sexual, aesthetic and utopian agenda of Hocquenghem and Schérer, is Fourier.

VI

The Baroque, Aesthetics and Politics: From Fourier to a New Gay Radicalism

Fourier (1772–1837) is the allegorist of the passions and of human happiness. Unlike his contemporary utopian socialist Saint-Simon, who identified the civilization that emerged from the eighteenth century and the French Revolution with progress, Fourier saw 'civilization' as an aberration, its rationality a mask for profound historical failure, notably the bourgeois rule of commerce and the subordination of women. Fourier's utopia is characterized by the maximizing of pleasure, the attainment of a life rich in gratified desire, the transformation of work into pleasure: 'happiness is having the greatest number of passions and being able to satisfy them all'.[38] His communities or *phalanstères* are units for co-operative consumption and production in which the basic twelve drives (sexual, but also olfactory) and their varying combinations (810 in total) are exquisitely associated, matched and satisfied in turn. All sexual preferences are legitimate. The point here is firstly that Fourier bases his concept of humanity not on an integral person or soul but on passions and the endless permutations of their exchange, not unlike the flows of *Anti-Oedipus*. Unlike Freud but like Deleuze and Guattari, the relationship between desire and society need not be one of sublimation but of fulfilment. His vision of Harmony associates singularities, such as flowers and animals, in an order of passions. He creates an allegory without ruling principle or personification, which simultaneously links and disperses its categories through a multiplicity of references, a play of *correspondances* (jasmine as the emblem of childhood ambition, the swan as that of futile virtue . . .), and an infinity of combinations.

Clearly, Hocquenghem's interest in the baroque, with its poetic resignifying of the world, has primarily aesthetic consequences. These are evident in the themes of his aesthetic works: in *L'Amour en relief* (Love in Relief), for example, a blind Tunisian perceives the world anew and falls athwart the power structures of the contemporary world, while in *La Colère de l'agneau* (The Anger of the Lamb), visits are made to the similar but different mappings of the world found in the first century AD, and, in the case of *Les Voyages et aventures extraordinaires du frère Angelo* (Brother Angelo's Extraordinary Journeys and Adventures), to those found in the sixteenth century. But they are also evidenced by the form of his novels. The imbrication of different narratives within each other, the variations of the relationship between narrator and narration, the proliferating detail as well as outrageously labyrinthine narrative structure (Deleuze linked the image of Borges's *Garden of Forking Paths* with a desanctified Leibnizian universe),[39] although not unusual fare in the modern novel, all suggest the baroque.

The consequences, as far as identity *politics* are concerned, of Hocquenghem's engagement with the baroque would seem less clear than its aethetic consequences. But whereas, early on in his theoretical itinerary, Hocquenghem discards the notion of identity and even the category of the human, he retained until his death a keen political sense. Indications of the uses to which his notion of the baroque may be put can be found in a late article in *Gai Pied* in 1987, 'L'homosexualité est-elle un vice guérissable?' ('Is Homosexuality a Curable Vice?').[40] 'There is therefore no definite, positive principle we can call "homosexuality"', he writes, 'if we understand by that everything social and intimate beyond the sexual relationship between two people of the same sex.'[41] Gay self-assertion is a defensive move like any other, like nationalism, and thus, contrary to the arguments of *Homosexual Desire*, enjoys no special status; it is no more 'real' than normative heterosexual self-repressive fantasms. Where Hocquenghem is still interested in 'homosexuality', however, is in the way it both exists and does not exist, how it undermines the very assurance of its own concept. Indeed, its disappearing act, appearing and reappearing according to historical and social change, or to the structures of secrecy and disclosure, is its strength. It constitutes a problem, or '*cyclothymie*', that state of veering from euphoria to melancholy. One of the Indo-European roots of 'gay' denotes excess. The provisionality of 'homosexuality' implies tension rather than fulfilment or taking for granted one's position or identity: 'Homosexuality is baroque, dramatic, it is an "effect" and not a principle. Rather than some inferiority to it, it undermines the concept's self-assurance.'[42] Still influenced by Foucault and Deleuze, Hocquenghem sees visibility and confession as traps, double binds of compulsory transgression that cannot be ends in themselves:

> 'Visibility' is the faculty of 'saying oneself', of being adequate to the idea of oneself, frankness, constancy of meaning, the unequivocal content of the message (gay [*homo*] and proud to be so). I was for visibility when it was emergence. Today . . . I find myself wishing for its disappearance. Without a play with invisibility, visibility is no more than pointless foolishness, a false problem, second-rate psychology.[43]

This play of absence and presence is expressed in two ways suggestive of the baroque. One is in the invocation of Leibniz. Hocquenghem is dissatisfied with the plenitudes of identity politics because they fail both to let in enough of the outer world and to embrace the variety within. As Deleuze wrote of Leibniz: 'No philosophy has ever pushed to such an extreme the affirmation of a one and same world, and of an infinite difference or variety in this world.'[44] Existence is an effort or tension, not a given, just as the world is the criss-cross of the effort each monad makes to exist. In addition, Leibniz's principle of indiscernibles, according to which 'there are no two points, two subjects, two people truly alike, because the space of their comparison is just the network woven between monads striving to exist',[45] is invoked to assert difference between those claiming an 'identity', but also to undermine the self-resemblance of the 'norm', since 'the homosexual', like the Jew, cannot easily be distinguished from the ('white', Christian, 'heterosexual') to whom he may be juxtaposed.

Secondly, it is music that becomes the privileged art form and metaphor for Hocquenghem's idea: 'I would "musicalize" ['*musicaliserais*'] the idea of homosexuality: it exists only in its rhythm, its intervals and its pauses, it exists only through its (dramatic) movement. It conjugates invisibility and visibility in this rhythm of emergence and disappearance.'[46]

Hocquenghem's final positions on gay politics had little to say about the construction of new hegemonies or about the 'popular', and he ran the risk of being confined to the role of dandy (a figure he was happy, like Baudelaire, to embrace). Both Judith Butler and Jeffrey Weeks have written of, respectively, the 'provisional unities'[47] and 'necessary fictions'[48] involved in the elaboration of an emancipatory sexual politics. What Hocquenghem does is, firstly, to stress one side, the provisionality and fictionality of these practices, in the name of a utopia. This is necessary work with a respectable historical ancestry. It enables him to correct the sometimes oppressive orthodoxies of gay 'identity', and to remind any militant (or consumer) that the 'unities', however 'necessary', must always be open to question. In addition, Hocquenghem's use of the baroque provides a purchase on the contemporary post-modern spectacle, in its renewed and distinct sense of history, and in the way that allegory can provide other ways of living and of seeing than the acceptance and even celebration of the cultural status quo. In the past ten years, the totalizations of 1970s sexual-identity politics have been very effectively modified, notably by Donna Haraway in her concept of the cyborg and Butler in her analysis of the performativity of gender. The renewal of interest in the baroque – and let us not forget the specificity of the French context – may run the risk of providing a catch-all concept, but it deserves to be put alongside the Anglo-American work. There is undoubtedly mileage in its historicity, its universalist ambitions, its transnationalism, and the invaluable effort by Buci-Glucksmann to gender it, particularly given Hocquenghem's reticence about engaging with concepts of femininity. Given the ambiguities of 'queer', a notion which could be regarded as either minoritizing or universalizing, the notion of the baroque as an unambiguous but anti-relativist challenge to the plenitude of identity would seem an important addition to our debates.[49]

Notes

1. S. Edge (1995), 'Consuming in the Face of Hatred: Lifestyle and the gay advance', *Soundings*, no. 1, p. 173.

2. Ibid., p. 166.
3. G. Hocquenghem (1985), 'Où en est l'homosexualité en 85, ou pourquoi je ne veux pas être un "écrivain gay"', *Masques*, nos. 25/6, pp. 111–13.
4. For a more comprehensive discussion of Hocquenghem, see B. Marshall (1996), *Guy Hocquenghem*, London.
5. G. Hocquenghem (1974), *L'Après-mai des faunes: Volutions*, Paris, p. 157.
6. G. Hocquenghem (1979), *Race d'Ep! Un siècle d'images de l'homosexualité*, Paris, p. 14: 'un processus graduel et invincible, fondé sur la progressive mise au jour d'une réalité préexistante et incoercible'.
7. G. Hocquenghem (1977), *La Dérive homosexuelle*, Paris, p. 17: 'Pendant que je dérivais dans un sens, tentant de rejoindre l'océan de l'informulé, explorant les marges à peine spécifiques des homosexualités, l'Homosexualité en passe d'être reconnue évoluait dans l'autre: s'organisant, se rationalisant, non seulement récupérée mais surtout fondatrice de nouvelles valeurs, et, pourquoi pas, de nouveaux empires. Se faisant héraut des nouvelles répressions, exigeant la punition des loulous agresseurs de pédés et l'intégration des homosexuels au sein de l'armée et de la police américaine, se donnant corps et culture.'
8. M. Foucault (1976), *Histoire de la sexualité. I. La Volonté de savoir*, Paris, p. 59.
9. G. Bazin (1964), *Baroque and Rococo*, London, pp. 6–7.
10. Hocquenghem, *L'Après-mai des faunes*, p. 8: 'une spirale très mobile . . . A un niveau il peut dire oui, oui je suis homosexuel, à un autre niveau non ce n'est pas cela, à un autre niveau c'est encore autre chose.'
11. G. Deleuze (1993), *The Fold: Leibniz and the Baroque*, trans. T. Conley, London, p. 25 (original emphasis): 'chaque monade comme unité individuelle inclut toute la série, elle exprime ainsi le monde entier, *mais ne l'exprime pas* sans exprimer plus clairement une petite région du monde, un "département", un quartier de la ville, une séquence finie' (*Le Pli: Leibniz et le baroque*, Paris, Minuit, 1988, p. 35).
12. Deleuze, *The Fold*, p. 53: 'Le prédicat, c'est "l'exécution du voyage", un acte, un mouvement, un changement, et non pas l'état de voyageant' (*Le Pli*, p. 71).
13. W. Benjamin (1977 [1923]), *The Origin of German Tragic Drama*, trans. J. Osborne, London, p. 161.
14. C. Buci-Glucksmann (1994), *Baroque Reason: The Aesthetics of Modernity*, trans. P. Camiller, London, p. 94: 'Cette image gravée au corps du flâneur, cette Passante baudelairienne juste entrevue dans l'ivresse des grandes villes, la multiplication des émotions, ne sont que des cas

particuliers de ce qui caractérise la modernité comme telle: le culte des images, la laïcisation-sublimation des corps, leur fugacité et leur reproductibilité', *La Raison baroque: De Baudelaire à Benjamin*, Paris, Galilée, 1984, p. 109.

15. Idem, *Baroque Reason*, p. 130: 'Mais le rien est tout. Par une sorte de conversion hérético-mystique, puis baroque, ce "rien d'être" se renverse en une infinitude de jouissance extatique, en un surcroît proliférant de formes' (*La Raison baroque*, p. 166).
16. Idem, *Baroque Reason*, p. 165: 'Faire de l'Un plusieurs, du Même un autre et les Autres: telle est l'alchimie imaginante, cette raison baroque de l'intersubjectivité où tout est matière à jouissance, à conversion et inversion, à captation par le fantasme et l'autre' (*La Raison baroque*, p. 230).
17. G. Hocquenghem and J.-L. Bory (1977), *Comment nous appelez-vous déjà? Ces hommes que l'on dit homosexuels*, Paris, p. 139: 'riche d'une poésie urbaine revivifiée, lieu naturel de l'extravagance nocturne'.
18. Ibid., p. 158: 'l'éclair catalytique entre des pôles éloignés'.
19. Ibid., p. 160: 'le mouvement qui prend de biais, à revers, par surprise, par l'érotisation indue d'une situation soustraite à son fonctionnement ordinaire'.
20. Ibid., p. 150: 'les percées qu'elles pratiquent dans le tissu social'.
21. In Michel de Certeau's work on everyday life, the *parcours* is associated with 'the microbe-like, singular and plural practices which an urbanistic system [associated with the *carte*] was supposed to administer or suppress, but which have outlived its decay' ('Walking in the City', in S. During (ed.) (1993), *The Cultural Studies Reader* (London and New York) p. 156).
22. Hocquenghem and Bory, *Comment nous appelez-vous déjà?*, pp. 165, 177, 197.
23. Ibid., p. 156: 'Peut-être sommes-nous les derniers témoins d'usages qui n'auront duré qu'un siècle ou deux, depuis le premier lampadaire ou la première pissotière jusqu'à l'éducation sexuelle.'
24. Ibid., p. 185: 'Notre passé damné vaut bien tous les avenirs normalisés.'
25. Ibid., p. 161: 'Les globes vaporeux des lampadaires formaient aussi deux arcs, halos symétriques.'
26. Ibid., p. 163.
27. Ibid., p. 158.
28. G. Hocquenghem and R. Schérer (1986), *L'Ame atomique: pour une esthétique de l'ère nucléaire*, Paris, p. 316.
29. Ibid., pp. 14–15.
30. Ibid., p. 27.

31. Ibid., p. 16: 'Aujourd'hui, le nivellement par la démocratie du trivial a nom culture de masse ou information médiatique; il s'exprime dans les sondages d'opinion, les recherches d'identité individuelles, ethniques ou raciales, où la "différence" banalisée devient un hommage à la norme.'
32. Ibid., p. 295: 'Un permanent retour au personnalisme est complémentaire, et non antagoniste, de la dictature des impératifs techniques.'
33. Ibid., p. 51: 'L'âme réduite à sa forme métaphysique, humaniste, est, comme le corps enfermé dans sa forme organique, abstraction réactive, limite à surmonter.'
34. Ibid., pp. 151–203.
35. See also Hocquenghem's contribution in *L'Europe des villes rêvées: Vienne avec Guy Hocquenghem* (Paris, 1986).
36. Hocquenghem and Schérer, *L'Ame atomique*, p. 194: 'La destinée du baroque, ce qui continue à faire pour nous sa grandeur, est de refuser la voie de la conciliation; il est pris dans une tension continuelle entre le vertige de l'infinité vide, a-cosmique et non signifiante de l'espace ouvert à toute fin, et la prolifération dense des images.'
37. Ibid., p. 178: 'En face du retour à soi, du repli et de la contraction identitaire, suscitée par le savant désordre moderne, l'allégorie élargit le champ, distend, donne de l'air, elle se détache, ombre animée, des messages et des mythes, des grands récits qu'elle était censée porter. Elle ne réduit pas tous les signes à l'incohérence et l'insignifiance, mais en reporte le sens dans une expérience toujours unique et toujours à renouveler, imprévisible et répétée, éternellement transitoire.'
38. R. Schérer (ed.) (1970), *Charles Fourier ou la contestation globale*, Paris, p. 69: 'le bonheur est d'avoir le plus de passions possible et de pouvoir les satisfaire toutes'.
39. Deleuze, *The Fold*, p. 61; *Le Pli*, p. 81. For more on the baroque and narrative, see G. Genette (1969), *Figures II*, Paris, pp. 195–222.
40. G. Hocquenghem (1987), 'L'homosexualité est-elle un vice guérissable?', *Gai Pied Hebdo*, nos. 278–9, pp. 64–5.
41. Ibid.: 'étant entendu que par là on entend tout ce qui est, au-delà du rapport sexuel entre deux personnes du même sexe, lié à lui socialement, intimement'.
42. Ibid.: 'L'homosexualité est baroque, dramatique, elle est un "effet", non un principe. Elle n'est pas par cela inférieure au concept: elle en mine l'assurance.'
43. Ibid.: 'La "visibilité", c'est l'aptitude à "se dire", à être adéquat à l'idée de soi, la franchise, la constance du sens, le contenu sans équivoque du message (homo et fier de l'être). J'étais pour la visibilité quand elle

était apparition. Aujourd'hui [. . .] je me prends à souhaiter sa disparition. Sans jeu avec l'invisibilité, la visibilité confine à l'inutile sottise, au faux-problème, à la psychologie du bazar.'

44. Deleuze, *The Fold*, p. 58: 'aucune philosophie n'a poussé si loin l'affirmation d'un seul et même monde, et d'une différence ou variété infinies dans ce monde' (*Le Pli*, p. 78).
45. Ibid.: 'Il n'y a pas deux points, deux sujets, deux personnes vraiment semblables, car l'espace de leur comparaison n'est que le réseau tissé entre les monades qui s'efforcent à être.'
46. 'L'homosexualité est-elle un vice guérissable' (1987): 'Je "musicaliserais" l'idée d'homosexualité: elle n'existe que dans son rythme, ses intervalles comme ses battements, elle n'existe que par son mouvement (dramatique). Invisibilité et visibilité se conjuguent en elle dans ce rythme d'apparition–disparition.'
47. J. Butler (1990), *Gender Trouble: Feminism and the Subversion of Identity*, London and New York, p. 15.
48. J. Weeks (1996), 'The Idea of a Sexual Community', *Soundings*, no.2, p. 83.
49. These debates are given by a further twist by a recent publication: M. Simpson (ed.) (1996), *Anti-Gay*, London.

– 3 –

Are Lesbians Women? The Relationship between Lesbianism and Feminism in the Work of Luce Irigaray and Monique Wittig

Renate Günther

Introduction

Since the 1970s, Luce Irigaray and Monique Wittig have become known primarily as feminists whose work presents a radical challenge to patriarchal society and discourse. The texts of both writers, furthermore, contain a clear lesbian dimension and reflect their views regarding the relationship between lesbianism and feminism. In the case of Irigaray, this aspect of her work is most evident from *Speculum of the Other Woman* (1985a [1974]) to *Le Corps-à-corps avec la mère* (1981) (The Bodily Encounter with the Mother), as throughout this period she argues for the importance of love between women as a basis for the constitution of a different female subjectivity and sexuality. But if this concern with lesbianism has been limited to a particular stage in Irigaray's writing, in the work of Monique Wittig it has been the most central element, both in her fiction and in her theoretical essays.

Given Wittig's reputation as a radical lesbian feminist, it came as somewhat of a surprise when, at the 1978 Modern Language Association Convention in New York, she ended her paper 'The Straight Mind' with the statement: 'Lesbians are not women.' This comment obviously has two serious implications: firstly, if lesbians are not women, how could one envisage any association between lesbianism and feminism, whose aims have been focused around women's rights and the struggle against women's oppression? Secondly, if the identity of lesbians as women is called into question, what does it mean to be a 'lesbian'? Does the term, as some post-structuralist critics have suggested, denote no more than yet another 'language effect', deconstructing lesbians as 'ontological beings' and presenting a reconstructed 'metaphorical lesbian, the lesbian-as-sign'?[1] By contrast, Luce Irigaray's insistence on the need to create a female identity which would be located beyond the patriarchal order looks, initially at least, a seductive proposition, particularly since this identity seems so closely linked to the idea of female bonding.

These apparently irreconcilable positions need to be situated and understood within the context of two opposing tendencies within contemporary French feminist thought. The work of Irigaray, on the one hand, is exemplary of the 'sexual difference' current in French feminism, and mirrors in many respects the concerns of 'cultural feminism', which first emerged in Great Britain and the United States in the mid-1970s. The principal aim of this tendency is to dismantle patriarchal concepts of femininity and to create a female culture grounded in a 'different', specifically female identity. Wittig, on the other hand, has consistently defended the view held by radical materialist feminists that the notion of 'sexed identities' is instrumental in maintaining the oppression of women and that the aim of feminism should, therefore, be the elimination of 'sexual difference'. It is my intention in this chapter to examine the lesbian dimension in the work of Irigaray and Wittig, with regard to their different interpretations and uses of the terms 'woman', 'lesbian' and 'feminism'. I will examine the implications of their respective positions for the future of lesbian existence, particularly in view of the relationship between lesbianism and feminism, and ask whether, in the light of Wittig's analysis, such a relationship can still be possible or desirable.

I

Luce Irigaray: From Women-Loving-Women to the New Heterosexuality

Throughout her work, Irigaray has maintained the view that patriarchal societies are not, in fact, founded upon a recognition of differences between men and women, but rather on the construction of an exclusively male model of subjectivity in which women are defined as the 'other' in relation to the male 'self', or as the object in relation to the male subject.[2] Within this hierarchically structured framework of binary oppositions, women become 'mirrors' for male self-identity, just as the construct of 'femininity' operates as a mere reflection of 'masculinity'. This is particularly evident in the dominant conceptions of the female body, which is perceived as another, albeit 'castrated', version of the male body. The mirroring function assigned to women is crucial to the maintenance of what Irigaray calls the 'specular economy' or 'the economy of masculine sameness', which erases female 'difference'. Irigaray's notion of 'difference', then, envisages the possibility of a female subjectivity and language beyond patriarchal gender divisions, one that would relate more appropriately to representations of the female body and sexuality outside the 'phallocentric economy'.

It was within this context that the subject of lesbianism was first introduced by Irigaray, as part of her deconstruction of Freud's theory of female psycho-sexual development.[3] She opens her critique by tracing Freud's investigations into 'how the child with bisexual tendencies *becomes* a woman'.[4] As Irigaray shows, the pre-oedipal 'child' in Freud is essentially the male child, whose development provides the normative model for his theory. The pre-oedipal girl, in so far as she has not yet become 'a woman', is assimilated to the male model and is, therefore, in Freud's view, like 'a little man'.[5] It is only via the 'castration complex' that this 'resemblance' gives way to 'difference', as the girl is now required to accept her 'lack' and occupy the position of 'woman/femininity' on the negative side of a series of binary oppositions.[6] The girl thus moves from the pre-oedipal 'virile' phase, where she was 'like a man', to the oedipal 'feminine' phase, where she is perceived as being 'unlike a man'. At no point in Freud's analysis is a woman described *as a woman*; hence, his discourse remains within what Irigaray calls 'the hom(m)osexual economy'. Her use of this term implies both 'the same' (homo-) and 'man' (*homme*), and indicates her view that, in patriarchal societies, all sexuality is constructed around a phallic model where the female body in its 'difference' is absent.

Equally significant for Irigaray is the fact that in Freud's model, this construction of femininity coincides with the girl's 'transition' from the pre-oedipal attachment to the mother as the first 'love object' to her subsequent oedipal involvement with the father. In fact, one of the consequences of the castration complex, Freud suggests, is that the girl repudiates the mother, as her initial love for the latter is transformed into hatred and rivalry around the father's attentions. 'Becoming a woman' thus involves both the negation of a positive female identity and the repression of a primary homosexuality in favour of heterosexuality. As Irigaray remarks, this 'transition' from mother to father signifies not simply a 'displacement' but rather 'an exile, an extradition, an expatriation from this (her) desiring economy'.[7]

Irigaray argues that, since Freud was working from within a phallocentric framework, he was incapable of imagining the possibility of love and desire between two women. Female homosexuality remained to him even more obsure than 'the dark continent' of femininity; hence, the only means by which he could conceptualize it was to re-absorb it into the specular structure of masculine sameness. Thus, he claimed that female homosexuality was simply a consequence of the girl's denial of her 'castration', which led her to develop a 'virility complex' and identify with the 'masculine' instead of the 'feminine' gender.[8] Since, according to Freud, female homosexuals choose as their 'love objects' similarly male-identified, 'virile' women, his construction of lesbianism is, like that of heterosexuality, part of the 'hom(m)osexual economy' (it is for this reason that Irigaray entitled the section in *Speculum of the Other Woman* (1985a) dealing with lesbianism 'female hom(m)osexuality'). In Freudian logic, then, being a woman and loving a woman are mutually exclusive propositions. The existence of lesbianism as a specifically female experience is a 'blindspot' in his dream of (masculine) symmetry. According to Irigaray, 'nothing has been revealed or expressed about the specificity of desire *between women*'.[9]

This erasure of love between women is not, however, exclusive to Freudian theory. In *This Sex Which is Not One* (1985b), Irigaray locates her previous discussion of Freud clearly within a wider analysis of relationships between women in patriarchal societies.[10] In such societies, she argues, all exchanges and transactions occur exclusively amongst male subjects, while women become the objects – 'the goods' – that are being exchanged. This system can only function on the condition that women remain separated from other women, to whom they can only relate as 'rivals' on 'the market'. The repression of the mother–daughter relationship in Freudian theory corresponds to the more extensive prohibition of emotional and sexual closeness amongst women. Irigaray concludes her analysis by asking what would happen if 'the goods' refused to go to the market and if, instead, they began to communicate with and to desire each other.

A powerful and poetic expression of this female-to-female communication comes in the last section of *This Sex*, 'Quand nos lèvres se parlent' ('When Our Lips Speak Together'), where Irigaray stresses the need for a new language, a '*parler-femme*', which would allow women to speak to each other outside the constraints of patriarchal discourse. 'When Our Lips Speak Together' is a lesbian lover's discourse, in which a female 'I' attempts to reach and enter into a dialogue with another woman, addressed as 'you', who is, however, still 'in exile' inside the dominant language and society. The feeling of alienation which results from this separation is contrasted with a longing for reciprocal closeness and identification. Thus, the boundaries between 'I' and 'you' are gradually dissolved, as Irigaray expresses the possibility of a different female inter-subjectivity and love between women. Similarly, the hierarchical opposition between 'subject' and 'object' is dismantled and replaced by a relationship in which both women are simultaneously 'subject' and 'object', 'self' and 'other'. Linguistically, this is suggested by the use of split subject and object pronouns, for example: 'I love you: your body, here, there, now. I/you touch you/me; it's quite enough for us to feel alive.'[11] As Carolyn Burke comments: 'In this text which attempts to embody female difference, [. . .] *tu* and *je* are not fixed persons. Fluid and changing, they are at once two lovers, two aspects of the self, and more, as the reader is gradually drawn into an exploration of plurality.'[12] The fluidity and ambiguity of Irigaray's *parler-femme* presents an alternative to the either/or logic of patriarchal language. Escaping from the pattern of binary oppositions, the women are described as being neither 'one', nor even 'two', but always 'several': 'From your/my lips, several songs, several ways of saying echo each other. For one is never separable from the other. You/I are always several at the same time. How could one dominate the other? Impose her voice, her tone, her meaning?'[13] The plurality inherent in the relationship between Irigaray's lovers means that, although they are inseparable, they do not merge with each other, since the possibility of fusion itself depends on a prior division between 'self' and 'other': 'They are not distinct, which does not mean that they are blurred.'[14]

It is worth noting at this point that the familiar anti-Irigarayan charge of 'essentialism' emerges as unjustified when considered in the light of this particular text. It is evident here that Irigaray does not posit the existence of a unified, clearly definable female identity. On the contrary, her aim is to free women from the categories of patriarchal language and replace them with multiple, limitless 'identities':

> You are moving. You never stay still. You never stay. You never "are". How can I say you, who are always other? How can I speak you, who remain in a flux that never congeals or solidifies? How can this current pass into words? It is multiple, devoid of "causes" and "meanings", simple qualities; yet it is not decomposable.[15]

But the fact that Irigaray refuses to enclose women within a single set of definitions, of 'simple qualities', does not mean that, for her, women do not exist. She suggests in this text, as elsewhere, that women are female human beings whose bodies have been appropriated, exchanged and distorted in a 'masquerade' of femininity.[16] If, as Irigaray believes, the oppression of women is centred on the female body, it follows that their freedom would begin with its liberation from the constraints which have been imposed on it in patriarchal societies. In 'When Our Lips Speak Together', love and desire between two women becomes crucial to this liberation of the body and sexuality. Christine Holmlund points out that lesbian relationships, both in *Speculum* and in *This Sex*, 'provide Irigaray with an alternative to the hegemonic phallocentric model she so harshly condemns'.[17]

Following her critique of Freud and her own vision of women-loving-women, Irigaray's concern with lesbianism reappeared in the context of her growing interest in the importance of mother–daughter relationships, particularly in *Le Corps-à-corps avec la mère* (1981). Here, as well as in her later book *Thinking the Difference* (1994), Irigaray reiterates her view that Western patriarchal cultures are founded on the symbolic obliteration of 'the mother', which enabled 'the father' to take control both in the family and in society at large. This 'matricide', according to Irigaray, went hand in hand with the suppression of the mother–daughter bond in favour of the patriarchal system of filiation: 'The beginnings of patriarchal power as we know it – which means the power of the man as the legal head of the family, tribe, people, state and so on – coincided with the separation of women from each other and especially the separation of daughters from their mothers.'[18] While mothers are required to renounce their identity as women to fulfil what Irigaray calls 'the desubjectivized maternal role',[19] daughters need to identify with 'the mother', but only to take her place by becoming mothers themselves. Like lesbian love, the creation of a resubjectivized mother–daughter relationship becomes a pre-requisite for the development of a different female identity.

In this respect I would only partly agree with Holmlund's interpretation that after *Speculum* Irigaray sees 'the reclamation of the mother and motherhood for women as a more urgent task than the reappraisal of the lesbian'.[20] While this may be true of some of Irigaray's work after *Le Corps-à-corps*, in this particular text she does not construct 'the lesbian' and 'the mother' as hierarchical opposites, as Holmlund's comment would imply. Firstly, Irigaray suggests that lesbian and mother–daughter relationships co-exist on a 'continuum' of experience that encompasses different expressions of love between women.[21] Although distinguishing between 'primary' and 'secondary' homosexuality, she claims that both are equally significant for women's discovery of themselves.[22] Secondly, there is a clear correlation between Irigaray's expression of lesbian love in 'When Our Lips Speak Together', her idea of a '*parler-femme*', and her representation of mother–daughter relationships, in so far as all three break down polarities and hierarchies. Thus, she suggests that the mother–daughter relationship should become a reciprocal one, whereby neither woman would remain fixed in her traditional position within the family structure.[23] Finally, the subversive possibilities of lesbianism as a mode of resistance, implicit in *This Sex*, are extended in *Le Corps-à-corps* to the mother–daughter bond, which, as Irigaray comments, 'constitutes an extremely explosive nucleus in our societies.

(Re)thinking and changing it means shaking up the patriarchal order.'[24]

From the early 1980s onwards, however, the lesbian dimension in Irigaray has become increasingly conspicuous by its absence. Christine Holmlund contends that this omission of lesbianism can be explained in terms of Irigaray's concern with exploring a variety of female figures, including 'the mother' and 'the heterosexual lover', all of which can be seen to 'question and extend each other'.[25] In the same context, Holmlund argues against any suggestions that 'the lesbian' represents no more than 'a stage' in Irigaray's reconceptualization of heterosexuality. It is this kind of interpretation, however, that is offered by Elizabeth Grosz who, not without some approval, claims that the function of lesbianism in Irigaray is merely 'strategic, perhaps even therapeutic', while its essential purpose is to provide 'a pre-requisite to viable, on-going relations between the two sexes'.[26]

In the light of Irigaray's most recent work, in particular *I love to you* (1996), my own view is that lesbianism represents neither a pre-requisite for, nor a female modality within, a new 'sexed culture'. I would suggest instead that lesbianism is absent from this culture because it is seen by Irigaray as fundamentally incompatible with it. Her vision of a new social order hinges on a perception of men and women as radically different, 'irreducibly other' to each other.[27] While patriarchal cultures have defined only women as 'the other', different *from* men, Irigaray constructs difference as an absolute, pure 'otherness' *between* men and women. However, even though she represents this otherness as non-hierarchical, it still remains entrenched in a binary structure of mutually exclusive categories maintained through a highly mediated and ritualized 'democracy', where language and the law constantly police 'the difference'. Female identity, then, can be conceptualized only in its 'otherness' with regard to an equally 'other' male identity. Irigaray's earlier model of a woman-identified female subjectivity, of which lesbianism was an important aspect, can no longer be accommodated within this dualistic framework. Similarly, the notions of plurality and multiplicity associated with the lesbian moments in her texts exceed the new binarism and are, therefore, no longer part of her conceptual system. Rather than being a 'pre-requisite' for Irigaray's latest vision, lesbianism is external to it, one might say 'radically different' from it. Paradoxically, her ethics of respect for 'otherness' does not seem to include the lesbian 'other', who has no place in the new culture. She is certainly not invited to 'question and extend' Irigaray's recent definitions of female identity. On the contrary, lesbians are presented as trapped in, and colluding with, the patriarchal 'economy of sameness': 'It is hardly surprising, therefore, that they [lesbians] might enjoy the actual support, either openly or indirectly, of authorities that at the same time refuse to bring in laws appropriate to female identity. Haven't these powers been structured, consciously or not, by homo-sexuality for centuries?'[28]

The various representations of lesbianism in Irigaray correspond to two different stages in her definitions of female identity and feminism. During the first stage, as I have shown, her aim was to dismantle patriarchal constructions of 'lesbians' and 'women', perceived as either 'like' or 'unlike' men and set against each other in a system of oppositions. Irigaray dissolved these oppositions in her representations of love between women as a basis for female inter-subjectivity, which would recognise diversity and plurality. Feminism, at this point, was conceived as a political and cultural movement in which women could create their own identities through their various relationships with other women. In Irigaray's culture of sexual difference, on the other hand, the only function of 'feminism' might be to define the nature of women's (and men's?) 'otherness' and to enshrine 'difference' in language and the law. By definition, such a culture needs to suppress 'same-sexuality', and it would thus erase both lesbians and gay men. It is difficult to imagine how any future alliance between lesbianism and the Irigarayan feminism of 'difference' can be sustained.

II

Monique Wittig: Lesbians in a Sexless World?

In the 1980s, Monique Wittig wrote a series of theoretical and political articles for the journal *Feminist Issues* that were subsequently re-published in *The Straight Mind and Other Essays* (1992).[29] Less well-known, perhaps, than her fictional work, these essays provide a clear account of Wittig's theoretical position and explain her disagreement with Irigaray and the adherents of the 'difference' current in French feminism. In the section that follows, I shall examine the central ideas presented in *The Straight Mind*, with particular reference to Wittig's critique of 'sexual difference' and to her views on women, lesbians and feminism.

Writing from a materialist feminist perspective,[30] Wittig argues that 'sexual difference' is not a 'natural' fact, based on biology or anatomy, but a social and ideological construct that is instrumental in maintaining the oppression of women. Any physical differences that exist between men and women are not significant in themselves, and may only acquire meaning within a particular social order. In Wittig's theory, patriarchal societies are founded on the division of human beings into two separate classes: owing to unequal socio-economic power relations, men are the dominant class, women the oppressed. This fundamental political difference becomes 'naturalized' through the ideology of 'sexual difference', which assumes that the categories male/female, masculine/feminine pre-exist patriarchal society. The latter becomes, therefore, only a logical extension of 'nature'. Wittig declares:

> For there is no sex. There is but sex that is oppressed and sex that oppresses. It is oppression that creates sex and not the contrary. The contrary would be to say that sex creates oppression, or to say that the cause (origin) of oppression is to be found in sex itself, in a natural division of the sexes preexisting (or outside of) society.[31]

However, Wittig's belief that 'sexual difference' is merely a socio-political construct leads to contradictions in her analysis of women's oppression. She argues, for instance, that the category of sex is the product of power relations through which 'men appropriate for themselves the reproduction and production of women and also their physical persons'.[32] The logic of this statement is circular, for how can men appropriate women if 'men' and 'women' are constructed as a result of this appropriation? Further, if the anatomical categories of 'male' and 'female' are themselves products of social relations, how would it be possible for women to be oppressed in their 'physical persons' prior to such categorization? A similar ambiguity emerges in Wittig's discussion of women, whom she considers to be a social class and not a 'natural group'. She argues that 'we [women] have been compelled in our bodies and in our minds to correspond, feature by feature, with the *idea* of nature that has been established for us. Distorted to such an extent that our deformed body is what they call 'natural', what is supposed to exist as such before oppression.'[33] While it is true that the deformed image of women's bodies has been presented as 'natural' by patriarchal cultures, Wittig's analysis does suggest that 'our bodies' exist prior to, and differ from, this distorted idea. Diana Fuss has also commented on this central paradox, arguing that while Wittig analyses 'the real, material oppression of women and the domination of women's anatomical bodies [. . .], as an anti-essentialist she seeks to abolish the category of sex and the notion that men and women constitute natural, anatomical groups'.[34] For, if the female body as such does not exist, what is the basis for any social construction of 'woman'?

Wittig's hyperconstructionist materialism, which does not acknowledge any possible distinction between anatomical/biological sex differences on the one hand, and social relations of domination on the other, has also shaped her views concerning the objectives of feminism. Drawing on the Marxist theory of revolutionary class struggle, Wittig envisages an analogous political struggle between 'the class of men' and 'the class of women', the outcome of which would be the abolition of both classes: 'And, as it had to happen in such a struggle, in destroying (abolishing) the One, the Other was also going to destroy (abolish) itself.'[35] However, since Wittig defines men and women exclusively in terms of antagonistic sex classes, the destruction of the latter would entail the simultaneous disappearance of men and women themselves, so that, in an analogy with the Marxist ideal of a classless society, Wittig's vision is that of a sexless society. In this society, individuals would exist simply as 'neuter', generally human, persons.

Closely linked to her deconstruction of 'sexual difference' is Wittig's critique of heterosexuality. It is significant that, throughout *The Straight Mind*, Wittig uses the concept of heterosexuality rather than that of patriarchy. While the term 'patriarchy' implies a monolithic, abstract social system, 'heterosexuality' refers to the relations between men and women within that system. Wittig does not see heterosexuality as a 'natural' relationship between the sexes, but as an institution that both reproduces and justifies the social domination of women. She argues, therefore, that heterosexuality is not a consequence of 'sexual difference', but that the 'category of sex is the product of heterosexual society that turns half of the population into sexual beings, for sex is a category which women cannot be outside of'.[36] In this context, Wittig distinguishes between 'woman' as a mythical, ideological construct, and the reality of women's existence as a class. Both, however, are meaningful only as part of the heterosexual 'regime', as the concept of 'woman' is defined with regard to its opposite 'man', while women as an oppressed class cannot exist outside their relationship with men as the dominant class.

Since Wittig envisages the ultimate disappearance of 'woman' as well as women, she does not seek to extend or redefine the constructs she criticizes. On the contrary, she implicitly accepts them by setting up a fundamental opposition between 'women', on the one hand, and 'lesbians', on the other. Thus, towards the end of her essay 'The Straight Mind', she comments on the current preoccupation with the question 'What is woman?' and concludes by saying that:

> Frankly, it is a problem that the lesbians do not have because of a change of perspective, and it would be incorrect to say that lesbians associate, make love, live with women, for "woman" has meaning only in heterosexual systems of thought and heterosexual economic systems. Lesbians are not women.[37]

Such a categorical statement requires further examination and raises a number of important questions. First, if Wittig believes that lesbians are not women, how then does she represent lesbianism elsewhere in *The Straight Mind*? Secondly, to what extent is it possible to maintain this oppositional construction when compared with the real existence of 'lesbians' and 'women'? And finally, taking into account the current political climate, in what sense can such divisions be helpful to either 'category'?

The first distinction introduced by Wittig to differentiate between 'lesbian' and 'woman' is at a conceptual level: 'lesbian' is theorized as a third term, neither 'man' nor 'woman', but 'the only concept I know of which is beyond the categories of sex . . .'.[38] While it is true that within the heterosexual conceptual system 'woman' is represented exclusively in terms of 'man', there is no reason why such definitions cannot be challenged and expanded to account for different ways of being a woman. In 1970, for instance, the American group Radicalesbians published an article entitled 'The Woman Identified Woman',[39] a concept which was then adopted by feminists, both lesbian and heterosexual, to signal their refusal to accept dominant constructions of 'woman'. Luce Irigaray's work, as I have shown, reflected a similar concern, as did that of Adrienne Rich.[40] Furthermore, as Diana Fuss has pointed out, if, in Wittig, 'lesbian' signifies a concept beyond heterosexual categories, why does she not extend this concept to include gay men?[41] If gay men are not beyond the categories of 'man' and 'woman', which category do they belong to and according to what criteria? Are they implicitly identified with 'man' as an anatomically male group? If this is so, then Wittig's view that 'sex' is purely a dominant social construct would no longer be tenable, and, by extension, lesbians would have to be defined, in one respect at least, with regard to their biological femaleness. It is precisely her radical denial of femaleness, however, that enables Wittig to set up an opposition between 'lesbians' and 'women'. If, on the other hand, she considers gay men to belong to the 'class of men', then lesbians must also be included in the 'class of women'. Thus, Wittig creates not only a division between lesbians and women, but also, as Fuss has argued, a 'new binarism' opposing 'lesbian' and 'male homosexual'.[42]

Alongside her own construct of 'lesbian', Wittig discusses the experiences of 'real' lesbians, both as individuals and as a group. Referring to the 'old days before the women's liberation movement', she reminds lesbians how 'totally oppressive [. . .] and destructive being "woman" was for us'.[43] Although it is true that the dominant concept of 'woman' was particularly oppressive for lesbians, heterosexual feminists also opposed it. Thus, Simone de Beauvoir's *The Second Sex* (1949) was devoted to a radical critique of *l'éternel féminin*, as was Betty Friedan's *The Feminine Mystique* (1964). Moreover, one of the principal concerns of the Women's Liberation Movement itself was to create different concepts of female subjectivity. However, as

Wittig herself remarks, even contemporary lesbians are still caught in the gender trap, where, in order not to be perceived as 'men', they want to become 'more and more feminine'. While this new trend towards 'femininity' may well be as alienating as the 'butch' stereotype,[44] its presence nevertheless suggests that lesbians are not altogether 'beyond' gender constructs and that Wittig's 'lesbian' is perhaps a (utopian) concept rather than a reality. Instead of seeing 'lesbians' in opposition to 'women', it might be more accurate to say that lesbians are perceived both as women and as not-women, and that their status in society is marked by this paradox. As Julia Penelope and Susan Wolfe have argued: 'Lesbians, after all, have been marginalized both as women, and therefore subsumed within the category of "the feminine", and as nonwomen, departing markedly from stereotyped ("constructed") femininity.'[45]

Her view that heterosexuality represents a class system leads Wittig to assert that lesbians are not part of the class of women, 'either economically, or politically, or ideologically'.[46] Lesbians, she argues, are able to escape from their class because they do not have a 'specific social relation to a man'. In my view, this definition of 'class', in terms of individual relationships rather than society as a whole, is limited and does not account for the position of lesbians within the overall structures of patriarchy. Economically, for instance, lesbians are subject to the same exploitation as other women, regardless of their sexual orientation. From a political and ideological perspective, it could be argued, for example, that violence against women, as well as dehumanizing constructions of 'woman', affect all women, as Wittig herself implicitly acknowledges in her analysis of pornographic discourse.[47] Elsewhere in *The Straight Mind*, however, she compares lesbians to 'runaway slaves' and thereby reinforces their separation from 'women' as a class: 'We are escapees from our class in the same way as the American runaway slaves were when escaping slavery and becoming free.'[48] The figure of the 'runaway', however, could also describe other groups of women, who are not (necessarily) lesbians. Thus, Wittig herself extends her term to include nuns and 'runaway wives', who would, therefore, not belong to the category 'women' either.

Despite the arbitrary and contradictory use of her own terminology, Wittig claims that her ultimate aim is the destruction both of 'woman' as a concept and of 'women' as a class, since both are products of 'heterosexuality as a social system'. Lesbianism, in so far as it provides the only alternative to heterosexuality, would not be included in this process of annihilation: 'To destroy "woman" does not mean that we aim, short of physical destruction, to destroy lesbianism simultaneously with the categories of sex, because lesbianism provides for the moment the only social form in which we can live freely.'[49] Contrary to Wittig's declared intentions, however, this statement does suggest that lesbianism could not survive in a sexless society. For if lesbianism represents a rejection of the categories of sex, then their very destruction would render the existence of lesbianism meaningless. Similarly, if 'woman' as a patriarchal concept were to be abolished, Wittig's alternative construct would no longer be necessary. On the other hand, if women do not exist as a class, lesbians cannot be 'fugitives' from that class. 'Short of physical destruction', then, Wittig envisages a revolutionary transformation of society that would entail the disappearance of all categories pertaining to 'sex' and 'sexuality'. This purely conceptual and political definition of 'lesbian' indicates that in *The Straight Mind* Wittig sees lesbianism as a provisional choice, based on a rejection of heterosexuality, rather than as a specific sexual identity.

In this context it is worth comparing the notion of 'political lesbianism' with the views put forward by Adrienne Rich in 'Compulsory Heterosexuality and Lesbian Existence'. Although her analysis of heterosexuality as an institution is similar to that of Wittig, Rich sees lesbianism not only as a form of resistance to patriarchy, but also as a positive expression of love between women. Commenting on the idea of a 'new bisexuality', a variation on Wittig's sexless future, Rich argues that this notion 'assumes that women who have chosen women have done so simply because men are oppressive and emotionally unavailable'.[50] For Rich, the compulsory nature of heterosexuality as 'the norm' and the repression of lesbianism are both part of the historical division of women in patriarchal societies. Love between women, on the other hand, represents both a refusal to accept this division and 'a profoundly *female* experience'.[51] Wittig's conceptual framework in *The Straight Mind* does not allow her to perceive lesbian relationships in this way, for to do so would be to acknowledge the existence of women, both physically and in terms of specific experiences. Furthermore, Rich's inclusive definition of 'lesbian' as a 'range of woman-identified experience', and her view that all women exist somewhere on a 'lesbian continuum'[52] contrast sharply with Wittig's assertion that no woman is a lesbian. The conclusion of Rich's analysis implies that she envisages the existence of a non-patriarchal society where heterosexuality would no longer be the compulsory norm, but one amongst other, equally valid choices of sexual identity.

The opposition constructed by Wittig between 'lesbians' and 'women' is difficult to substantiate, moreover, when examined in the light of work carried out by feminist historians.[53] Drawing on research in this area, Penelope and Wolfe point out that, until the nineteenth century, love and 'romantic friendships' between women were not only socially acceptable, but actively encouraged as 'practice' for heterosexuality and marriage. It was only when women, following the emergence of the feminist movement, began to seek economic independence and relationships with other women beyond heterosexual marriage, that 'romantic friendships' were prohibited. A significant aspect of this repression was the construction by sexologists, in particular Havelock Ellis and Krafft-Ebbing, of 'the lesbian', a term not previously used. Their theories 'pathologized' lesbians as 'congenital inverts', as 'men' trapped in a female body.[54] Such views are, of course, analogous to Freudian discourse, with its construction of lesbianism as a consequence of 'the virility complex'. Sexology and psychoanalysis can, therefore, be seen as part of an anti-feminist backlash that aimed to suppress female solidarity by creating an artificial distinction between 'women' and 'lesbians'. Ironically, given Wittig's objections to psychoanalysis as being exemplary of 'straight' discourse,[55] the polarization inherent in her own theory could be construed as reinforcing such discourse.

The woman/lesbian opposition constructed by Wittig has significant implications for her views on any possible future allegiance between lesbianism and feminism. Her objective of creating a society in which all manifestations of sexual difference will have been eliminated is incompatible with any cultural expression of women's identities as female subjects. Thus, Wittig cannot accept either 'cultural feminism' or the idea of lesbian cultures and identities, other than as provisional strategies, as political counter-cultures, which will necessarily vanish after 'the revolution'. I would disagree in this respect with Diane Griffin-Crowder, who claims that Wittig's vision of an 'Amazonian culture' does not demand that we 'abandon the hard-won affirmation of women we find in women's music, books, art'.[56] In the light of Wittig's political essays I would suggest that this is precisely what she demands. Commenting on different interpretations of the term 'feminist' within the Women's Movement itself, Wittig states that 'for many of us it means someone who fights for women as a class and for the disappearance of this class. For many others it means someone who fights for woman and her defense – for the myth, then, and its reenforcement.'[57]

If neither women as a class nor 'woman' as a concept are to survive in Wittig's utopia, then anything that might be considered specific to women, whether in terms of 'identity', the body, language or culture will surely also be destined to disappear. At a time when women, both lesbian and heterosexual, are beginning to affirm their own subjectivity, they are being asked to abandon this search for self-expression and to abolish themselves in the very act of liberation. Wittig herself seems to acknowledge this paradox when she argues that women, once they have become conscious of their oppression, need to recognize that 'one can become *someone* in spite of oppression, that one has one's own identity'.[58] While admitting that 'there is no possible fight for someone deprived of an identity', the nature of this identity is not elucidated, except with reference to women's subjective awareness of their oppression. 'Real' subjectivity, for Wittig, can only be attained through a universalizing concept of the 'generally human' which lies beyond the categories of sex.[59] As Christopher Robinson has remarked, if 'lesbian' is already a concept 'beyond sex', in Wittig's 'new state' 'all the citizens [. . .] are lesbians, because they have achieved *sameness*; the oppositional values of heterosexual society have been eliminated'.[60] However, as Robinson rightly points out, how would such 'sameness' be recognizable without a concept of 'difference'?

In Wittig's theoretical essays, then, the term 'lesbian' is ultimately a metaphor for a different way of being and relating, outside gender dualities, but unconnected to biological sex. She has moved to a perspective from which, potentially, everybody will be 'a lesbian' and thus the history of lesbianism as a female experience, existence and struggle has, once again, been erased. As Penelope and Wolfe have argued, lesbians have been excluded 'from the category "woman" by feminist as well as patriarchal discourse'.[61] Wittig's new categorizations, however, reinforce this exclusion and the continuing marginalization of lesbians in society. The impact of her statement on the feminist movement, moreover, is likely to exacerbate already existing divisions between lesbians and heterosexual women, thereby undermining the sense of unity needed to tackle together problems and issues affecting all women. Although at first glance the theories presented by Irigaray and by Wittig seem diametrically opposed, their implications for the future of lesbian existence are similar. For Irigaray's resolutely heterosexual universe, based on rigid definitions of 'identity' in terms of 'sexual difference', has no more room for lesbians than does Wittig's sexless world, in which the abolition of heterosexuality would render lesbianism as a political strategy superfluous. Homosexuality as an emotional and sexual choice, whether for men or for women, cannot be accommodated in either Irigaray's or Wittig's utopias. However, in the current political climate there is little evidence that either patriarchy or compulsory heterosexuality are about to disappear. On the contrary, both are constantly reinforced by dominant cultural discourses, at the same time as gay men and lesbians have been subjected to new forms of legal and political repression. The suggestion that either a 'post-feminist' sexless society, or one respectful of 'difference', is imminent, represents, in my view, an illusion which detracts from the realities of oppression experienced by both lesbians and gay men in the 1990s.

Notes

1. B. Zimmerman (1992), 'Lesbians Like This and That: Some Notes on Lesbian Criticism for the Nineties', in S. Munt (ed.), *New Lesbian Criticism*, Hemel Hempstead, pp. 1–15, p. 4.
2. See L. Irigaray (1974), *Speculum, de l'autre femme*, Paris, pp. 165–83. All page references given here relate to the French original, and all translations are mine.
3. See ibid., pp. 9–162.
4. Ibid., p. 19, 'comment l'enfant à tendances bisexuelles *devient* une femme'.
5. Ibid., p. 25.
6. Ibid., p. 20.
7. Ibid., p. 47: 'un exil, une extradition, une expatriation hors de cette (son) économie désirante'.
8. Ibid., p. 120.
9. Ibid., p. 125: 'Car de la spécificité du désir *entre femmes* rien n'a été dévoilé, énoncé'.
10. L. Irigaray (1977), *Ce sexe qui n'en est pas un*, Paris, pp. 189–93. All page references given here relate to the French original, and all translations are by C. Burke, *Signs*, vol. 6, no. 1, pp. 69–79.
11. Irigaray, *Ce sexe*, p. 208, 'Je t'aime: ton corps là ici maintenant. Je/tu te/me touches, c'est bien assez pour que nous nous sentions vivantes.'
12. C. Burke (1980), 'Introduction to Luce Irigaray's "When Our Lips Speak Together"', *Signs*, vol. 6, no. 1, pp. 66–8.
13. Irigaray, *Ce sexe*, pp. 208–9: 'Entre tes/mes lèvres plusieurs chants, plusieurs dires, toujours se répondent. Sans que l'un, l'une, soit jamais séparable de l'autre. Tu/je: font toujours plusieurs à la fois. Et comment l'un, l'une, dominerait-il l'autre? Imposant sa voix, son ton, son sens?'
14. Ibid., p. 209: 'Elles ne se distinguent pas. Ce qui ne signifie pas qu'elles se confondent.'
15. Ibid., p. 214: 'Tu bouges. Tu ne restes jamais tranquille. Tu ne restes jamais. Tu n'es jamais. Comment te dire? Toujours autre. Comment te parler? Demeurant dans le flux, sans jamais le figer. Le glacer. Comment faire passer dans les mots ce courant? Multiple. Sans causes, sens, qualités simples. Et pourtant indécomposable.'
16. Ibid., p. 132: 'la mascarade de la féminité'.
17. C. Holmlund (1991), 'The Lesbian, The Mother, The Heterosexual Lover: Irigaray's Recodings of Difference', *Feminist Studies*, vol. 17, no. 2, pp. 283–308, p. 287.

18. L. Irigaray (1994), *Thinking the Difference: For A Peaceful Revolution*, trans. K. Montin, London, p. 13.
19. Luce Irigaray (1981), *Le Corps-à-corps avec la mère*, Montreal, p. 27: 'le rôle [. . .] maternel désubjectivé'.
20. Holmlund, 'The Lesbian', p. 290.
21. See also A. Rich (1977), *Of Woman Born*, London.
22. Irigaray, *Le Corps-à-corps*, pp. 30–1.
23. Ibid., p. 86.
24. Ibid., p. 86: 'La relation mère/fille, fille/mère constitue un noyau extrêmement explosif dans nos sociétés. La penser, la changer revient à ébranler l'ordre patriarcal.'
25. Holmlund, 'The Lesbian', p. 304.
26. E. Grosz (1988), 'The Hetero and the Homo: The Sexual Ethics of Luce Irigaray', *Gay Information*, nos. 17–18, pp. 37–44, p. 41.
27. L. Irigaray (1996), *I love to you*, trans. A. Martin, London, p. 47.
28. Ibid., p. 5. For further commentary on Irigaray's privileging of an order of (hetero)sexual difference and its consequences *vis-à-vis* her theorization of female homosexuality, see M. Whitford (1991), *Luce Irigaray: Philosophy in the Feminine*, London and New York, p. 154.
29. M. Wittig (1992), *The Straight Mind and Other Essays*, Hemel Hempstead.
30. See also C. Delphy (1975), 'Pour un féminisme matérialiste', *L'Arc*, no. 61.
31. Wittig, *The Straight Mind*, p. 2.
32. Ibid., p. 6.
33. Ibid., p. 9.
34. D. Fuss (1990), *Essentially Speaking: Feminism, Nature and Difference*, London, p. 50.
35. Wittig, *The Straight Mind*, pp. 52–3.
36. Ibid., p. 7.
37. Ibid., p. 32.
38. Ibid., p. 20.
39. Radicalesbians (1970), 'The Woman-Identified-Woman', *Notes from the Third Year*, pp. 240–5.
40. A. Rich (1984), 'Compulsory Heterosexuality and Lesbian Existence', in A. Snitow *et al.* (eds), *Desire: The Politics of Sexuality*, London, pp. 212–41.
41. Fuss, *Essentially Speaking*, p. 46.
42. Ibid., p. 46.
43. Wittig, *The Straight Mind*, p. 12.
44. Ibid., p. 12.

45. S. J. Wolfe and J. Penelope (1993), 'Sexual Identity/Textual Politics', in S. J. Wolfe and J. Penelope (eds), *Sexual Practice/Textual Theory: Lesbian Cultural Criticism*, Oxford, pp. 1–24, p. 3.
46. Wittig, *The Straight Mind*, p. 20.
47. Ibid., p. 26.
48. Ibid., p. 20.
49. Ibid., p. 20.
50. Rich, 'Compulsory Heterosexuality', p. 217.
51. Ibid., p. 228.
52. Ibid., p. 227.
53. See L. Faderman (1985), *Surpassing the Love of Men: Romantic Friendship and Love between Women from the Renaissance to the Present*, London; S. Jeffreys (1985), *The Spinster and Her Enemies: Feminism and Sexuality 1880–1930*, London.
54. Wolfe and Penelope, 'Sexual Identity', pp. 17–20.
55. Wittig, *The Straight Mind*, pp. 21–32.
56. D. Griffin-Crowder (1983), 'Amazons and Mothers? Monique Wittig, Hélène Cixous and Theories of Women's Writing', *Contemporary Literature*, vol. 24, no. 2, pp. 117–44, p. 143.
57. Wittig, *The Straight Mind*, p. 1.
58. Ibid., p. 16.
59. Ibid., pp. 19–20.
60. C. Robinson (1995), *Scandal in the Ink: Male and Female Homosexuality in Twentieth-Century French Literature*, London, p. 188.
61. Wolfe and Penelope, 'Sexual Identity', p. 3.

– 4 –

The Outlaw Returns: *Homos* vs. Tradition in the New Work of Leo Bersani

James S. Williams

In the fourth and last chapter of *Homos* (1995), a devastating study of the current political risks in the United States of both increased gay visibility and 'desexualizing' queer critiques of homosexual identity, Leo Bersani suddenly turns to the topos of the gay outlaw in modern French literature, specifically André Gide's *The Immoralist* (1902) (*L'Immoraliste*), Marcel Proust's *Cities of the Plain* (1921–2) (*Sodome et Gomorrhe*), and Jean Genet's *Funeral Rites* (1944) (*Pompes Funèbres*). Bersani argues that these three texts propose in different ways an ethics of 'homo-ness', or a new way of structuring our relations to ourselves and to others, based on what he calls 'expansive narcissism'. These authors, he writes, are drawn to 'the *anti-communitarian* impulses they discover in homosexual desire',[1] and 'otherness is articulated as relay stations in a process of self-extension'.[2] Gay desire thus reveals itself as a desire for the same from the perspective of a self already identified as different from itself. According to Bersani, desire so defined can free us from an oppressive, Lacanian psychology of desire as lack, a psychology that grounds sociality in trauma and castration. A new reflection on homo-ness, he concludes, 'could lead us to a salutary devalorizing of difference – or, more exactly, to a notion of difference not as a trauma to be overcome [. . .] but rather as a nonthreatening supplement to sameness'.[3]

The polemical energy and idealist drive of *Homos* has, in sharp opposition to the current, prevailing mood of AIDS-inspired fatalism, an almost old-fashioned, gay liberation ring to it. The title of Chapter 4, 'The Gay Outlaw', is itself provocative, for if it recalls in the first instance the American world of John Rechy's *The Sexual Outlaw* (1977) – an age of promiscuity-as-revolution prior to AIDS – it also harks back further to the general pre-war culture of the homosexual exile wandering abroad (metaphorically and sometimes literally) in search of freedom and pleasure.[4] In fact, the main impression created by *Homos* is of analytical rigour merging into fundamentalist joy. The very neatness – not to say tweeness – of the recurring duosyllabic term 'homo-', used in one case at the end of Chapter 3 to reclaim Freud's 1914 essay on the Wolf Man as a caring boy–father scenario that voids the castrating figure of the father (this is Bersani's counter-response to Foucault's conception of a happy gay sexuality excluding fantasy), is extended by the symmetrical structure of the book itself, which could not, on a superficial level, be more perfectly self-contained. In a series of parallel inversions – Chapter 1, 'The Gay Presence'/Chapter 2, 'The Gay Absence'; Chapter 3, 'The Gay Daddy'/Chapter 4, 'The Gay Outlaw' – gay presence is reversed into gay absence, and the gay father is rediscovered as the gay outlaw. Furthermore, the short opening prologue subtitled 'We' sets into play the utopian notion of a shared identity between author and reader. Bersani imagines, somewhat fancifully, that even a 'black, economically disadvantaged gay man will find what he [Bersani] has to say about Genet resonant with his own experience', since it is possible that 'the most varied, even antagonistic, identities meet transversely'.[5] A 'pleasing instability' is claimed for the 'we' of *Homos*: 'my "we"', Bersani asserts, 'frequently defines a perspective that is at once mine and not mine'.[6]

I do not intend in the short space available here to establish whether Bersani is justified in invoking a utopian form of transverse identity while at the same time chastizing queer theorists and anti-identitarian activists for refusing to acknowledge sufficiently that their homosexuality is, above all, a sexual practice. Such work has already been undertaken by David Halperin, who accuses Bersani of being more communitarian and queer than his commitment to go beyond the social would seem to allow.[7] Nor do I wish to assess how abstract and compromised Bersani's terms of 'homo' and 'homo-ness' may actually be, in comparison, say, with the more directly oppositional terms of 'queer' and 'queerness'. Tim Dean has eloquently shown how *Homos* may ultimately 'degay' gayness, since in Bersani's scheme 'homo-ness', while inherent in gay sexuality and signifying 'a revolutionary inaptitude for heteroized sociality',[8] can also be found more generally in forms of 'anti-redemptive' art where the reader is irremediably excluded, notably the work of Beckett.[9] (In *Arts of Impoverishment: Beckett, Rothko, Resnais* (1993), Bersani examined, in collaboration with Ulysse Dutoit, how certain 'impoverished', 'anti-modernist' artistic practices can inhibit our approach and movement towards the work of art at the very moment we try to take its critical measure.) But nor, finally, do I intend to uncover the latent redemptive qualities of Bersani's extensive critique of 'the culture of redemption' (his term for the ways in which art and culture can erase, repeat and redeem life).[10] This would be a natural if predictable critical move, although one fast gaining ground. Gidean moments of memory and nostalgia are uncovered, for instance, by Michael Lucey in his analysis of the rhetorical structures at work in Bersani's controversial 1987 article on gay desire and gay activism, 'Is the Rectum a Grave?'. This is where Bersani attacked for the first time anti-essentialist gay critics and activists such as Simon Watney who, he claims, empty gayness of all substantive attributes, and thereby participate in society's sweeping redemptive, or 'pastoralizing', project. For Bersani, a moralizing discourse about promiscuity serves only to transform the concrete, sexual practice of anal *jouissance* into the cerebral tensions of courtship.[11]

What interests me most, in fact, about *Homos* is the formal aspect of Chapter 4, that is to say, its incongruous position and disjunctive status in relation to the book as a whole. For readers not only of the previous tightly woven and aggressively argued chapters of *Homos* but also of Bersani's general work in art and psychoanalysis, the style of 'The Gay Outlaw' comes as rather a shock. It is an uncharacteristically loose piece of writing with a defiantly rough edge, basically juxtaposing three separate chunks of literary analysis and resorting at times to disarmingly casual expressions such as 'radical slumming'.[12] As some rather puzzled critics have commented, the chapter is inadequately signposted,[13] despite Bersani's warning in the Prologue that Chapter 4 is no mere 'addendum of literary criticism' but 'absolutely crucial to the persuasiveness' of the preceding arguments.[14] Even the statement made on page 99 that the discussions of Gide and Proust should be seen as initial responses to the psychoanalytic challenge of dissociating masochism from the death-drive is couched in the form of a parenthesis, as though the final chapter were significant only for what has come before. And while Bersani is razor-sharp in exposing the effects of gay (in)visibility in the US, he completely elides the particular cultural context of his chosen French writers. Moreover, not only does he resolutely avoid giving anything like a blueprint for reversing the political and theoretical problems that he raised in earlier chapters with such vigour and clarity (his ideas are, to all intents and purposes, unfeasible in concrete political terms), but also he refuses to supply any form of theoretical self-reflection on, or justification of, the structure and style of Chapter 4. Clearly his is not a comparative discussion of French gay male writers of the kind, for example, once attempted by Gerald Storzer, who sought to establish homosexual paradigms.[15] Yet in sharp contrast to the first three chapters, where he identifies gay/queer critics and patiently takes them to task one by one, Bersani provides little or no perspective on the current state of play in Gide, Proust and Genet studies as he heads directly to the sexual core of his chosen novels. Finally – and this is perhaps the most untypical aspect of Bersani's work in *Homos* – he never articulates explicitly the intellectual wager of the chapter, which is to oppose gay/queer cultural and political self-erasure with what he proposed earlier in the book as '*a nonsuicidal disappearance of the subject*'.[16]

What, then, are we to make of such an internally divided and awkwardly proportioned text as *Homos*? Why does Bersani suddenly return to the high modernist, French literary tradition that he had studied at length in previous works such as *Marcel Proust: The Fictions of Life and Art* (1965), *A Future for Astyanax: Character and Desire in Literature* (1976), and *Baudelaire and Freud* (1977)?[17] Nothing seems more outdated and inappropriate at the present time than a return to the Romantic figure of the social outcast, particularly in Genet (by Bersani's own admission the least 'gay-affirmative' author he knows[18]) whose early prose, according to Christopher Robinson in his recent overview of twentieth-century gay and lesbian writing, *Scandal in the Ink*, offers a completely negative portrait of homosexuality because locked in a straitjacket of criminality, betrayal, treason and collaboration.[19] Could it be that Bersani is acting as the self-appointed 'outlaw' of gay and queer studies by returning narcissistically (understood in the most conventional sense), in a kind of critical vacuum, to former sites of personal critical triumph? Certainly, in the very 'inadequacy' of the fourth chapter – its refusal to deliver direct answers to social and political questions and its absorption in issues of narcissism and the body – *Homos* could be said to embody a key issue of ideological difference formalized by Lee Edelman in *Homographesis*: the difference between, on the one hand, the political rhetoric of (normalizing) gay activism, and, on the other, what it defines itself against, namely gay narcissism and passivity (for example the perceived self-indulgence, regression and even masochistic self-identification of drag queens and transvestites).[20] Yet is it perhaps also the case that Bersani is using the modern French tradition as an outer limit, or 'limit-relation', for his overtly political work, in the process confirming his earlier interest in those death-like states of 'radically unsettled being' that he traced in his 1982 study, *The Death of Stéphane Mallarmé*?[21] After all, of the two prefaces used as epigraphs in *Homos* – one by Joyce, the other by Gide – the latter reads simply: 'Familles, je vous hais!' ('Families, I detest you all'). (We recall also that Pascal's phrase, 'Le *moi* est haïssable . . .' ('The self is to be detested . . .'), served as an epigraph for 'Is the Rectum a Grave?'.)[22] If so, does Bersani stand accused of simply subscribing to the French tradition of *belles lettres* and the literary topos of the social outlaw?

I want to explore these different questions by entering into the textual void of *Homos* opened up by Chapter 4 and its deployment of the outlaw theme. My focus will not be on the critical worth of Bersani's interpretations of Gide, Proust and Genet, but rather on the chapter's performative aspects, specifically its process of 'friction', an idea presented by Bersani in vague and suggestive terms in the opening paragraph. He writes there: 'some useful friction – and as a result some useful thought – may be created by questioning the compatibility of homosexuality with civil service'.[23] Bersani uses this term also in Chapter 3 to describe the movement of resistance produced in any exercise of power, stating: 'as power moves toward, and against its objects, it inevitably produces frictions that thwart its movements'.[24] These frictions are placed in the context of Freud's account of sadism and masochism:

> The subject seeks to repeat an excitement to which the object to be appropriated has become irrelevant and which may consist, most consequentially, in the dissolution of the appropriating ego. Appropriation has been transformed into communication, a non-dialogic communication in which the subject is so obscenely 'rubbed' by the object it anticipates mastering that the very boundaries separating subject from object, boundaries necessary for possession, have been erased.[25]

Bersani further extended this movement of friction to Freud's case of the Wolf Man, which he presents as 'a fascinating model of frictional confrontations' and 'powerful thrusts'. He is referring by this not simply to the repeated penetrations of the father's penis, but also to what he terms 'the interpretive aggressions of Freud's insistent, curiously unsupported theory of castration'.[26] The latter, Bersani argues, 'is effectively turned back by all the "memories" of the child's concern for the father's loss of power', since the son's power is improvised as a response to the vulnerability inherent in the very position and exercise of power'.[27] As we enter Chapter 4, the question is thus already posed of what type of friction (if any) is generated for the reader by Bersani's critical encounter with Gide, Proust and Genet. As we shall see, this question bears directly on the nature of Bersani's overall theoretical project and raises general issues of gay critical practice. It will be my contention that Bersani's charged return in *Homos* to the modern French canon constitutes above all a powerful, and timely, reflection on the development of gay/queer literary studies as a new critical tradition. Let us first review in brief the individual parts of Chapter 4.

After raising the question of the compatibility of homosexuality with civic service, Bersani immediately launches into a discussion of the strange anomaly of *The Immoralist*, namely Michel's 'sexual preference without sex'.[28] According to Bersani, Gide preempted Foucault's unmasking of the classificatory processes that reify bodily behaviour as psychic essences by taking one of those essences and rendering it, as a category, incoherent.[29] Michel thus becomes a bodily ego driven by a revolutionary eroticism, seeking to touch inaccurate extensions, or 'replications', of himself in the young Arab boys he encounters. As his body reaches out in chaste promiscuity 'to find itself beyond itself', Michel experiences pederasty as a narcissistic expansion of his desiring skin, while his homosexuality 'glides' into an impersonal sameness.[30] In such a way, the risks taken in 'cruising'[31] the other as the same in homo-ness provide an opportunity, 'at once insignificant and precious',[32] for narcissistic pleasure. Bersani affirms in a delicately poised formulation that narcissistic expansion constitutes a 'renunciation of narcissistic self-containment',[33] resulting in an erotic moment of self-divestiture.

From here Bersani proceeds directly to a discussion of sexual inversion in Proust. His virtuoso move is to find a radical 'homo'-edge to Proust, claiming that at the very moment the narrator of *Cities of the Plain* most insistently represents homosexuality as a distorted relation of difference, he lays the groundwork for an authentic homo-ness.[34] Focusing again on depersonalizing and dehumanizing modes of human behaviour, Bersani argues that Proust's comparison of Jupien and Charlus cruising each other to a bee cross-fertilizing a rare orchid serves to establish the idea of a universal, 'natural' community, one that encompasses other races, generations and species – even the inanimate – in 'a vast network of *near-sameness* characterized by relations of inaccurate replication'.[35] Here, too, Bersani treads a very fine line: to desire in others what we already are is really a 'self-effacing narcissism constitutive of community in that it tolerates psychological difference because of its very indifference to psychological difference. *This* narcissistic subject seeks a self-replicating reflection in which s/he is neither known nor not known'.[36] On the question of the radicality of this episode within the context of the first part of *Cities of the Plain*, Bersani, rather strangely, does not consider how far he has revised his earlier thoughts on the topic expressed in *The Culture of Redemption*, ideas with which Eve Kosofsky Sedgwick subsequently took issue in *Epistemology of the Closet*.[37] It might be argued, in fact, that Bersani is over-compensating in *Homos* for his initial dismissal of Proust's examination of *la race maudite* as a banal, reductive, even romantic thematization of homosexuality, which he opposed to the later, more elaborate meditations on desire in Proust's novel focused around the figure of Albertine.[38]

Nothing prepares the reader, however, for the conceptual switch from a discussion of what might be valuably human in the human community to the section on Genet which begins: '*Betrayal is an ethical necessity*'.[39] Bersani draws us into an ever more rarefied, ascetic world of evil, betrayal and specialized sexuality. In Genet, he writes, 'evil, the ethical corollary of [. . .] penile aggression, is an antirelational thrust',[40] and solitude, emptied of all value, is the logical extension of betrayal, since it consists merely 'in a movement out of everything'.[41] As for homosexuality, it stands as the prototype for all relations that break with humanity and elevate waste and the reduction of difference to sameness and the requirements of pleasure. In an astonishing and quite unprecedented alignment of theory and sexuality, Bersani argues that the night-time fucking scene between Erik and Riton on the roof-tops of Paris during the Liberation of Paris, when the two fantasy figures face in the same direction and 'come not with each other but, as it were, *to the world*',[42] serves ultimately to 'restart' relational activity. Thus, if the main impression of *Funeral Rites* remains the closed, onanistic monumentality of gestural beauty that Bersani critiqued at length in *A Future for Astyanax* (although once again no reference is made during Chapter 4 to that earlier analysis), Genet also points the way to 'a curative collapsing of social difference into a radical homo-ness, where [all relations with the other having been abolished] the subject might begin again, differentiating itself from itself and thereby reconstituting sociality'.[43]

The force and scale of Bersani's dynamic approach to *Funeral Rites* should not be underestimated. Never has he entered more comprehensively, and more unnervingly, into the realm of the sexual, arguing that at its most extreme, Genet's 'cherished' practice of sexual rimming presents an amalgam of life and fecund waste from which can emerge new literary landscapes. In Genet, he declares, dying must be conceived as *jouissance*, and sublimation should be understood more as an activity of consciousness accompanying a particular sexual activity whose original, erotic exaltation is always forcefully present ('murderous betrayal generalizes and socializes rimming without losing any of rimming's erotic energy').[44] Bersani rounds off Chapter 4 by considering Genet's own partial dismissal of his work and his refusal to establish the usual, culturally consecrated communication between an author and his novel (he quotes Genet on *Funeral Rites*: 'this book is sincere and it's a joke').[45] Genet, like Beckett, is the sign for Bersani of a radical modernity anxious to save art from the preemptive operations of institutionalized culture.

If we now step back a little from this heady and disturbing excavation of sexual desire, we can see clearly that the provocatively 'aberrant' and essentially disconnected appreciations of Gide, Proust and Genet serve primarily 'to repeat, expand, and intensify the same',[46] i.e. to demonstrate homo-ness, rather than to develop or elaborate a particular line of argument. In fact, it is the very lack of a teleological approach that makes the final comparison between Genet and Beckett in terms of modernity and culture seem impossibly over-general. Moreover, if, following Genet, Bersani exposes and exploits the potential of culture's dominant terms, particularly its ethical and sexual categories, to erase cultural relationality (for Bersani, 'the very precondition for subversive repositionings and defiant repetitions'),[47] he also invokes a physical world of rimming that cannot entirely escape the negative effect of Genet's 'moral abstractions' – abstractions that he is at pains throughout to criticize.[48] Yet as he turns his back on America and goes back in time to re-experience more directly than ever he dared in *A Future for Astyanax* illegitimate acts of French rimming, Bersani never stops to acknowledge these particular problems and complications. Still less does he inform the reader of his theoretical intentions. As a result, the reader is left adrift, forced him/herself to make the difficult, and often quite unpredictable, connections both between the different parts of Chapter 4, and between it and the previous three chapters. (This feeling is further increased by our knowledge that the Genet section of the chapter has remained almost unchanged since its first appearance as an article in *Diacritics* entitled 'The Gay Outlaw'.)[49] It is certainly hard to agree with Bersani's statement in the Prologue that the last chapter is 'absolutely crucial' to the rest of the book. Having virtually demolished the new American generation of queer culture and what he sees as its misguided sense of social revolt, it is as though Bersani were casting into doubt, and even undermining, the carefully laid foundations and structures of his own theoretical and psychoanalytical project, which has sought to trace the self-erasing contours and erratic formalisms operating in modernist and anti-modernist art. One can perhaps understand – without necessarily wishing to endorse – Halperin's complaint that the Bersani of *Homos* is a 'politically non-aligned exponent of French avant-garde thought who surrounds the calculated outrageousness of his refined scholarly exegeses with an incomparably glamorous aura of transgressive chic'.[50]

How, then, are we to view Bersani's explosive treatment of the outlaw theme in the modern French canon? The question can best be explored, I think, by turning to Bersani's earlier study, *The Culture of Redemption*, where he speaks about his general theoretical ambitions. To prepare the reader there for his argument that the culture of redemption is dependent on fundamental assumptions about authoritative identities and on identity as authority, Bersani included a prologue very different in style from that of *Homos* in which he carefully introduced the form, structure and objectives of the book, emphasizing in particular its conceptual mobility. In addition, he made the following, highly personal statement: 'I recognize that [. . .] I also confirm a slightly dispiriting consistency in my own work [. . .] I have perhaps been less restlessly self-dismissive in my own criticism than my work suggests I should be [. . .] I have for some years now repeatedly circled around the question of the relation between cultural authority, selfhood, and sexuality.'[51] He confesses: 'the questions I ask in reading literary texts (or visual art) constitute a kind of moral criticism [. . .] this involves a certain indifference to criticism anxious to teach the difference between the literary and the nonliterary'.[52] Bersani describes his version of moral criticism as an 'ethical-erotic project',[53] and speaks in terms of an aesthetics of narcissism, offering by way of example those early moments in Freud's 1914 essay 'On Narcissism' where narcissism is treated more as 'a self-*jouissance* which dissolves the person and thereby evades – at least temporarily – the sacrosanct value of selfhood'.[54] Bersani explains:

> If sexuality is socially dysfunctional in that it brings people together only then to plunge them into a self-shattering and solipsistic jouissance that drives them apart (a jouissance somehow 'figured' in writers as different as Baudelaire, Bataille, and Flaubert), it can also be thought of as our primary, hygienic practice of nonviolence, and even as a kind of biological protection against our continuously renewed efforts to disguise and to exercise the tyranny of the self in the prestigious form of legitimate cultural authority.[55]

Bersani's principal aim in *The Culture of Redemption* is revealed as a desire to trace the narcissistic retreats and intensities of literature.[56] In the particular case of Freud, that means determining 'the necessary implication of [the] psychoanalytic theorizing itself in disturbances that, while ostensibly the subject of its discourse, more profoundly *agitate* that discourse'.[57] In a later chapter of *The Culture of Redemption* entitled 'Erotic Assumptions: Narcissism and Sublimation in Freud', Bersani will prove convincingly that Freud's reaffirmation of theoretical authority in his essay on narcissism takes place by way of reinforcements in the theory of the ego, 'an exercise all the more unexpected because [Freud's] discussion begins by suggesting that the ego is born as an already shattered totality, as an agency seduced into being by the very prospect of being shattered'.[58]

It is fair to say that the radical desire for self-delegitimation expressed in the Prologue of *The Culture of Redemption* is not totally realized in the main body of the work itself, any more than in its eight-page Epilogue, which, as a piece of literary exegesis of Genesis, is not immeasurably different in style and approach from the book as a whole. Indeed, the kind of 'persistent subversion of authority'[59] that Bersani admires in Genesis, notably in the wandering, nameless and deviant figure of Ishmael, finds no direct formal echo in his own masterfully controlled and perfectly measured critical text. The key theoretical demand made in the Prologue not simply to avoid cultivating a legitimate cultural or theoretical authority but also, more fundamentally, to destroy that pretension, has still, therefore, to be met.

Indeed, in a critical project like Bersani's, which proclaims itself so profoundly anti-redemptive, the lack of a decisive move towards textual self-dismissal and self-delegitimation becomes directly apparent.

The vital need for such a move accounts for the particular value and significance of Chapter 4 of *Homos*, which, I would claim, 'undoes' what has already been accomplished by Bersani in his previous work. Incomparably neat and polemically smooth for three-quarters of its length, *Homos* is shattered out of its conceptual coherence by the very 'deviance' of Chapter 4, which leaves wide-open the gap between the various discourses set in play. That is to say, at this particular stage of his 'ethical-erotic' project, Bersani allows his work to be 'lured' by the outlaw tradition within French *belles lettres* in order precisely to create the formal, textual conditions for self-*jouissance*. What we witness in Chapter 4 is a spectacular, erotic exercise in 'turning back' on oneself at the very moment a display of the law of critical authority – or what Bersani calls in *Arts of Impoverishment* 'a hyperbolic (personal and cultural) ego'[60] – is most called for. By turning away from America, sexual politics and queer theory, and by effectively 'desublimating' his former work on the French tradition, Bersani produces in *Homos* a textual form of the extreme sexual excitement that he has defined elsewhere as 'both a turning *away from* others and a dying *to* the self' (my italics).[61]

Rather than being a mere 'addendum', then, Chapter 4 of *Homos* can be experienced as a massively extended *punctum* in the erotic sense provided by Barthes in *Camera Lucida*, i.e. of a mysterious, unpredictable 'tilt', 'the passage of a void'.[62] Certainly, if *Homos* represents Bersani's most personal work, it is not because he reveals there his own sexual and political tendencies, but rather because he presents his theoretical ego 'destroying' itself in its own narcissistic, sexual intensity, assisted in part by the often blistering force of his rhetorical technique (in particular, his combustive reliance on superlatives and absolutes such as the recurring formula, 'nothing can'). By denying any real form of narrative closure to *Homos*, Bersani cancels himself out as an omniscient psychoanalytic (and now cultural) critic and, in the process, transforms his book into a work of art according to the definition given in *Arts of Impoverishment*: that of a movement towards an impoverished and dispersed self. We could go even further and say that Bersani's text possesses what, in the opinion of Richard Howard, is the essential quality of French gay writing of the last twenty-five years, namely, that 'the homosexual writer is born simultaneously with his text: or rather [that] his text brings him into being'.[63] If a gay signature is inscribed in *Homos*, it is, however, only in that intense moment of friction when Bersani all but 'signs away' his own well-established authorial power.

Crucial, of course, to the production of textual friction in *Homos* is the reader, who is forced to enter the process of signature by 'counter-signing' Bersani's text in the most radical way possible. Having lured 'us' into expecting a narcissistic reaffirmation of his critical authority founded in the French literary tradition – an authority that we might willingly and narcissistically wish to endorse – Bersani forces us to contemplate our own appetitive critical desires precisely by shattering them. In the charged, erotic, textual encounters of *Homos*, and particularly in the case of Genet, where the narratee is vicariously 'rubbed', Bersani generates a fundamental drive towards dis-identification even at the risk of losing the reader, i.e. of ourselves 'losing ourselves' as readers. Hence, a potentially static bond of gay identification between author, book and reader becomes what we might call a mutual 'self-outlawing', Bersani's aim clearly being that his readers review and redefine their own textual/sexual subjectivities. At the very least, Bersani's pushing of the limits of critical 'deficiency' confounds any expectations the reader may have of a happy 'cruise' with Bersanian theory. This is inferred by Bersani himself in a recent interview, where he presents *Homos* in terms of an individual challenge: '[o]ne of the great virtues of writing and thinking is to test how you can go against yourself, not simply for dilettante aesthetic reasons, but because it's the obligation of every human being to test their limits. And for me that means testing the limits of my relations to others [. . .].'[64] To return again briefly to Barthes, the effect of *Homos* may be compared to that of 'Soirées de Paris', a posthumously published, 'post-theoretical' work by Barthes written in the form of a personal diary, where the lack of a plural agreement on the French reflexive verb '*se tirer*' in the opening epigraph – a line by Schopenhauer rendered as: 'Eh bien, nous nous en sommes bien tiré' ('So, we're well out of it') – sets up a whole problematics of narrative relations that affects not only the narrator and his subject (a gigolo) but also the author and reader.[65]

But there are other aspects to Bersani's adversarial, self-shattering work in *Homos* that make it more than just a narcissistic and ahistorical experiment in gay textuality, and that prevent 'homo-ness' from remaining a strictly personal, esoteric term. Already the description by Bersani of his critical project as 'ethical-erotic' indicates an ambition to go beyond the idea of simply rescuing the erotic from the domain of the ethical. As Dean has persuasively argued, Bersani's de-idealization of sex is strategic, since a collective and individual sense of gay selfhood is no longer appropriate in the current context of AIDS, where the boundary between ego-annihilating *jouissance* and exciting – but ultimately suicidal – risks of unsafe sex is liable to become blurred.[66] Yet in *Homos*, where Bersani turns his back, as it were, on cultural/social/political theory and returns to fiction, and where the gay theme becomes the basis for a new 'poetics' (as opposed to 'politics') of style, the personal 'rimming' of the modern French canon has immediate and unexpected repercussions for the current debate on the relations between art and theory. For while *Homos* may be compared with other recent attempts to create a form of personal, gay criticism, notably D. A. Miller's imaginary 'encounter' with Barthes across cultures and generations in *Bringing Out Roland Barthes* (1992), its erotic, textual vibrations offer a unique vantage point from which to consider the nature and future direction of queer theory. Its underlying message, delivered with acute force in its very refusal to articulate links between modernist French literature and contemporary, postmodern American culture, seems to be this: that if queer theory is not simply to be applied imperialistically as Theory to national literatures and cultures, and if it is not therefore to congeal institutionally as part of the critical *doxa* but instead generate new and fertile textual and cultural convergences, then – to paraphrase Bersani's notion of homo-ness – it will need to approach art less phobically as an object to be 'overcome' in the interests of a preset political agenda, and more as another form of itself, i.e. as a different form of critical practice. Paradoxically, this will only be possible if theory and practice are maintained in a mutual state of tension and resistance, that is to say, in a mode of friction that avoids the all-too-easy blurring of formal distinctions. (Compare in this regard Bersani's implicitly self-critical text, which serves to provoke and contest the reader's critical position and desire, with Miller's overly self-conscious and self-preoccupied blend of literary criticism and fantasized relations.[67]) Indeed, the 'formative', intertextual non-relations of *Homos* are quite at odds with certain self-idealizing forms of queer community where one writes in complicity with a chosen audience, an obvious case in point being the Duke school of queer theory led by Sedgwick and Michael Moon.[68] Finally, if we bear in mind that Bersani strongly endorsed *Bringing Out Roland Barthes* when it first appeared, *Homos* can be read specifically as Bersani's theoretical self-differentiation from himself in order to reconstitute the very nature of theoretically informed gay writing and reading.

What Bersani is ultimately saying in *Homos*, like Genet with his novel, is not to pursue theory too 'seriously', too 'exclusively'. In the terms used to describe sexuality in his article 'Is the Rectum a Grave?', the value of theory is precisely to demean the seriousness of efforts to redeem it.[69] What this means is that we should approach theory more as the work of the imagination, or, better still, as the 'hard work' of art. A 'strong' writer like Gide, with his unswerving belief in the power of art always to provide 'the sufficient solution' (Preface to *The Immoralist*),[70] provides an obvious and valuable point of reference. Yet there is also the more pertinent, contemporary example of Loïc Chotard's 1994 novel about gay sexual cruising, *Tiers Monde*, which, like *Homos*, raises in its very 'weakness' major questions about the relations between theory and fiction, although in reverse. As Michael Worton has shown, Chotard's novel 'disappoints' in terms of traditional narrative intrigue, and its anti-hero narrator Gérard even 'forgets' to describe the 1980s Paris setting (it also comes complete with a final 'Note' revealing that some of the men who inspired the novel have since died). By presupposing an active, 'questing' reader who will work through theories that are absent from the text but necessary for its readerly construction (for example, Baudelaire's concept of the *flâneur*), *Tiers Monde* becomes a site of intertextual speculation, 'establishing itself (temporarily) as theory and theory as fiction'.[71] Similarly, the experimental, ethical-erotic project currently being developed by Bersani allows us to reconceive the relations between theory, sexuality and artistic practice, and, in so doing, to imagine what increasingly throwaway notions like gay writing, gay theory, and the gay reader might most radically mean. We await with thrilling, open anticipation the next confrontation.

Notes

1. L. Bersani (1995), *Homos*, Cambridge, Mass., p. 7.
2. Ibid.
3. Ibid.
4. I am drawing here on Jonathan Dollimore's fine analysis of the relationship between homosexuality and death, 'Sex and Death', *Textual Practice*, vol. 9, no. 1 (1995), pp. 27–53, where he discusses the urban confinement of homosexual transgression in post-war gay culture. He quotes as an example of Rechy's revolutionary ethos the following statement: 'Promiscuous homosexuals (outlaws with dual identities [. . .]) are the shock troops of the sexual revolution. The streets are the battlegrounds, the revolution is the sexhunt [and] a radical statement is made each time a man has sex with another on the street' (J. Rechy (1978 [1977]), *The Sexual Outlaw: A Documentary*, London, p. 301). Dollimore concludes his article, which also focuses on Foucault's life and work, with a discussion of the value of Barthes's 'wise' conception of the sexual, and non-sexual, casual, erotic encounter, or 'trick', as formulated in his preface to Renaud Camus's 1979 novel *Tricks*. The

trick, Dollimore explains, enacts 'the possibility of a simultaneous identification/disidentification in which I cease to be the fixed, tyrannized subject and become – become what?' (p. 46). As we shall see, the claims made by Dollimore for the trick – that it is 'a liberation *from* self, from a self-oppressive identity – especially the subordinated identity' (p. 45) – are quite different from Bersani's radical notion in *Homos* of an anticommunitarian, even 'dehumanized', form of cruising.

5. Bersani, *Homos*, p. 9.
6. Ibid.
7. See D. Halperin (1996), 'More or Less Gay-Specific' (a review of *Homos*), *London Review of Books*, 23 May, pp. 24–7. Halperin describes Bersani as a fundamentalist who 'refuses to deviate from the literal truth of object-choice' (p. 26). He also, quite correctly, attacks as unjust, even insulting, Bersani's accusation that queer activists harbour an 'aversion to – homosexuality' (p. 26). Kevin Kopelson, in his review of *Homos* in *SubStance*, no. 79 (1996), argues along similar lines that Bersani's special pleading on behalf of gay male sameness is readily dismissible as utopian, essentialist and humanist. He attributes to Bersani's 'phallocentrism' and 'lawyerly zeal' a wish to find in Proust sameness where there isn't any (male inversion), and an inability to see sameness where there is (lesbianism).
8. Bersani, *Homos*, p. 7.
9. See T. Dean (1996), 'Sex and Syncope', *Raritan*, vol. 15, no. 3, pp. 64–86. Bersani himself explains that homosexuality is only 'a privileged vehicle for homo-ness [. . .] which designates a mode of connectedness to the world that it would be absurd to reduce to sexual preference' (*Homos*, p. 10). In fact, 'homo-ness' is potentially universal, 'an anti-communal mode of connectedness we might all share, or a new way of coming together' (ibid.).
10. In his 1990 book, *The Culture of Redemption*, Cambridge, Mass., Bersani examines first 'the corrective will' (in Proust, Freud, Benjamin, Baudelaire, Nietzsche, Malraux, Bataille) then 'encyclopedic fictions' (Flaubert, Melville, Joyce, Pynchon), in order to show that literary repetition is an annihilating salvation, both for life and art. Put in its simplest terms, '[t]he redemptive aesthetic asks us to consider art as a correction of life [. . .] A redemptive aesthetic based on the negation of life (in Nietzschean terms, on a nihilism that invents a "true world" as an alternative to an inferior and depreciated world of mere appearance) must also negate art' (p. 2).
11. See L. Bersani (1987), 'Is the Rectum a Grave?', *October*, vol. 43, pp. 197–222 (p. 220). Michael Lucey's discussion of the article in *Gide's*

Bent: Sexuality, Politics, Writing (Oxford and New York, 1995), pp. 38–41, focuses in particular on the last sentence: 'Male homosexuality advertises the risk of the sexual itself as the risk of self-dismissal, of *losing sight* of the self, and in so doing it proposes and dangerously represents *jouissance* as a mode of ascesis' (p. 222). Lucey argues persuasively that the 'shattering' force of the present participle 'losing sight' is undermined by other verbs in the present tense ('advertises', 'proposes', 'represents') which promise a forward-looking, utopian campaign as well as a 'hoisting' up of the presented past, wholesale and undamaged, into the present of representation (p. 40). Hence, Bersani's present tense, a key element in his strategy to represent *jouissance* outside memory, carries with it the structure of its own nostalgia (ibid.). Dean also discusses this sentence in 'The Psychoanalysis of AIDS', *October*, vol. 63 (1993), pp. 83–116, where he claims that words such as 'advertise' give Bersani's analysis the simple charms of an advert. Dean argues further that Bersani's appeal to the ego, even an appeal for it to solicit its own shattering, must count as a non-psychoanalytic solution, for phrases such as 'our primary practice of nonviolence' implicitly advocate a redemption of subjectivity, if not of selfhood. The problem, according to Dean, is that Bersani, because he derives his usage of *jouissance* from Bataille and not Lacan, cannot distinguish between the terms 'ego' and 'subject' (i.e. a subject founded in the ego and an ego founded in – and therefore split by – the unconscious). Dean's approach is to be compared with that of John Champagne (1995) in *The Ethics of Marginality: A New Approach to Gay Studies*, Minneapolis and London, where Bersani is attacked precisely for his use of psychoanalytical paradigms, which, according to Champagne, render his work acultural and ahistorical (p. 52; p. 56). Finally, in an article '"All the Sad Young Men": AIDS and the Work of Mourning' (in D. Fuss (1991) (ed.), *inside/out: Lesbian Theories, Gay Theories*, London and New York, 1991, pp. 311–23), Jeff Nunokawa criticizes the rhetorical strategies in 'Is the Rectum a Grave?' which, he claims, ultimately evade the question of death. For Nunokawa, Bersani's 'morbid troping of gay men's self-dissolution in anal intercourse as a kind of death' subscribes to a long and lethal tradition of representing gay men', and moreover, Bersani's 'imagination of this fatality is a renaissance conceit in which the casualty is death itself' (p. 323).

12. Bersani, *Homos*, p. 127.
13. See, for example, R. Canning (1995), 'Faulty constructions' (a review of *Homos*), *New Statesman and Society*, 21 April, p. 39.
14. Bersani, *Homos*, p. 7.

15. See G. H. Storzer (1979), 'The Homosexual Paradigm in Balzac, Gide, and Genet', in G. Stambolian and E. Marks (eds), *Homosexualities and French Literature: Cultural Contexts/Critical Texts*, Ithaca and London, pp. 186–209. A measure of the increasing inappropriateness of such an approach is gained by Storzer's own concluding remark that, owing to changing views about the nature of the self – and thus about the very notion of 'definitive sexuality' – in literature since 1960, the homosexual paradigm appears to lose all significance and value (p. 209). He adds that already in Balzac, Gide and Genet, there is a gradual erosion of the assumptions upon which such a literary construct is based.
16. Bersani, *Homos*, p. 99.
17. In *A Future for Astyanax: Character and Desire in Literature*, Boston and Toronto (which includes studies of Racine, Flaubert, Stendhal, Lautréamont, Rimbaud and Artaud), Bersani already engages with Genet and Proust. In the case of Genet, he analyses the masturbatory powers of omnipotence and uncompromised desire present in *Funeral Rites*, which, he claims, remains Genet's 'most impressive performance of self-annihilating and world-devouring power' (p. 291). He adds that the 'violent and rather cheaply obscene images of a theatricalized self' (p. 291) are leavened only by a dose of humour. As for Proust, Bersani examines *In Search of Time Past* from the perspective of memory and the energies of a 'prospective self'.
18. Bersani, *Homos*, pp. 160–1.
19. C. Robinson (1995), *Scandal in the Ink: Male and Female Homosexuality in Twentieth-Century French Literature*, London, pp. 59–67 (p. 59).
20. See L. Edelman (1994), 'The Mirror and the Tank: "AIDS", Subjectivity, and the Rhetoric of Activism', in *Homographesis: Essays in Gay Literary and Cultural Theory*, London and New York, pp. 93–117. Edelman points out that narcissism and passivity figure the place of gay male sexuality in the Western cultural imaginary. Like Bersani, Edelman raises the question of address, stating that the use of the first person plural is always propelled by specular fantasy (p. 116). He concludes: 'at a moment when the "activist" interpellation of the oppositional subject invokes the logic of ascesis that underwrites the dominant subject's authority, such "luxuries" as analysis and narcissism, both figured by the mirror, may themselves prove necessary as instruments of defence that can disclose the possibility of a politics in whose name the mirror need not be cracked – a politics whose lineaments no mirror as yet has ever fully shown' (p. 117).
21. See L. Bersani (1982), *The Death of Stéphane Mallarmé*, Cambridge, p. 19. Bersani explores both Mallarmé's ironic treatment of negativity

in poems such as *Igitur* and the continually renewed disappearances of the poet's own individual personality. Mallarméan death is defined as a 'continuous moving away from stabilizing (and obsessive) images'.
22. Bersani, 'Is the Rectum a Grave?', p. 197.
23. Bersani, *Homos*, p. 113.
24. Ibid., pp. 99–100.
25. Ibid., p. 100.
26. Ibid., p. 111.
27. Ibid., p. 112.
28. Ibid., p. 118.
29. Ibid., p. 122.
30. Ibid., p. 125.
31. Ibid., p. 129.
32. Ibid.
33. Ibid., p. 120.
34. Ibid., p. 145.
35. Ibid., p. 146.
36. Ibid., p. 150.
37. See 'Proust and the Spectacle of the Closet', in E. K. Sedgwick (1990), *Epistemology of the Closet*, Berkeley and Los Angeles, pp. 213–51 (pp. 215–16). Sedgwick points out that the Charlus–Jupien relationship constitutes the one exception to the pattern of relationships in *In Search of Lost Time*, precisely because it works and lasts.
38. See 'Death and Literary Authority: Marcel Proust and Melanie Klein', in Bersani, *The Culture of Redemption*, pp. 7–28 (p. 24).
39. Bersani, *Homos*, p. 151.
40. Ibid., p. 169.
41. Ibid.
42. Ibid., p. 166.
43. Ibid., p. 177.
44. Ibid., p. 160.
45. Ibid., p. 180. This is Bersani's translation of: 'Ce livre est sincère et c'est une blague.'
46. Ibid., p. 149.
47. Ibid., p. 153.
48. Ibid., p. 160.
49. L. Bersani (1994), 'The Gay Outlaw', *Diacritics*, vol. 24, no. 2/3, pp. 5–18.
50. Halperin, 'More or Less Gay-Specific', p. 26.
51. Bersani, *The Culture of Redemption*, p. 3.
52. Ibid.

53. Ibid.
54. Ibid., pp. 3–4.
55. Ibid., p. 4.
56. Ibid.
57. Ibid., p. 3.
58. Ibid.
59. Ibid., p. 208.
60. L. Bersani and U. Dutoit (1993), *Arts of Impoverishment: Beckett, Rothko, Resnais*, Cambridge, Mass., p. 8.
61. Bersani, *The Culture of Redemption*, p. 45.
62. See R. Barthes (1984), *Camera Lucida: Reflections on Photography*, London, p. 49.
63. R. Howard (1989), 'From Exoticism to Homosexuality', in D. Hollier (ed.), *A New History of French Literature*, Cambridge, Mass., pp. 836–42 (p. 841).
64. G. Kelly (1995), 'Queering the pitch', interview with Leo Bersani, *Times Higher Education Supplement*, 26 May, pp. 18–19 (p. 19).
65. J. S. Williams (1995), 'The Moment of Truth: Roland Barthes, "Soirées de Paris" and the Real', *Neophilologus*, vol.79, pp. 33–51. The article argues that 'Soirées de Paris' enacts a violent, 'self-complete textual fantasy' (p. 45).
66. See Dean, 'Sex and Syncope', p. 78. According to Dean, Bersani's particular account of art appropriates the philosophy of 'rapture' for those whose participation in high cultural practices may indeed be life-saving. Drawing on the work of Catherine Clément in her 1990 study, *La Philosophie du ravissement*, Dean himself proposes the notion of syncope as a sexual practice, which, he claims, would represent the best resource for dealing with AIDS and sexual politics, since syncope bears an imitative yet apotropaic relation to death. For a very different approach to the value of art in the face of AIDS, see L. Hammer (1995), 'Art and Aids; or, How Will Culture Cure You?', *Raritan*, vol. 14, no. 3, pp. 103–18. Taking as his model the poetry of James Merrill, Hammer argues that art 'communicates' AIDS, breaking down in the name of love the boundaries separating stage and audience.
67. Bersani grandly proclaimed in his blurb on the dust-jacket of *Bringing Out Roland Barthes* that, by means of a 'tenderly uncompromising uncloseting' of Barthes's work, Miller 'develops Barthes's gay muscle', thus rescuing him 'from the dreary repetitiveness of hustlers and hangers-on'. In the aforementioned article 'The Moment of Truth', I consider the implications of Miller's attempt at once to expose Barthes's 'phobic' relation to the act of gay self-nomination, and to 'band' with him,

quite literally: the University of California press packaged *Bringing Out Roland Barthes* with Richard Howard's translation of Barthes's *Incidents* to produce a two-volume set.

68. I am thinking, for example, of Sedgwick's 1993 book *Tendencies* (published by Duke University Press), which includes a chapter co-authored by Moon entitled: 'Divinity: A Dossier, A Performance Piece, A Little Understood Emotion'. Originally delivered as a performance piece in 1990, the chapter aims to 'explore the powerful condensation of some emotional and identity linkages – historically dense ones – between fat women and gay men' (p. 218). My use of the term 'formative' refers to E. Wilson (1996), *Sexuality and the Reading Encounter: Identity and Desire in Proust, Duras, Tournier, and Cixous*, Oxford, a probing study of the reading encounter which shows how certain modern texts draw attention to the strategies by which identity is constructed textually, most often by disrupting, frustrating and misrepresenting the reader.
69. Bersani, 'Is the Rectum a Grave?', p. 222.
70. 'A vrai dire, en art, il n'y a pas de problèmes – dont l'œuvre d'art ne soit la suffisante solution' (A. Gide (1975 [1902]), *L'Immoraliste*, Paris, p. 8).
71. See M. Worton (1995), 'Labyrinths of Desire and Loitering (into) Literature: On Reading Theory – and Loïc Chotard's *Tiers Monde*', *Canadian Review of Contemporary Literature*, vol. 22, no. 2 (June), pp. 223–39 (p. 237). Referring to Ross Chambers's notion of 'loiterature', or marginal(ized) literature, where the writer/narrator performs the failure of writing, Worton shows that *Tiers Monde* (Paris, 1994) is a kind of anti-*Bildungsroman*, 'a novel about gay practice which has no theory of gay sexuality or gay desire [. . .] a novel about wandering which goes nowhere' (p. 237). See also Worton's chapter 'Cruising (Through) Encounters' in the present volume.

PART II

Narrative Articulations

– 5 –

Commodifying Queer: Violette Leduc's Autobiographical Homotextualities

Alex Hughes

Introduction

In 'The Production of Belief: Contribution to an Economy of Symbolic Goods', Pierre Bourdieu charts that economic process whereby creative artefacts are consecrated as bearers of Value by cultural entrepreneurs (publishers, theatre managers, art dealers etc) and critics, thus becoming 'cultural commodities'; goods with a guaranteed right of circulation within the cultural field.[1] Measured against the notion that to be recognized as the producer of such commodities constitutes the acme of writerly achievement, the chequered literary fortunes of Violette Leduc (1907–72) hardly attest to a success story. Before the publication in 1964, by Gallimard, of her first autobiographical *récit*, the novels she had been writing since 1946 had found favour with Simone de Beauvoir and her circle and had attracted a small following of readers, but had failed to enter fully into what Bourdieu labels the 'cycle of consecration' (that system wherein key players in the cultural market sanction works and their creators as value-laden).[2] *La Bâtarde* changed Leduc's situation dramatically. When the *récit* made its appearance on the French literary stage, accompanied by a highly 'consecratory' preface by Beauvoir, Leduc and her work were catapulted into the public and critical consciousness, acquiring a degree of cultural commodification that had previously eluded them. Praised by numerous reviewers for the daring sincerity it displayed, panned by conservative critics for its sexual explicitness – *Minute*, for instance, slated it as scandalous, while the more 'moderate' Bernard Pivot confined himself to deploring its incursions into immodesty[3] – *La Bâtarde* was the literary sensation of 1964. Nominated for the *Prix Goncourt* and the *Prix Femina*, it won neither, but sold 120,000 copies immediately after publication. This notwithstanding, Leduc's texts did not accrue, in the 1970s and 1980s, the commodity value of the autobiographies of her mentor Beauvoir. While her work continued to interest a limited number of academic critics,[4] obscurity became once more the essence of her lot. In the 1990s, however, the situation appears to be changing. A Violette Leduc archive has been established at the *Institut Mémoires de l'édition contemporaine*, in Paris. Two studies of Leduc's writing were published in 1994: René de Ceccaty's *Eloge de la bâtarde* (In Praise of *La Bâtarde*) and my own *Violette Leduc: Mothers, Lovers and Language*.[5] Finally, an issue of the Lille-based review *nord'* devoted exclusively to Leduc came out in June of 1994, and the first international conference on her work was held at the University of Lille in March 1995.

Violette Leduc would seem, then, to be rising from the ashes of critical neglect, or, in Bourdieuian terms, to be achieving a kind of belated (re)consecration. Various factors have contributed to her revival, not least the vogue that autobiographical discourse is presently enjoying in France and elsewhere. Leduc's 'recommodification' coincides with – and should, in future, be facilitated by – a sea-change currently occurring within literary critical practice, in particular Anglo-Saxon, as it pertains to female-authored writing. An exploration of this phenomenon will enable us to establish how it might inflect Leduc's literary renascence. Additionally, and more importantly, it will provide a point of entry into a reading of the ambivalent literary gender acts and gender crossings – the focus of the central section of this chapter – that Leduc operates, and will help to insert them into a broader sexual/political context.

I

In the late 1970s and 1980s, decades that saw the publication of key theoretical texts by Hélène Cixous and Luce Irigaray, gynocentric literary analysis tended to focus on women writers' transcription of woman's sexed subjectivity. Concomitantly, discussions of feminine-specific forms of language linked with the female body and libido came into prominence.[6] Latterly, however, readers of women's texts have shown signs of abandoning practices that engage – in however deconstructive a fashion – with identity politics, in favour of what are arguably more challenging literary-analytical procedures. An indication of this epistemological shift is provided by the use feminist critics are currently making of the work of Judith Butler.[7]

Butler's radical analyses frame gender as an enactment compelled by a prohibitive Law of (heterosexual) identity, and as involving an imitative, regulated, *bodily* citation of that law. Gender performances in no way reflect a 'voluntarism which presumes a subject intact, prior to its gendering', but are expressive, rather, of constraint.[8] Born out of a disciplinary regulation of the flesh – Butler is nothing if not resolutely Foucauldian – gender performances are 'mimes', which are inscribed on the surface of the body, but which appear as the effects of an *inner essence.*[9] Because they are compelled by the dominant sexual regime, gender performances mostly approximate, moreover, 'the intelligible grids of an idealized, compulsory heterosexuality'.[10] The disciplinary production of gendered being effects, in other words, what Butler describes as a false stabilization of gender, which works in the interests of the heterosexual construction of sexuality. This stabilization generates a binary system wherein, generally, sexual practices, gender identities and anatomical sex mesh together 'cohesively'. Gender performances can, of course, lapse into 'incoherence'. That this is so is evidenced, says Butler, by those 'discontinuities which run rampant within heterosexual, bisexual and gay and lesbian contexts where gender does not necessarily follow from sex, and desire, or sexuality generally, does not seem to follow from gender – indeed where none of these dimensions of significant corporeality express or reflect one another'.[11] For Butler, 'queer' disorganizations of/within the gendered field of bodies disrupt the regulatory model of heterosexual coherence, exposing it as a constructive norm and as a fiction. However, the strategic performance, on the part of the collectivity, of 'coherent' gender acts serves to marginalize such disorganizations. It serves also to produce the appearance of fixed, primary, and naturally binarized gender 'cores'.

In her essay 'Toward a Feminist Poetics', Elaine Showalter evokes the image of a youthful woman critic (Critica by name) racing into the British Museum past a trio of (male) professors, in order to embark upon the business of producing innovative readings of female-authored writings.[12] These days, the chances are that Showalter's Critica will be turning to 'queer' studies such as Butler's *Gender Trouble* (1990) and *Bodies that Matter*, (1993b) for analytical inspiration, rather than to Cixous's 1976 essay 'The Laugh of the Medusa' (which foregrounds the multi-pleasurable female body and its relation to discursivity). She is likely moreover, in her search for source-texts, to be in pursuit not of textual articulations of feminine specificity or sexual difference, but rather of literary productions that chart the workings of gender as an acculturated product or process, 'constructed through relations of power and, specifically, normative constraints that not only produce but also regulate various bodily beings'.[13] What, though, is the relationship between the phenomenon Critica embodies and the commodity potential of Violette Leduc's *oeuvre*? The point, here, is that Leduc's writings – given their emphasis on the plasticity of sexed positionalities and their avoidance of an essentializing perspective – invite, very obviously, precisely the kinds of interpretation to which Critica is currently drawn. Specifically, they lend themselves to readings driven by a focus on gender as a contingent, denaturalized bodily style, as an entity whose manifestations possess the potential to contest that 'notion of coherence assumed to exist among sexed bodies, gender identities and sexuality', and as a '[potentially] multiple phenomenon for which new terms must be found'.[14] Such critical incursions into Leduc's creative universe have, on the whole, as yet to take place.[15] It is highly probable that they will occur, and imperative that they should. Consequently, it seems safe to assume that the Leducian revival that now appears to be happening will receive additional impetus – a fact that can only enhance the (re)commodification of Leduc's *oeuvre*.

That Leduc's writings leave the reader with the sense that, within them, it is the representation not of the Feminine but rather of gender, in all its proliferating, normative and 'abject' modalities, that is primordial, is intimated by remarks contained in René de Ceccatty's *Eloge de la bâtarde*. De Ceccatty comments that in Leduc's texts there is, 'in spite of [a] stubborn repetition of sexual labels', a negation of the notion of 'tendance sexuelle'.[16] This negation, he suggests, turns upon the fact that: 'neither lesbian nor heterosexual nor bisexual by nature or by education [. . .], [Leduc] is an unspecified, label-free subject of pleasure and desire'.[17] De Ceccatty's remarks are interesting in so far as they lend support to the argument – a key tenet of this discussion – that Leduc's writings emphasize, centrally and 'denaturalizingly', the absence of an abiding, essential gender core, as well as the potentially fragile, fluid character of gendered being and doing. That this is the case is evidenced by Leduc's multiple metamorphoses of her sexual/textual self, metamorphoses that punctuate both her directly autobiographical *récits* and her autobiographical fictions. The following sections of this chapter will focus on these metamorphoses, specifically in their homosexual form and especially in *La Bâtarde*, a text 'covering' the formative years of Leduc's childhood, adolescence and early adulthood.[18] Tracing their trajectory will make it possible to frame them in terms of that phenomenon of 'disloyal' gender performativity whose subversive potential Judith Butler (among others) dissects so pertinently.

II

If Leduc is 'known' as any kind of writer, it is probably as a lesbian writer. Her reputation reflects, obviously, the central place female same-sex love occupies in her textual recreations of her past. Her second novel, *L'Affamée* (The Famished Woman) (1948), records a lesbian epiphany relating intimately to Leduc's infatuation with Simone de Beauvoir. Violette, the autobiographical self-projection Leduc creates in *La Bâtarde*, has two female lovers: her initiatrix, the exciting Isabelle, and the more prosaic Hermine, who seeks to enclose her partner in a stifling union, in which Violette must play the 'petite femme'. The 'real-life' Violette/Hermine and Violette/ Isabelle relationships charted in *La Bâtarde* mirror 'fictional' lesbian bonds chronicled in Leduc's third novel *Ravages* (1955), and in her novella *Thérèse et Isabelle* (1966). This last work began life as the prologue to *Ravages*. However, Gallimard – which became in the 1960s the first mainstream house to publish sexually explicit texts, but which was not, in the mid-1950s, ready to defy France's draconian censorship laws[19] – expurgated it, citing as justification the explicit evocations of adolescent lesbian eroticism it contained. This mutilation, which helped to impel Leduc into a nervous breakdown, was never fully made good. When Gallimard brought the text out in revised form, in 1966, much of the erotic force of the original had been attenuated.[20]

Within and via the baroque world of her own writing, Leduc 'performs', then, as lesbian autobiographical creatrix and as lesbian protagonist. Hence, to frame her as an exemplary – and martyred – feminine homoerotic literary voice would seem to be wholly appropriate. The innovatory nature of Leduc's female homosexual writing, suggested as it is by the parallels binding elements of the original version of *Ravages* with Monique Wittig's *The Lesbian Body* (1973), reinforces the validity of such a categorization. So, too, does Elaine Marks's comment, in her 1979 essay 'Lesbian Intertextuality', that in Leduc's autobiographies, for the first time in French literature, 'the lesbian is no longer the object of literary discourse seen from an outside point of view. She is her own heroine.'[21]

However, Leduc herself – for all her sense of belonging to a continuum of women writers bent on achieving a 'necessary opening up of a [female] sexuality too long concealed'[22] – would probably have been less than happy at being categorized in this (de)limiting way. Her autobiographical account, in *La Chasse à l'amour* (In Pursuit of Love) (1973), of her uneasy encounter with a pair of lesbian readers – readers impassioned by the Sapphic passion of *L'Affamée* – reinforces our sense of this fact. Confronted with these women's enthusiasm for her lesbian writing, and with their determined sexual openness, Leduc's narrator Violette is left to wonder to herself whether in fact she actually dislikes lesbians ('Est-ce que, par hasard, je détesterais les lesbiennes?').[23] Amongst other things, this unexpected observation hints obliquely at the fact that the sexual practice which, in Leduc's writing, is idealized above any other is not lesbianism at all, but rather *male* homosexuality. Leduc's work reveals a passion for masculine homoeroticism on the part of its creator and her textual projections. Evidence of it is provided by the series of male homosexual love objects – starting with the writer Maurice Sachs – who provoke in Leduc's autobiographical heroine a destructive infatuation. The lengthy disquisition on male homoeroticism contained in her *récit de voyage Trésors à prendre* (Treasures For the Taking) (1960) – beginning as it does with a categorical 'I am for male homosexuality' ('Je suis pour l'homosexualité masculine')[24] – leaves the reader in no doubt as to Leduc's penchant for gay men, which, amongst other things, leads her to 'homosexualize' the heterosexual males who feature in her novels and *récits*.

Numerous factors explain the privileged position male homosexuals occupy within Leduc's texts. In their company, her self-creation Violette feels immune to pregnancy, the fear of which her unwed mother instilled in her. The outsider status that is hers within their erotic universe means that the lack of desire gay men feel for her – unlike that of their heterosexual counterparts – need not humiliate her, and it even, in fact, permits her to indulge her masochistic passion for the impossible. Most importantly, homosexual men appeal, because, surprisingly, they recall her adored grandmother Fidéline, who cared for her in her childhood:

> Fearful of my mother [. . .], I turned to a woman who resembled neither a man nor a woman. Her face, captured on the one old photograph I have of her, isn't beautiful. It is virile. I've thought hard about what I am about to write: my grandmother (who got married, had two children) will have been the first homosexual with whom I fell passionately in love as I took refuge in the skirts of her secular cassock [*soutane de laïque*]. She was a man in a dress [*homme en robe*], who protected me when she shielded me from my mother and showed no fear of her.[25]

This extraordinary passage from *Trésors à prendre* intimates that Leduc's passion for male homosexuality has as its particular focus the 'grandmotherly' or 'priestly' homosexual, the 'homme en robe'. Avatars of this cross-gendered being who people her textual universe are, variously, Maurice Sachs – portrayed in *La Bâtarde* as possessed of 'pudgy prelate hands' ('mains potelées de prélat'), day-robes, mules and silken socks – and the seemingly interchangeable, camp figures of the '*folle*' (queen) and the '*travesti*' (drag queen).[26] Leduc's third autobiographical volume, *La Chasse à l'amour* (1973) records the pitying detachment she experiences as she observes a parade of 'dames affligées de ne pas l'être' on the stage of the Carrousel, a Parisian transvestite nightclub.[27]

Trésors à prendre, however, reveals that she is in fact deeply attuned to the similarities that bind her own situation to that of the '*folle*', the self-feminizing queen. '*Folles*', asserts Leduc, are the products of authoritarian mothers, mothers whose role as consorts in the reproductive process remained minimal. Having taken Woman as their patron saint, they are the reincarnation of their masculinized mothers: mothers who were not, and could not be, attractive to men and who, like the '*folles*' themselves, are caught in limbo between the 'weaker' and the 'stronger' sex.[28] Their lot, in consequence, suggests Leduc, involves a kind of 'hell on earth' ('un enfer sur terre').[29] These observations apply only too well to Violette herself. She too, as *La Bâtarde* indicates, is the child (and the reflection/projection) of an authoritarian woman, of a single ('phallic') mother who, on every level save the biological, 'produced all alone' her progeny. She, too, lives out 'un enfer sur terre', primarily due to her physical unattractiveness. If, in other words, Leduc's autobiographical protagonist is drawn not only towards male homosexuals in general but also, specifically, towards '*les folles*', this is arguably because these last not only remind her of her grandmother, 'l'ange Fidéline', but also stand in some kind of parallel relation to herself.

In Leduc's textual universe, empathy or the awareness of affinity leads regularly to identification. Consequently, the fact that Leduc's autobiographies contain instances of a kind of (bodily) 'self-homosexualization' on the part of her self-creation Violette should come as no surprise. In *La Bâtarde*, recalling how she obliged Gabriel, her future husband, to penetrate her anally (p. 289), Leduc's narrator explains that she was motivated not by a fear of pregnancy, ultimately, but rather by the desire to have a pair of homosexuals in her bed ('le souhait d'un couple d'homosexuels sur ma couche').[30] In *La Chasse à l'amour*, in an erotic encounter with another lover, René, Violette – after deliberating as to whether or not she wishes to be sodomized – opts to adopt a more active, penetrative 'homosexual' stance, creating a reversed reiteration of the homosexual couple scenario of *La Bâtarde*.[31] This episode is not only staged by Leduc as a male/male coupling but is also framed, tacitly, as the antithesis of – and an improvement upon – lesbian sexual interaction. In the same *récit*, after her encounter with her lesbian readers, Violette comments 'lesbians make me gloomy. They aren't gay, but rather frenetic',[32] imputing to herself a judgement which, in *Trésors à prendre*, she sets up as that typically proffered about lesbians by male homosexuals.[33]

Violette's male-homosexualizing self-metamorphoses may be taken to constitute so many performative gender acts: acts which, if they are rendered dissonant and 'incoherent' by her biological femininity, acquire nonetheless their own logic in the textual world of sexual flexibility and illegitimacy created by Leduc's autobiographical writings. Ultimately, and perhaps inevitably, these acts transport Leduc's self-projection into the camp universe of the '*folle/travesti*', the cross-gendered, cross-dressed homosexual. The process whereby this incursion occurs is complex, and requires careful delineation.

In *La Bâtarde*, the adult Violette embarks upon liaisons with a man, Gabriel, and a woman, Hermine. With Gabriel, in the earliest phase of their dealings, Violette – suited, booted and sporting a cravat – plays (heterosexual) man to the 'woman' she intermittently wishes him to play (p. 167). As her lesbian relationship with the exigent Hermine develops, however, she (apparently) trades mannishness for an intense insertion into feminization, effecting one of the many corporeal crossings chronicled in Leduc's *récit*. The following extract, in which Violette narrates herself through the routine of physical transmogrification she follows before going to parade around the boulevards of Paris clad in the designer finery Hermine has offered her, records a typical, if extreme, manifestation of this phenomenon:

> It is pleasant, drums, to hear you catch exactly the right tone. I am playing too, I am patting the dark-toned makeup on my Nordic-skinned face. I pat, I slap the makeup on, I slap my skin. Those are the instructions. [. . .] Imagine a tiny porthole of pink lacquer, a circle of pink swooning with its own pallor, inside which there lies a disc of paste, a concentrate of timidity. [. . .] Several circles on the left cheek, several circles on the right cheek, for it must be patted in before you spread it out, that is the secret of a natural base, of perfect makeup, the saleslady told me so quite clearly. [. . .] You know you're getting ready for your circus act, smudged clown in the glass. Drums, into training, all fatigue forbidden. I am about to do my circus act, and my ring is to be the wide boulevards of Paris (p. 202).[34]

The process Violette submits to in episodes such as this has been read in a variety of ways by Leducian critics. Shirley Neuman interprets it as evidence of Violette's inability to resist the constraining force of patriarchy's 'cultural script of femininity': an inability signalled by her involvement in 'a series of invitations and losses each of which stages her body as [female] spectacle'.[35] Neuman's reading of the compelled nature of the Leducian heroine's womanly masquerade – a masquerade she views as 'produced' by Hermine's normative demands and as 'sewn into [Violette's] flesh'[36] – is convincing. However, it obscures the highly ambivalent nature of the 'feminine' state Violette actually slips into in those parts of *La Bâtarde* typified by the extract cited above.

In these sections, Violette does not achieve, by means of the vestimentary and bodily modifications she effects, a gender performance properly consonant with what Neuman terms 'the ideology of femininity/hetero-sexuality'.[37] She is propelled, rather, into a form of theatrical display that recalls what Kim Michasiw has termed the monstrous semiosis of the feminine intrinsic in gay camp performativity, and gives birth to something close to the hyperbolic femininity of drag.[38] Violette's flirtation with feminization, then, which is truncated when she is mocked for her ugliness by a woman passer-by encountered on the Pont de la Concorde (p. 222), incorporates and disguises a flirtation with a quite other type of gender performance: the melancholic performance of the gay drag artist who, Butler suggests, forever grieves, and endlessly pursues, the uninhabitable Feminine.[39]

The masculine/feminine ersatz nature of her 'circus act' is implied by the comments proffered by the men who observe her Parisian parade: comments that draw attention to her not-so-very-feminine 'half-boyish femininity' ('féminité d'androgyne'), her 'sculptured bullfighter's buttocks' ('fesses sculptées de toréro'), the Dietrich-like huskiness of her voice (pp. 204–10). Its 'homosexualized' dimension is highlighted by the connections binding the account offered in *La Bâtarde* of Violette's engagement with beautification to Leduc's dissection, in *Trésors à prendre*, of the activities and practices of '*folles*'. '*Les folles*', suggests *Trésors*,[40] crave and covet all the dresses they see models wearing, all the fur-wraps glimpsed in theatre foyers, all the silky underwear spotted in mail-order catalogues, so desirous are they of access to an iconic Womanhood that permanently eludes them.

In the central chapters of *La Bâtarde*, Leduc's Violette – as she remoulds her face and figure, desperately accumulating the emblems of femininity (including a Joan Crawford hairdo) – manifests markedly similar tendencies (pp. 212–13). This parallel helps to confirm our sense that, in this particular phase of her sexual/textual trajectory, the identity category into which Violette is inserted is not (at least, not entirely) that of normative, culturally conscripted femininity, but pertains rather to that cross-gendered, 'paradigmatic' enclave within male homosexuality adulated by her creatrix. Violette may be taken, in other words, to be 'performing' here in tandem with, if not as, the doubly sexed, highly ambiguous figure of the gay cross-dresser, that figure that Leduc, in *La Chasse à l'amour* and *Trésors à prendre*, associates with saintliness. We can 'read' her as accessing a kind of gendered performance for which the compelling gender model proffered by her grandmother had, perhaps, always already destined her.

In *La Bâtarde*, then, Leduc constructs her autobiographical self-projection in such a way that Violette can be seen to 'inhabit' (i) a lesbian identity incorporating the femininity of the domestic concubine/'little woman' (p. 187); (ii) the passive sexuality of the submissive gay male; and (iii) the theatrical, ambivalent gender comportment of the *travesti/folle*; as well as

(iv) the normative category of heterosexual femininity. Clearly, some of these variant modalities of gendered experience – which offer ample confirmation of Butler's contention that the inner truth of gender is (in both senses of the word) a fabrication[41] – are negotiated by Violette more seriously and more enduringly than others. That said, in the light of their combined textual presence, it is hard to justify de Ceccatty's suggestion that, in the work of Violette Leduc, male and female homosexual modalities remain distinct and discrete.[42] In fact, male and female homosexuality, together with the male (homosexual) practice of drag, are connected in Leduc's writing by virtue of the gender *péripéties* of her protean autobiographical heroine. What, though, are we to make of Violette's sexual metamorphoses? Can we, more particularly, interpret her shift into the parodic (non)femininity of drag – a femininity which, as Butler notes, has been viewed as degrading to women[43] – as anything other than a problematic appropriation of what may be a misogynistic, ridiculizing masculine practice? In order to address these questions, it will prove helpful to return to Judith Butler's analyses of gender-as-performance in the specific context of drag.

In Chapter 4 of *Bodies that Matter*, 'Gender is Burning', Butler theorizes gender as the result of an interpellation. She suggests that gendered being involves repeated acts of performative obedience to the call of the symbolic, heterosexual "law", an obedience generated by the fear of punishment. She goes on to point out, however, that the Law of Gender 'calls up' not only gender states and acts that are expressive of the obligatory frame of reproductive heterosexuality, but also 'pathologizing practices' or 'sites of ambivalence'.[44] Produced 'at the limits of [. . .] legitimacy' and characterized by a failure to respect that unity of sex, sexuality, gender and desire required by and for heterosexual coherence, these illegitimacies serve to consecrate the status of heterosexual performativity as originary and proper.[45] Butler's point is that hegemonic heterosexuality requires and creates a space of gender 'otherness' – a space constituted by 'abject' gender performances – in order to establish itself as that which is natural, normal, and 'right'.

The 'pathologizing' activity on which Butler focuses in 'Gender is Burning' is drag. Her point of reference is the cross-dressing practised by the black and latino homosexuals and transsexuals who feature in Jennie Livingston's documentary film *Paris is Burning* (1990). Butler argues that Livingston's film-text shows how drag does indeed, on the one hand, support hegemonic heterosexuality, because it represents an exaggerated reconsolidation of heterosexual gender norms. On the other hand, Butler suggests, drag – resting as it does upon an equation of gender and mime – possesses the potential to 'unmask' and *denaturalize* the gender performances of hegemonic, heterosexual 'normality'. Drag offers a kind of clue to the fact that these 'coherent' performances are neither essential nor originary, but are themselves constructed and compelled acts of *mimicry*. In other words, drag, for Butler at least, may well idealize dominant heterosexuality and its norms, but simultaneously it 'reveals the imitative structure of [heterosexual] gender itself – as well as its contingency'.[46] It exposes 'the impersonations by which ideal heterosexual genders are performed and naturalized, and undermines their power by virtue of effecting that exposure'.[47] The struttings of the drag queen hint, according to Butler, that even normative, 'natural' gender rests upon 'a constant and repeated effort to imitate its own idealizations',[48] an effort that betrays its actual, fabricated unnaturalness.

How, to come back to the focus of the present discussion, does all of this relate to Violette Leduc? Can we use Butler to interpret, in a 'political' fashion, the performative gender shifts charted in *La Bâtarde*? If we transpose the gender acts performed by Leduc's autobiographical heroine on to a Butlerian grid, we can, in fact, construe them as possessing a denaturalizing impact analogous to that effected by the cross-dressers discussed by Butler, but one that is actually more subversive. Like the mimicries of Butler's/Livingston's drag queens, Violette's performances can be taken implicitly to expose the contingent character of hegemonic gender enactments.

They do not, however, function in the service of heterosexual norms. The particular drag artist who 'stars' as the heroine of Livingston's film, and of Butler's analysis of it, Venus Xtravaganza, is a homosexual transvestite and pre-operative transsexual. In his/her hyperbolic miming of a 'real' woman, Venus certainly – on one level – contests binary gender norms, by reworking their 'natural' cohesion of anatomical sex, gender identity and gender performance. However, as Butler indicates, Venus's imitative acting out of 'whole womanhood' clearly cannot be viewed as entirely contestatory. The end point of his/her trajectory is, after all, heterosexual gender performance. S/he may – through ambiguous mimicry – denaturalize that performance, but his/her imitative activities involve also an adulatory reinforcement of it.

Leduc's Violette, on the other hand, incarnates a kind of limit-point of gender denaturalization; her crossings of gender and sexuality are 'disloyal' in a way that Venus's are not. This is because, instead of moving from the margins towards the hegemonic, Violette does the opposite. She transmutes herself not towards conformism but toward the modalities of what Butler terms 'abjection'. The gender crossings she enacts in *La Bâtarde* take her, intermittently, out of a womanhood (whether heterosexual or lesbian) on which her purchase is always less than solid, and into a mime of maleness that incorporates not only the heterosexual and the homosexual Masculine but also, on occasion, a feminized, 'illegitimate', wholly *un*natural masculinity, the masculinity of the 'folle'. If, in other words, Livingston's Venus 'cites' heterosexually ideal gender norms in such a way that they are ultimately validated, Violette's proliferating and misplaced gender acts cannot possibly be said to support what Butler describes as the heterosexual project.

III

In her explorations of gendered subjectivity, Butler invokes texts by Willa Cather, Nella Larsen and Luce Irigaray as works that, like the film *Paris is Burning*, stress the need to effect 'repetitions of hegemonic forms of power which fail to repeat loyally'.[49] In the autobiographical universe created by Violette Leduc, 'disloyal' performativity is palpably evident, specifically within the realm of gender and sexuality. Leduc produces texts in which gender norms are reiterated in such a bizarre, fluid, and 'treacherous' way that what emerges in the end is a 'gender trouble' to which the reader cannot lightly remain impervious, and which implicitly sets gender up as a multiple phenomenon, 'a kind of becoming or activity that [. . .] ought not to be conceived as a noun or a substantial thing or a static cultural marker'.[50]

In the light of this, it seems justifiable to categorize Violette Leduc's autobiographical writing as a decidedly 'queer' – or, to borrow Lee Edelman's term, 'homographic' – production, wherein any notion that sex/gender categories can, and should be, fixed is resisted, leading to the negation of 'natural', dualizing delimitations/identities.[51] It is for this reason, to return to the question of Leduc's cultural commodification, that we can assert with reasonable conviction that, in and after the late 1990s, her work will attract new readers, new readings, and, more importantly, a newly-valorized symbolic status – in the Anglo-Saxon world, at least, where 'queer' is commercially 'hot'. If, as a consequence of the emergence of queer theory as a valid and valuable reading tool, Violette Leduc's writing, with its extraordinary, kaleidoscopic chroniclings of sexual/gender possibilities, does acquire a more powerful stake in the cultural marketplace, this is surely all to the good. Devotees of her work have long been in no doubt that Leduc deserves her place in the sun. It is worth remembering, however, that 'revivals' that rely too heavily on the vagaries of market forces – forces whose favours are notoriously fickle – tend to prove impermanent, offering perhaps less than wholehearted cause for celebration.

Notes

1. P. Bourdieu (1986), 'The Production of Belief', trans. R. Nice, in R. Collins *et al.* (eds), *Media, Culture and Society*, London, pp. 131–63 (pp. 132–3). I am most grateful to Andrea Noble for drawing my attention to this essay.
2. Leduc herself was acutely aware of her own marginal status within the literary field, entry to which is likened by Bourdieu to acceptance by a select club (see 'The Production of Belief', p. 133). This is evidenced by her reaction to Gallimard's decision to publish her first novel, *L'Asphyxie* (Asphyxia), not in their 'Collection blanche' but in the seemingly less prestigious 'Collection Espoir'. In her second autobiographical *récit*, *La Folie en tête* (Mad in Pursuit) (Paris, Gallimard, 1970), she recounts her disappointment at what she took to be a signal of Gallimard's unwillingness to valorize her writing (p. 105) and indicates, with habitual mordant humour, the gloom her inclusion in the 'Espoir' series instilled in her (p. 63).
3. 'Cette Violette ne sent pas bon', *Minute*, 30 October 1964; B. Pivot, 'Les Tares de la bâtarde', *Figaro Littéraire*, 22–8 October 1964.
4. In this context, the groundbreaking work of Isabelle de Courtivron – notably her *Violette Leduc*, Boston, 1985 – must be cited.
5. R. de Ceccatty (1994), *Eloge de la bâtarde*, Paris; A. Hughes (1994), *Violette Leduc: Mothers, Lovers and Language*, London. A biography of Leduc, by Carlo Jansiti, is due out in 1998.
6. It is impossible here to provide a comprehensive survey of the multifarious modes of, and influences upon, 1970s and 1980s feminist criticism. My summary, inevitably, elides key questions of cultural, epistemological and political difference. For a useful account of the development of feminist literary critical practice from the 1960s to the 1990s, see M. Humm (1994), *A Reader's Guide to Contemporary Feminist Literary Criticism*, New York and London.
7. One way of understanding this shift – which must not be generalized, inappropriately, as indicative of a 'mass exodus' away from 'outmoded' practices of interpretation – is to view it as a transition on the part of critics from 'Feminist Theory' to 'Queer Theory'. For an interesting account of the relationship between these two methodological domains, one which problematizes and contests stereotypical notions of what each may be said to explore, see J. Butler (1994), 'Against Proper Objects', *Differences*, vol. 6, no. 2/3, pp. 1–25.
8. J. Butler (1993a), 'Critically Queer', *GLQ: Journal of Gay and Lesbian Studies*, vol. 1, pp. 17–32 (p. 21).

9. One of the most interesting aspects of Butler's work is that it reassociates the categories of gender and sex – categories that much feminist theory seeks to keep separate – via the notion that gender constitutes a mode of bodily performativity, or corporeal stylization, i.e. constitutes something that is acted out at the level of the anatomical as opposed to something that society attributes to beings with a particular anatomical make-up, and overlays upon anatomy.
10. J. Butler (1990), *Gender Trouble*, New York, p. 135.
11. Ibid., pp. 135–6.
12. 'Toward a Feminist Poetics', in E. Showalter (ed.) (1985), *The New Feminist Criticism: Essays on Women, Literature and Theory*, New York, pp. 125–43. Showalter borrows this image – which I, in turn, am borrowing from her – from Leon Edel's 1977 essay 'The Poetics of Biography'.
13. J. Butler (1993b), *Bodies that Matter*, New York, p. x.
14. Butler, *Gender Trouble*, p. 123; Butler (1986), 'Sex and Gender in Simone de Beauvoir's *Second Sex*', *Yale French Studies*, 72, pp. 35–49 (p. 47).
15. The exception here is S. Neuman's excellent Foucauldian/Butlerian piece, '"An appearance walking in a forest the sexes burn": Autobiography and the Construction of the Feminine Body', *Signature*, vol. 2, 1989, pp. 1–26, which explores Leduc's account of the formative engagement with 'the cultural script of femininity' (p. 15) experienced by her autobiographical heroine. Given the nature of their content, it is surprising that Leduc's tales of sexual metamorphosis have not, in recent times, been more widely 'taken up' by contemporary French critics. According to Ginette Vincendeau, such critics belong to a 'culture des années 80' that is less than receptive to artefacts that politicize sexual difference and gender, but is, however, fascinated by sexual ambiguity and by phenomena such as androgyny, transvestism, and transsexuality. See G. Vincendeau (1989), 'Vu de Londres: mais où est passée la théorie féministe en France?', *CinémAction*, vol. 47, pp. 95–9 (p. 98).
16. '. . . malgré la répétition obstinée de ses désignations sexuelles', R. de Ceccatty, *Eloge de la Bâtarde*, p. 79 (my translation).
17. 'Ni lesbienne, ni hétérosexuelle, ni bisexuelle de nature ou d'éducation [. . .], elle est sujet non spécifié et non désigné du plaisir et d'amour' (ibid.).
18. Extracts from the 1965 translation of *La Bâtarde*, by Derek Coltman, and page references to it, will be contained in the body of my chapter. This translation was published in London, by Peter Owen, and retains

the French title in preference to a clumsy English equivalent such as 'The Female Bastard'. The equivalent extracts from the French original, plus page references, will be contained in the Notes. The French edition used is the Gallimard *édition blanche*, published in Paris in 1964.

19. See C. Brécourt-Villars (1985), *Ecrire d'amour*, Paris, p. 50.
20. For an account of the fortunes of Leduc's third novel, see C. Jansiti (1994), 'Ils ont refusé le début de *Ravages*', *nord'*, vol. 23, pp. 77–89.
21. E. Marks (1979), 'Lesbian Intertextuality', in G. Stambolian and E. Marks (eds), *Homosexualities and French Literature*, Ithaca and London, pp. 353–77 (p. 373).
22. '. . . la mise à jour nécessaire d'une sexualité trop longtemps maintenue secrète': Interview with Pierre Descargues, *Tribune de Lausanne*, 18 October 1964, p. 8.
23. *La Chasse à l'amour*, Paris, Gallimard, 1973, p. 303. Beauvoir published this last volume of Leduc's posthumously, after Leduc's death from breast cancer in 1972. It has not been translated into English. All translations relating to it are mine.
24. *Trésors à prendre*, Paris, Gallimard, 1960, p. 113. This text has not been translated into English. All translations are mine.
25. 'Craignant ma mère [. . .] je me suis tournée vers celle qui ne ressemblait ni à un homme, ni à une femme. [. . .] Son visage, que je revois sur l'unique et vieille photographie n'est pas beau. Il est viril. [. . .] Je réfléchis à ce que je vais écrire: ma grand-mère (qui se maria, eut deux enfants) aura été le premier homosexuel auquel je me sois attachée avec passion pendant que je me réfugiais dans les plis de sa soutane de laïque. C'était un homme en robe qui me protégeait lorsqu'elle m'enlevait à ma mère et qu'elle n'avait pas peur d'elle' (ibid., p. 116).
26. It is important to note that 'folles' and 'travestis' should not automatically be placed on a continuum that elides the significant differences between them. Leduc, however, tends to do so, perhaps because camp, as Daniel Harris explains, given its status as 'something that can be donned like formal wear for occasions of state and similarly doffed when the situations demands', implies always a kind of 'cross-dressing' (see D. Harris (1991), 'Effeminacy', *Michigan Quarterly Review*, vol. 30, no. 1, pp. 72–81 (p. 78)). In *Trésors à prendre* (pp. 120–1), for instance, Leduc makes it clear that she considers '*les folles*' ('children who have taken Woman as their patron Saint'/ 'des petits enfants qui ont choisi la femme pour sainte patronne') to possess transvestite tendencies. Further, she perceives both '*folles*' and '*travestis*' to be haunted by a sense of exile *vis-à-vis* their 'enrobed' sexual organs (see *Trésors*, p. 121; *La Chasse à l'amour*, p. 121) – a fact that reinforces our sense that she views them as

somehow identical. Consequently, the terms '*folle*' and '*travesti*' will be used interchangeably in the rest of this discussion. We need also to take note of the problematic, politically fraught character of Leduc's generalizing equation of homosexuality and (the desire for) '*travestissement*'. In fact, as Butler points out, 'cross-gendered identification is not the exemplary paradigm for thinking about homosexuality, although it may be one. [. . .] Not only are a vast number of drag performers straight, but it would be a mistake to think that homosexuality is best explained through the performativity that is drag' (Butler, 'Critically Queer', p. 25).

27. *La Chasse à l'amour*, p. 121.
28. A 'folle' suggests Leduc, is the fruit of 'une femme autoritaire qui a fait toute seule le fils, mais comme il lui manquait le sperme personnel, ce fils est encore elle-même, exacerbée, écartelée entre le sexe faible et le sexe fort' (*Trésors*, p. 120).
29. See *Trésors*, pp. 120–1 for full details of Leduc's views on 'les folles'.
30. *La Bâtarde*, p. 287.
31. See *La Chasse à l'amour*, pp. 213–14, p. 289.
32. 'Les lesbiennes m'attristent. Elles ne sont pas gaies: elles sont frénétiques' (ibid., p. 303).
33. 'Les homosexuels qui ont l'horreur des femmes sombres, découragées, évitent la société des lesbiennes parce que, disent-ils, elles sont tristes' (*Trésors*, p. 121).
34. 'Tambours, c'est plaisant, avec vous c'est le ton juste. Moi aussi, je joue: je tapote la crème rachel sur mon visage de Nordique. Je tapote, je gifle le produit, je gifle l'épiderme. C'est recommandé. [. . .] Imagine un hublot minuscule de laque rose, d'un rose éperdu de pâleur à l'intérieur duquel se trouve un disque de pâte, un concentré de timidité. [. . .] Plusieurs pastilles [de fard] sur la joue gauche, plusieurs pastilles sur la joue droite puisqu'il faut tapoter avant d'étaler, c'est le secret d'un maquillage naturel, précisait la vendeuse. [. . .] Tu le sais, tu te prépares pour un cirque, clown effacé. Tambours, à l'entraînment, défense de se fatiguer, je vais entrer dans le cirque, ma piste sera les grands boulevards. . .' (*La Bâtarde*, p. 201).
35. S. Neuman, 'An appearance walking in a forest', pp. 11, 15.
36. Ibid., p. 19. Neuman is privileging here that equation of femininity and masquerade favoured by psychoanalysis.
37. Ibid., p. 17.
38. In an interesting discussion of gay male camp, Kim Michasiw frames this phenomenon as involving acts of identification with those elements of the masculine construction of femininity that are indicative of the

way in which 'masculine desire shades over into terror'. According to this critic, underlying camp is 'an increasingly panicked defense against what the female might signify [that] produces monsters of semiosis': K. Michasiw (1994), 'Camp, Masculinity, Masquerade', *Differences*, vol. 6, no. 2/3, pp. 146–73 (p. 162).

39. In 'Critically Queer', Butler offers a convincing account of the connection between drag on the one hand and melancholia on the other. Butler defines melancholia in its Freudian mode, as 'the effect of an ungrieved loss (a sustaining of the lost object/Other as a psychic figure with the consequence of a heightened identification with that Other, self-beratement, and the acting out of unresolved anger and love)'. Her point, in other words, is that drag issues from an introjection by the male subject of a insufficiently mourned maternal object, who becomes the focus for identification. See 'Critically Queer', pp. 24–5.
40. See *Trésors*, p. 121.
41. See *Gender Trouble*, p. 136.
42. De Ceccatty's point is that, just as 'Gomorrha has a very different signification from Sodom in Proust's writing, in the same way, male and female homosexuality have different functions in the work of Violette Leduc, and are never set up as parallel' ('Gomorrhe [a] un sens bien différent de Sodome dans l'œuvre de Proust, de la même manière, les deux homosexualités, masculine et féminine, ont chez Violette Leduc deux fonctions distinctes: elle ne les a jamais rapprochées') (*Eloge de la Bâtarde*, p. 162).
43. See Butler, *Gender Trouble*, p. 137 and *Bodies that Matter*, pp. 126–7.
44. Butler, *Bodies that Matter*, pp. 124–5.
45. Ibid.
46. Ibid., p. 137.
47. Ibid., p. 231.
48. Ibid., p. 125.
49. Ibid., p. 124.
50. Butler, *Gender Trouble*, p. 112.
51. Edelman defines 'homographic' writing as involving, on one level, 'a mode of strategic or analytic resistance to the logic of regulatory identity', and an 'inscription of homosexual possibilities [which] deconstructs the binary logic of sexual difference on which symbolic identity is based'. See L. Edelman (1994), *Homographesis: Essays in Gay Literary and Cultural Theory*, New York and London, pp. 12–13.

– 6 –

'Hardly Grazing', Josiane Balasko's *Gazon maudit* (1995): The *mise-en-textes* and *mise-en-scène* of Sexuality/ies

Susan Hayward

Film synopsis: Marijo, a butch-lesbian, drives south leaving Paris and a broken relationship. Her van breaks down and she turns up at the middle-class home of Loli and her philandering husband Laurent. A love relationship develops between Loli and Marijo that Laurent finds impossible to accept. However, having neglected his wife for aeons and having had his philandering exposed to his wife, he is in no position to play the hard-done-by husband when Loli installs Marijo as her lover and consigns her husband to the couch. Eventually, at Marijo's instigation, and as a result of Loli's sense of fair play, a love triangle is established in which Loli shares herself with both her husband and her lover. Laurent, however, is determined to win Loli back, and when an ex-lover of Marijo's turns up at the house he seizes his chance to play on Loli's «volatile» temperament (she is after all Spanish!). It works. Loli runs away and says she no longer wants to see Marijo. Faced with this seeming impasse, Marijo agrees to leave, but on one condition: that Laurent make her pregnant. Eight months later, on a train to Paris, Loli bumps into Marijo's ex-lover and finds out what happened. At first outraged by what she perceives to be a further deception of Laurent's, she insists she and her husband find Marijo (now back in Paris). Furthermore, she reinstalls Marijo and thus the former triad back into her home – to which has been added a new baby, Marijo's daughter. Laurent, the reformed loving parent, father and husband, goes in search of a larger home for the extended family. The man whose property Laurent is interested in purchasing is a Barcelonan like Loli, and shows his evident attraction to Laurent. Laurent in turn is clearly taken with the new possibilities – perhaps a *ménage-à-quatre* is in the air.

Introduction

Although Josiane Balasko is relatively unknown outside her own country, her work as a comedian of film and theatre and as a film-maker is very popular in France. *Gazon maudit*, her fourth film to date (as film-maker), is consistent with the nature of her three preceding ones, in that marginality is once again a central theme. Similarly, this film follows the others generically in its designation as a social comedy.

As a performer and director, Balasko emerges from the *café-théâtre* tradition of the 1970s – a tradition which, in its turn, emerged after the May '68 'revolution'. She was part of the *troupe du Splendid*, many of whom (including Coluche and Bertrand Blier) went on to work in the cinema as actors or film-makers. The comic tradition of the *café-théâtre* is one of anarchy, of complete disrespect for the establishment and for societal rules – including those governing sexuality. The 1970s was a period of sexual freedom and experimentation, in France as elsewhere, and a constant theme of the *café-théâtre*'s work was sexual utopia, often in the form of a triangular relationship encompassing homosexual as well as heterosexual relations.[1] This comedy also broke away from France's comic tradition of farce, boulevard comedy and vaudeville, and – partly drawing on the work of Antonin Artaud – established a new kind of comedy that was aggressive and hard-hitting (even though it did not entirely lose its misogynistic dimension) and appealed enormously to young audiences.

It is important to draw attention to Balasko's heritage, since genre and sexuality are two key elements of her film *Gazon maudit*. In both areas, Balasko breaks new ground, and, because films about lesbianism in French cinema are extremely rare, she is clearly in the vanguard. Her film marks her attempt to write a text that is generically and 'genderically' situated in the feminine: one that is written and staged from a woman's point of view. In an interview,[2] Balasko, who scripted the film, speaks of the difficulty of writing comedy without referring to a model, since, as she says, the models for comedy, specifically French comedy, are consistently male. In representing female sexuality and lesbianism on screen, she also wanted at all costs to avoid voyeurism and the pornographic script of the lesbian/heterosexual triangle which, in her opinion, are purely male manifestations of fantasy and desire. The purpose of her film becomes, then, the writing of a female text on desire between two women. In Balasko's own view, *Gazon maudit* involves an attempt to talk about female homosexuality to a larger audience, and to counter stereotypes of lesbianism as melodramatic and doomed.[3]

This essay will investigate how Balasko sets out to achieve this. First, I shall examine how she inserts comedy into the feminine through language, the body and the comic structures she creates – the *mise-en-textes* of sexuality/ies. Second, I shall analyse her *mise-en-scène* of sexuality/ies, which, although frameworked within the comedy genre, nonetheless delivers some strong messages about sexual desire, exchange and repression, and advocates using the body – as Balasko herself puts it – as '*une instance de liberté*'.[4] Obviously, there is considerable overlap between the concepts of *mise-en-textes* and *mise-en-scène*; however, they do suggest a different set of strategies, or a distinction where the first emanates from the principle of scripting and the second from that of staging. Finally, throughout this essay I shall be bearing in mind how Balasko's undertaking raises a number of problematic questions, starting with a fairly crucial one: namely, given that its authorial voice is not that of a lesbian, can *Gazon maudit* be deemed to relay a gay signature? For, as we shall see, ambiguity surrounds the lesbian status of Balasko's text. Although the film is about sexuality (heterosexual and homosexual), with, as its central character, a lesbian whose lesbianism is a catalyst for change in its three main protagonists (a married couple and the lesbian herself), it is nonetheless a film scripted and directed by a woman, Josiane Balasko, who stars as the central lesbian figure but/and who possesses 'a public image in France (that) includes the knowledge of her as a heterosexual woman and a mother'.[5] Implicit in this positioning and knowledge is a form of reassuring play around gender, both in relation to Balasko as *auteur* and for the spectator. And, of course, part of the comedy of *Gazon maudit* emanates from this knowledge.

I

Mise-en-textes of Sexuality/ies

The part-title of this essay, 'hardly grazing', bears a direct reference to the homophobic resonances of the film's title: *Gazon maudit*. Originally a sporting term, used in football to signal a jinxed pitch (literally translated, it would mean 'cursed turf'), it is also used as a slang term to designate derogatorily the 'cursed turf' of the lesbian. 'Gazon' refers to the female pubic hair around the genital area, while 'maudit' signifies that a particular turf, the lesbian's, is off-limits (to heterosexual males, that is) and is therefore to be cursed. French audiences going to see this film would be in no doubt of the meaning of its title, or (because it is signed Balasko) of its status as a comedy. And it is with the notion of comedy that I would like to begin.

Balasko's film is deliberately polemical, although she insists that it is not political[6] – a view with which it is difficult to concur, given that *Gazon maudit* not only has gender issues on its agenda but also raises questions of genre, contesting thereby both mainstream French comedy and the representation of heterosexual desire as a logical imperative. Despite the fact that its political resonances are denied by its creator, it is clearly the case that, in *Gazon maudit*, parody is used to powerful effect in both the *mise-en-textes* and *mise-en-scène* of sexuality/ies. Indeed, the very authorial act of contesting, through the use of parody, the viciously misogynistic tradition of French farce is a first *mise-en-texte* of sexuality, or, better, a *remise en contexte*. Balasko herself speaks of wanting to challenge this very masculine genre, by inserting as central a lesbian character, and a butch-lesbian at that. As I shall indicate in a moment, this is the starting-point of her generic (and therefore textual) subversion.

But first a little contextualizing of my own. To indicate where my thinking around this film has 'arrived', I must invoke the work of others who have helped me to framework my approach: Judith Butler's *Gender Trouble* (1990) and *Bodies that Matter* (1993); Laura Mulvey's *Fetishism and Curiosity* (1996); Tamsin Wilton's *Lesbian Studies* (1995); and Chris Straayer's *Jump Cut* article 'The Hypothetical Lesbian Heroine' (1981). And I would like to start by citing Straayer's article on lesbian desire and film, which helps us to appreciate the importance of Balasko's undertaking. Straayer argues that:

> Feminist film theory based on sexual difference has much to gain from considering lesbian desire and sexuality. Women's desire for women deconstructs male/female sexual dichotomies, sex/gender conflations, and the universality of the Oedipal narrative. Acknowledgement of the female-initiated active sexuality and sexualized activity of lesbians has the potential to re-open a space into which straight women as well as lesbians can exercise a self-determined pleasure.[7]

In terms of self-determined pleasure, the reception of Balasko's film by French audiences alone would attest to the considerable pleasure derived from it by women, straight and lesbian – as well, of course, as by other audiences. It came second in the French box-office listings in 1995, and remained in the top four for much of 1996. Lesbian audiences in France on the whole approved of the film – and welcomed the placing of lesbianism on the mainstream agenda.[8] There can be little doubt that it is the focus on the lesbian character that is a source of the pleasure generated by *Gazon maudit*.

Let us take a closer look at Straayer's discussion of sexuality and the lesbian heroine, and see how her analysis connects with Balasko's subverting tendencies. Generally speaking, in mainstream cinema, narrative serves to contain sexual pleasure and to displace it into a particular construction of sexual desire; that is, heterosexual desire. It is also the case, Straayer argues, that 'within the construction of narrative film sexuality, the phrase "lesbian heroine" is a contradiction in terms'.[9] Now, in *Gazon maudit*, Marijo (the lesbian) is very much the heroine. Balasko herself says as much, adding that Marijo is the only one who does not lie.[10] Thus, Marijo is doubly marked as different in relation to the textual practices of narrative film: first, in relation to sexuality (she is a lesbian) and second, in relation to language (she does not lie). This suggests that the body of Balasko/Marijo points to (and occludes) certain problems of enunciation, subjectivity and gendered subjectivity. I want now to explain how this might be the case.

In the act of enunciation (making a speech act), two entities are at play: (i) the 'enunciator' (the person who makes the speech act) and (ii) the 'enounced' (in French, the '*énoncé*') or verbal result of it. Enunciation is, additionally, a time-bound speech act, and the '*énoncé*' comes to be non-coincident with the moment of utterance. Thus, in terms of time-scale, enunciation and '*énoncé*' are not the same. Consequently, a central question that enunciation sets in motion is: who is the subject of the speech act? Who is represented in the act of utterance, and who is the speaking subject? When I say 'I', which 'I' am I referring to? The 'I' who has spoken and, temporally, has moved on? Or the 'I' who is spoken for, and remains a speech act? These questions suggest that a split subject emerges in the act of enunciating, and that a gap in subjectivity exists between the enunciator (or utterer), and the subject of the enunciation. In his *Problems in General Linguistics*,[11] Emile Benveniste illustrates this gap by addressing the paradox of the liar: if the enunciator says 'I am lying', then the subject of the '*énoncé*' cannot also be lying. Only one of the split subjects – because they are, precisely, split subjects – can be telling the truth about lying: subject I or subject II. In other words, the temporal difference between speech acts (enunciation and '*énoncé*') incorporates subject difference, too.[12]

In saying that Marijo is the only one who does not lie, Balasko hints at the fact that *Gazon maudit* mobilizes some interesting possibilities for subject positioning. A first relates to the split between character and author that Balasko's film-text incorporates, and to the tensions between scripting and *mise-en-texte* – particularly of sexuality – arising from it. Author and character occupy the same body (Balasko's). This notwithstanding, if the film's character (the subject of its '*énoncé*', Marijo) is not lying, then this implies that the subject of the enunciation (its author) may well be. And, as we know, Balasko's embodiment of the lesbian Marijo is, indeed, a lie. In the gap between script and *mise-en-texte*, between author and character, there occurs, then, in *Gazon Maudit*, an exposure of the process of subject division evoked above. I will pick this point up in a moment. But if we now enter the diegesis with the notion in mind that Marijo is the one not to lie, then it is tempting to engage with the possibility that something *else* is also occurring in *Gazon maudit*. If she does not lie, then, in terms of enunciation, this suggests that Marijo may occupy both enunciatory 'places' simultaneously, and may also occupy, therefore, the space *between* the two subject positions. Further, within the terms of this reading at least, Marijo's not lying suggests, too, that in recognizing herself as a subject of *desire* who is likewise doubly positioned, she does not *mis*recognize herself. For she certainly recognizes herself as she is: as lesbian *and* as mother. And in so doing (that is, in not rejecting the female/female intersubjective realm even though she turns to the masculine other in order to acquire a child), Marijo confounds gender stereotypes, subjecting the female Oedipal narrative trajectory to a considerable degree of destabilization. After all, what she eschews is an either/or model of subjecthood fundamental to univocal heterosexism, the heterosexual imperative that constructs subjectivity according to gender divisions, and within the parameters of an all-embracing Oedipus-continuous – in other words, patriarchal – law.

In a film whose sources of humour are many and varied, Balasko seems to be playing with the comic tradition to produce textual tensions that suggest that the Oedipal narrative could be done away with and that space should be made for agencings of desire which do not require subject and gender fixity either in language or performance. Viewed in this light, Balasko's performance as Marijo does play with the idea of multiplicity, since she embodies simultaneously such sexual modes as: «heterosexual-female-mother» and «homosexual-female-mother». This is not to deny that such a positioning has its problems (I will address these in my next section). However, the clashes and tensions that she sets up as author do challenge the accepted script of French farce and its heterosexist assumptions.

In parenthesis, before returning to the comic tradition of French farce, I want to touch on other ways in which Balasko subverts film genres that stage the Oedipal narrative – specifically, those of the road movie and the western. Typically, the narratives of both of these genres are of a moralistic nature, and both exemplify nostalgia for the myth of American frontiersmanship. Although on first appearance they appear counter-Oedipal, their function is, arguably, to secure patriarchy, the heterosexual imperative, and Western capitalism. The 'hero' of the western rides into town and cleans it up and then leaves (presumably to go to another town that needs its corrupt morals tidying up). He never marries or settles down, nor does he have kids. But he cleans up the town, ridding it of corrupt capitalism, so that good capitalist and reproductive practices may safely prevail. In a road movie, the 'hero' goes on the road to escape the restrictions and repressions of Western capitalism, now seen as corrupt, or sets off to find a better way of life in an imagined good, capitalist state. As with the western's hero, he, too, wants to escape the heterosexual imperative of marriage and reproduction. During his travels, he experiences encounters that either improve his self-knowledge or add to his already disabused state of mind. In *Gazon maudit*, Marijo is the character who is on the road. She emblematizes the road movie and western aspect of the movie: driving into town, acting as the catalyst for change *and* exchange (for the better), and then leaving town. But, in contrast with the traditional narratives of road movies or westerns, she is brought back to 'settle' by the very persons whose lives she has helped radically to change. Marijo 'saves' Laurent and Loli's marriage, but instead of becoming subsequently marginalized, she becomes central once again. Within the farce genre, then, in *Gazon maudit*, other generic texts of masculinity (the western and the road movie) are at once inscribed and challenged.

But how else does her film contest the tradition of French farce? Adultery is a mainspring of this comedy, as is sexual innuendo and a play with heterosexuality. Laughter is at the expense of the 'outsider', either in the form of the woman (the 'other woman' in a triangular relationship) or the homosexual (also represented as the other woman – the woman-other). Triangles abound in French farce, but all is resolved in the end in favour of safely-contained heterosexual marriage. In *Gazon maudit*, however, triangles get reasserted, with Loli as the desired apex of the triangle. And, as we know, at the very end of the film, it appears that the triangle may reconfigure itself quadrilaterally. Laughter in this film does not occur at the expense of the outsider, Marijo, precisely because it is through her character that the original assumptions about sexual desire come to be questioned.

By placing Marijo as absolutely central to the narrative, as agent, through her sexuality, for change and exchange – she and Loli do, after all, fall in love and experience other pleasures – Balasko casts the outsider as insider. She thus undermines the traditional vaudeville triangle. Furthermore, at the end of the film, it is not heterosexuality that is ultimately reaffirmed, but choice ('une instance de liberté', as Balasko puts it). Indeed, all of the attempts by Laurent, the husband, to separate the two women's bodies physically and to interrupt their desire fail. *Gazon maudit* thus shows that desire is no longer containable and displaceable into safe constructions of heterosexual desire. The film also challenges the assumption that heterosexuality and coherent selfhood are indissolubly linked (a point I will develop in Section II). Further still, the stereotypical trope of the lesbian/homosexual as 'threat' (to a marriage that is eventually saved by its brush with 'danger') is given little credence here. Marijo *does* effect change, but this is more because she exposes – or, rather, allows to be exposed – her co-protagonists' vulnerable spots. Laurent, in particular, comes to realize the errors of his ways. Yet Marijo, for her own part, as catalyst for change, represents no mere cypher. She too learns to accept the idea that she does not need to remain fiercely independent but can let others nurture her.

II

Mise-en-scène of Sexualities

Filmically, one of the ways Balasko achieves generic and 'genderic' subversion is through a *mise-en-scène* of sexualities via pairings. Throughout *Gazon maudit*, Balasko sets up mirroring scenes that work to comic effect and as parodic comment. She achieves this primarily through the pairing of Laurent's sexual exploits – i.e., a *mise-en-scène* of his machismo, which persists until the very end of the film – alongside Loli and Marijo's gradually emerging love-affair. Laurent, a real-estate agent, performs his sexual fantasies with the different women he takes to various houses he has been engaged to sell. His seductions are highly 'scripted'. He picks up women by means of the oldest of tricks: lighting their cigarettes and employing the banter of macho cruising. All moves with incredible haste. This contrasts with the encounters between Marijo and Loli, which proceed in a leisurely manner. One such pairing of seduction scenes comes at the beginning of the film, and sets the tone. It shows Laurent first getting rid of one woman (whom, as he says, he has just 'screwed'), then picking up another for what we imagine will be a future tryst, and then finally taking a third to a deserted mansion (on sale, naturally) for a 'fantasy fuck'. This is intercut with shots of Marijo, Loli, and their long-drawn-out first seduction scene. Here they are seen lighting not cigarettes but cigarillos and naming in French and Spanish (with great hilarity) the slang versions for the female genital area. Loli plucks a hair from Marijo's chin, and the first kiss comes literally hours later.

Another exemplary pairing occurs a little later in the film when Laurent, now aware that his wife 'fancies' Marijo, proceeds to get very drunk on an outing with his friend Antoine. The two men, we should note, are cycling off to their Saturday afternoon tryst with two Englishwomen in the country. Laurent ends up first in a pig-pen caressing a pig and then in a tin bath being bathed clean. He is deeply unhappy, deeply dirty and still deeply hypocritical, since he fails to see anything wrong with his own behaviour, and can only blame that of his wife and therefore of all women, whom he calls 'pouffiasses' ('ugly bitches'). Meanwhile, the scene cuts to Loli and

Marijo, who, by way of contrast, are 'en volupté' in *their* bath, having obviously just made love. The *mise-en-scène* here is clear: male stridency contrasts with the voluptuousness of the two women embraced in the bath, kissing and speaking softly, with Loli caressing Marijo's breast. There is no suggestion here that we are witnessing female bonding as a containment for lesbian desire – bodily pleasure is wholly explicit. For Laurent, the opposite is true: his lot is pure bodily discomfiture.

I want now to return to the idea of performance, and to Laurent's playing out of sexual fantasies, in order to develop further, in relation to gender performativity, identity and the body, the notion that sexualities are enacted. This will provide some useful ways of reading Balasko's film, and will enable us to see how normative gender performativity is set on its head in this subverting and subverted farce. But first a brief overview of the concept of gender performativity, and of its hegemonic function.

Pointing to the repressive nature of the patriarchal law, and to the ways in which it structures the world by suppressing multiple meanings and positionalities, Judith Butler explains how, under patriarchy, sex and gender are compelled to be the same, to the effect that gender – which she broadly defines as sexual and corporeal *performance* – comes simply to encompass the cultural meanings that the sexed body assumes.[13] That is, in the face of the multiplicity of meanings that sexuality potentially bears, patriarchy institutes univocal and discrete meanings in its place, so that sex and gender come to be seen as one. This, Butler suggests, represents a limiting of gender to a binary opposition (masculine/feminine), and helps to conflate sex, gender and desire into a single, 'cohesive' chain that mirrors – and secures – the logic of the heterosexual imperative. For Butler, then, it is the case not only that patriarchy's regulation of gender as a binary relation confirms 'a compulsory and naturalized heterosexuality', but also that a key process whereby the differentiation between the masculine and the feminine terms of the gender binary is accomplished is the practice of heterosexual *desire*.[14] In other words, heterosexuality serves to separate us off into the discrete gender-unities that patriarchy requires. The stability of these unities is maintained, indicates Butler, by the fact that through the process of gender performativity, sex itself – never, for Butler, a 'simple fact or static condition of a body' – is retroactively 'materialized', and materialized in a 'natural' (that is to say, binary) form. Indeed, the heterosexual imperative requires, she suggests, that performances of gender (including the heterosexual act of intercourse) be reiterated as a way of *regulating* sex, of sedimenting it so that its dualized mode acquires a 'naturalized effect'.[15] So, heterosexuality serves to reinforce the binary divide between the sexes, just as that divide serves to reinforce heterosexuality.

The masculine/feminine binary opposition sets in motion other oppositions, the most significant of which – for patriarchy's sake – is same/other, a concept of sexual difference that allows the patriarchal regime to stay in place. Within the male/female dyad, under patriarchy, the function of the female is to secure male subjectivity. It is her difference from the male, her visible otherness (signalled by the absence of the penis), that assures him of his sexual identity. She returns a reflection to him that, through its difference, confirms his sameness (i.e., she confirms that his body, reflected in the mirror she represents, is the same as his and different from hers). The patriarchally-marked female, therefore, 'performs her sex' only in order to affirm male subjectivity. Within patriarchal law, she functions as the object of male desire and the site of reproduction, while the male represents the agent, the subject of desire and the preserver of the law. Clearly, gender/sexual performances that are 'other' than, or dissonant with, the heterosexual imperative threaten the logic of that imperative. However, as Butler explains, in order to contain this threat, the hegemonic order of patriarchal performativity establishes which 'performing' bodies matter, laying down what counts as a valuable body in the world and what does not.[16] And, in this logic, a body that 'matters' (i.e., has materiality and value) is an intelligible, sexed body; a body that is rendered intelligible by the (patriarchal) discourses that support it and signify its value.

In *Gazon maudit*, Laurent believes and acts out the idea that he is a body that matters (at a prime level, literally, through his constant reenactment of the sexual performance of intercourse). Loli's body is also permitted to be a body that matters, but only in so far as it is a reproducing body (we note that Laurent avoids having sex with her at all costs, until she is 'lost' to him). Marijo, however, who is outside the heterosexual imperative, may be considered to be and to have a body that does not matter – a body that is abject, 'unintelligible'. This is because queerness, which Marijo's body incarnates, disrupts sex's stability, by pointing to the instability of its dyadic, gendered form,[17] and is consequently excluded and demarcated in language and discourse as abject, i.e. as belonging to the domain of delegitimated sex. In one sense, of course, heterosexuality needs queerness in order to enforce its own sense of legitimacy. As Butler argues: 'if the materiality of sex is demarcated in discourse [as it is within patriarchal law], then this demarcation will produce a domain of excluded and delegitimated sex' (my parenthesis).[18] As we know, in patriarchal law the subject is always already constructed through the phenomenon of exclusion – a position of otherness occupied by the gendered feminine other (the female other of the heterosexual matrix). So the lesbian is doubly devoid of a place to occupy, is doubly denied a 'legitimate' space within the hetorosexist matrix of power.

She lives, as Butler argues, squarely under the sign of the unliveable.[19]

But what happens when the lesbian, the *un*intelligible body that does not matter, occupies, as the heroine, the central position of the narrative? In *Gazon maudit*, we note that Marijo is demarcated in discourse as abject (she is labelled as *gouine*/diesel dyke), and that language, in the mouths of Laurent and Antoine, consigns her – or attempts to consign her – to the domain of abjected bodies. She, however, through her own particular form of performativity, refuses to occupy that domain. In the face of the male discourse that demarcates her as dyke, Balasko's heroine responds by appropriating its language, just as she appropriates 'male' dress codes (suits, shirts, etc.). Her cross-dressing code is, moreover, an appropriation that *threatens*. As Balasko says, Marijo disturbs: 'a woman who dresses up as a man is disturbing, she becomes a threat because she is treading on male territory [. . .]'.[20] The interior of her van, which we see at the very beginning of the film, signals a further way in which she appropriates the iconography of maleness. Its windscreen is adorned with objects (girlie transfers and so forth) normally associated with male truck-drivers, and its driver lights her cigarillo with a zippo lighter. This all works to hilarious effect, but reinforces our sense that Marijo's appropriation of the masculine is a threatening phenomenon, to which we respond by laughing, but laughing differently than if we had been watching a male truck-driver driving and lighting up. Her appropriation, in other words, makes a difference. She appropriates macho iconography, and in so doing usurps its original value. She also points up the foolishness of male rhetoric about lesbians. Laurent categorically states that 'The ugly dyke has to go for women because she can't get a man.' So what does this say about him and about the sort of discourse he employs, once Marijo 'appropriates' (as he sees it) his wife Loli?

As lesbian body, Marijo is the outlaw of culture and its inscriptions of gender. As such, she 'performs' a sex that the heterosexual binary divide refuses to see 'as one'. Because, however, she is also crucial to Balasko's narrative, the result is that that narrative, within which Marijo's body materializes the unliveable (of which her sexual body is the sign), serves to visibilize the unintelligible, the 'invalid'. It does so, specifically, by focusing on Marijo's role as a usurper within the heterosexual matrix of desire. Her usurpatory status is exemplified by the lesbian look of exchange that passes between herself and Loli. Marijo looks to Loli for a returning look of desire, and she gets it.[21] Her body, as abject body, thus enters the limits of the socially hegemonic. Through the exchange of looks (traditionally, in the patriarchal order, the exchange of looks is male-to-female-to-male), the outsider comes to occupy a place *inside*. By so doing, Marijo disrupts from within, and she re-eroticizes denied areas of sexual pleasure. As usurper within the heterosexual desiring realm, she is transgressive: she embodies the language of usurpation – she usurps the male prerogative – but does not replicate it. Her repudiated, abject body is not there to secure the heterosexual imperative through a materialization of gender performativity as prescribed by patriarchal law. It remains in the heterosexual/patriarchal domain, but it does something else: it liberates the erogenous body. Judith Butler reminds us that the heterosexual order denies a multiplicity of pleasures.[22] The re-eroticization of the body that Marijo introduces, through visibilizing her body and making it matter, is exemplified by Loli's pleasure, which, visibly displayed on her face and body, derives from Marijo's body and from the mutual pleasure she and Marijo share. The bath scene constitutes one example of it. Another occurs at the restaurant, where they sit together and stroke each other under the table, much to Laurent's fury and much to the subversive pleasure of the viewer.

Marijo's lesbianism – her sexual performance – permits the visibilization of another sex, and of a difference that makes a difference. It does so because it is invested not in reflecting male subjectivity back at itself but rather in self-reflexivity, *and* because it reveals thereby the constructs put in place by the heterosexual imperative (a point I will develop a little later). Marijo's usurpation of the heterosexual matrix is compounded by the fact that not only does she embody the lesbian body, thereby signalling the falsity of the sex/gender binary privileged by heterosexual logic, but she also comes to embody the maternal body, and uses that body as a site of exchange (she will leave Loli and Laurent to their relationship, if Laurent can provide her with a baby). In other words, Marijo gives her body – as a lesbian *and* a maternal body – value. In terms of gender construction, there is 'double trouble' here. To explain how, let us return to Judith Butler and her remarks, offered in *Gender Trouble*, on the issue of the maternal body and its value.[23]

According to patriarchal law, as theorized by Butler (amongst others), entry into the Symbolic is possible only if the subject repudiates the mother's body. The relinquishing of the breast and the rupture from the maternal body are the conditions for subjectivity and identity. And, within the terms of patriarchal discourse, when woman occupies the position of the maternal body, that body occupies a 'prediscursive' space. The reasoning goes as follows. The maternal body is, as we know, a body that 'matters' because it is in a state of reproduction. The child inside it is not yet born, and so is in a prediscursive state (as, by implication, is the mother). In that the maternal body is constructed as prediscursive – is not, in other words, *in* the space of the Symbolic – it is momentarily and potentially subversive of patriarchal law. However, as Foucault makes clear, sex is part of culture's hegemonic strategy, and motherhood may be viewed as a hegemonic construct like any other. In fact, it is useful for patriarchy to let women believe that they are having their moment of subversion, particularly since, after their brush with maternal outlawry, they are returned *post partum* to the law. Put another way, the construction of maternity as prediscursive must be acknowledged as a patriarchal one, whose subversive potential is containable. Further, this construction is deeply imbricated in that process whereby the female body is normalized and *in*visibilized as a vehicle for the reproductive function.

So, with Marijo and *Gazon maudit*, there cannot help but be double trouble about. The first order of trouble is due to the fact that Marijo, as a putatively abject body that does not matter, chooses to occupy a body that *does* matter (the maternal, reproductive body). However, and this is the second order of trouble, since her body – as lesbian – is always already outlawed, she remains out of the law not just as maternal body but also *afterwards*. 'Worse' still, in exchange for making a baby, it is she, not patriarchal law, who restores the heterosexual imperative (by leaving Loli and Laurent), even though, as she warns Laurent, he cannot ultimately hope for the two women to end their relationship ('we will always end up finding each other', she declares). And indeed the heterosexual unit is only briefly restored. In both of her positions, therefore, as lesbian and as mother – that is, as an abject body that matters (an oxymoron if ever there was one) – Marijo points to the instability of culture's hegemonic strategy. First, she ensures that the distinction between bodies that matter, and bodies that do not, collapses. Second, her lesbian body gives agency to her maternal body, pointing to a contradiction within heterosexuality's single chain of logic (sex/gender/desire). Finally, Marijo, by being so visible first as lesbian (as suggested above, she has already 'visibilized' herself prior to the moment of conception) and then as mother and lesbian, exposes that process of *in*visibilization of the female body as reproductive function that is effected by the heterosexual matrix of power.

There are, however, problems with all of this. Whilst the *character* Marijo may well embody a difference that (ultimately) *does* matter, the person who embodies Marijo, namely Josiane Balasko, is, of course, not lesbian, and so occupies, in terms of visibility, a different place. And I want to ponder this issue for a moment, before returning to the diegesis of *Gazon maudit* and concluding with a discussion of other issues of performativity.

In the film, a heterosexual feminine and maternal body (a body that matters: Balasko) is masquerading as a lesbian and maternal body (a body that does not: Marijo). Further, the heterosexual feminine body is masquerading as a butch, cross-dressed, unintelligible body that, within the confines of patriarchal law at least, does not matter. But that original masquerading body (Balasko's) is always already, because feminine, a masquerading body of another kind, whose sexual difference serves to assert male subjectivity, and is represented as so doing (through clothing, for example). So a double masquerade is at play here: the masquerading feminine is masquerading as lesbian. Here is the problem: because the woman, within the heterosexist matrix of power, acts as an affirmatory mirror for male sexuality (with the result that it is not her sexuality that is subject), she is already invisibilized as female. By performing as a lesbian body, however, and by cross-dressing as an assertion of that performance as lesbian, the woman (here Balasko) confronts us with a series of masquerades. Whose body are we watching? Whose is the cross-dressed body, in a scenario where one invisible body is enacting another invisible body? It is here, it seems to me, that cracks start to appear; cracks that generate questions of authenticity around the authorial voice performing as a gay signature, and thus provoke a certain discomfiture, for some lesbian spectators at least.

Another way of approaching this problem is to look at the question of cross-dressing in relation to its practice within film genre. Cross-dressing is usually a reassuring element within mainstream cinema, particularly comedy. We all know that underneath the skirt, in a cross-dressed male, there is the penis. His performance will draw attention to his masculine sexuality – that is, after all, part of the comedy. We know also, conversely, that the cross-dressed female has to suppress her sexuality in order for 'problems' of homosexuality not to pose a threat. A male cross-dressed as a woman can manifest desire for a female on screen; we know it is safe, although the hints of lesbianism make us laugh (apparently). A cross-dressed female, however, takes a risk in making evident her desire for her (real) male counterpart, because of its homosexual connotations. For the lesbian viewer, there are two sources of discomfiture around Balasko/Marijo's specific form of cross-dressing (which takes in both Balasko's performance as a lesbian and Marijo's self-ironizing performance as a butch lesbian whose foil is the Spanish femme Loli). First, the cross-dressed female is flirting not with heterosexual desire but with lesbian desire, thus usurping the position traditionally occupied by the cross-dressed male. In a sense, she is playing the cross-dressed game the wrong way round, because she cannot uncover the safety-valve, the penis, and all of a sudden reveal herself as male – which would make it all 'all right'. Second, this cross-dressed female is 'really' a heterosexual woman masquerading as lesbian, flirting with lesbian desire and thus usurping the place traditionally occupied by the lesbian (butch, cross-dressed or not).

In her essay 'Outside In, Inside Out', Trinh Minh-ha makes the point that those who 'seek to reveal one society to another' claim that their objective is to 'grasp the native's point of view' and 'to realize *his* vision of *his* world'.[24] Admittedly, Trinh Minh-ha is talking here about questions of 'Third Cinema' and post-colonial discourses. However, her thoughts are useful for my considerations of the motivation of Balasko's film, of which the film-maker herself states: 'I wanted to talk about female homosexuality to a large audience.'[25] In her article, Minh-ha addresses the way in which the ex-colonialist (in this instance, the ethnographic film-maker) recolonizes the 'Other' through *his* claim to objectivity, authenticity and to seeing things from the native's point of view (through, in other words, giving the native a voice). But, as she says, 'to put oneself into someone else's skin is not without difficulty'.[26] We know that Balasko, in order to inhabit the part of Marijo, visited lesbian bars and observed lesbians for their outward appearance (clothes, hair etc).[27] As for the inward dimension, she says 'I tried to reach inside myself to find my masculine side. And I found it, which was amusing.'[28]

Balasko certainly gives the lesbian a central voice, but it is she, as film-maker, who is *talking* about female homosexuality. The problem Balasko creates is that the authenticity of the gay signature does not, arguably, hold – despite some lesbian audiences' pleasures in the film. By endeavouring to get inside an outsider's place – the lesbian 'I' – Balasko gives the illusion of knowledge. Lesbians, after all, recognize the butch type, and the lesbian bar scene at the end of the film does have 'authentic resonances'. It is as if the 'straight film-maker' has come to talk about 'the female homosexual' – pursuing an anthropological study (an 'outing') with *difference* in mind. And so her film runs the risk of undermining its own project, which is to expose and subvert the securing effects of essential difference.[29]

However, I do not myself wish to adopt a position that essentializes a straight film-maker playing a lesbian character, although I readily acknowledge an ambivalence in my reading of this film. Thus, whilst I lodge these reservations, I also recognize that, within the film's diegesis at least, Marijo's persona and performance *do*, as I have argued above, undercut binary oppositions. Furthermore, she moves ('drifts', as Minh-ha would put it)[30] between outside/inside, invisible/visible, unliveable/liveable. She embodies what I would term a *livisibilization*[31] of the self, and, as such, unsettles every definition of otherness arrived at. And it is with these thoughts in mind that I would like to frame my concluding remarks.

III

Issues of Gender Performativity

By way of a conclusion, I would like to reflect on the value of Balasko's film as a comedy and as a subversion of the tradition of French farce, and to develop the idea of gender and performance in another way: that of gender parody. In so doing, I want to turn once more to Judith Butler. Butler makes the point, after Foucault, that gender is an *effect*; that is, that the gendered body is performative.[32] Words, acts, gestures and desire 'produce the effect of an internal core or substance', creating 'the illusion of an interior and organizing gender core'.[33] In other words, the interiority is as much an illusion as the outer performance – an illusion discursively maintained for the purpose of the regulation of sexuality. Re-writing Nietszche, Butler states: 'There is no gender identity behind the expression of gender, [. . .] identity is performatively constituted by the very "expressions" that are said to be its results.'[34] She goes on to suggest, and this is the key point, that 'if the inner truth of gender is a fabrication and a true gender is a fantasy instituted and inscribed on the surface of bodies, then it seems that genders can be neither true nor false, but are only produced as [. . .] truth effects [. . .]'.[35] In other words, gender is a form of mimicry, of pastiche – and, as pastiche, is a 'neutral'/naturalized form of imitation, which means that gender performativity becomes a 'naturalized' construction masquerading as an original, or masquerading as having an original.

Although within cultural theory there is some debate as to the viability of Butler's claims regarding drag's subversive potential to disrupt (from within) the heterosexual imperative, nonetheless, within film studies and film theory, the ideological functions and counter-hegemonic potential of drag and cross-dressing have been widely discussed since the mid-1980s at least. Annette Kuhn shows quite clearly that the co-opting of cross-dressing into mainstream cinema constitutes a way of neutralizing its threat, and Richard Dyer has explicated the subversive force of female cross-dressing in films starring Judy Garland.[36] To my thinking, Butler usefully advances the debate around issues of representation and masquerade, at least within the context of film studies. In *Gender Trouble*, Butler explains how drag – and I would add, in the context of this essay, cross-dressing – reveals most completely that performing a gender is like repeating a copy of a copy. Drag, she says, 'implicitly reveals the imitative structure of gender itself'.[37] Drag and cross-dressing are both potentially forms of gender parody, therefore, because they reveal the imitative structure, and do not just reproduce it (this would be pastiche). Gender parody distinguishes itself from pastiche, in that it is a parody of the *idea* of the natural and the original. It reveals that 'the original identity after which gender fashions itself is an imitation without origin'.[38] And in that lies the creativity, the subversive potential of cross-dressing and drag, particularly as these practices are represented on screen.

Cross-dressing, as exemplified by Marijo in *Gazon maudit,* is the parody of the pastiche of gender identity. Marijo's own performance – her lesbian body, her cross-dressed appearance that challenges and parodies discourses of sexual difference as binary – not only subverts gender coherence, but exposes gender performativity for what it is: a copy. Her body and her bodily performance counter the 'various forces that police the social appearance of gender'.[39] And the subversion they effect also impinges on the codes and conventions of French farce, which, like so many other cultural artefacts, rests on, and incorporates, a cultural policing of gender. If we compare Marijo's performance with Laurent's, we can see that while hers (as described above) is parodic, his embodies the pastiche mode to the hilt. The repetition of his sexual fantasies that he enacts with all his women underscores the importance of reiteration for the materialization of heterosexual sex. This reiteration eventually sucks in his wife Loli, once their sexual relationship is resumed and they 'cheat' on Marijo with their daytime trysts.

Since *Gazon maudit* is, however, a film of utopia and a comedy – a combination flavoured by Balasko's 1970s background – we need always to bear two points in mind. The first is that the film is a comedy of stereotypes, and that laughter emerges from the realization that, all along, the original is derivative. In this regard, gender itself is a stereotype and the parodic mode is consequently a more 'realistic' one to inhabit. The second point is that the film represents a *mise-en-abyme* of the disappearing sense of the normal, within which Laurent in particular shifts from the idea of sex as compulsory heterosexuality to an understanding that identity, which includes sexual identity, is a complex and plurivocal matter. Given all of this, it is strange that Hollywood should want to do a remake, but not so strange that Balasko wants nothing to do with it.

Notes

1. Film examples of this sexual utopia include Coline Serreau's *Pourquoi pas!* (1977) and Claude Faraldo's *Themroc* (1972).

2. F. Strauss (1995), 'L'empire des sens', interview with Balasko in *Cahiers du cinéma*, no. 489, pp. 60–3, p. 62.
3. G. Vincendeau (1996), 'Twist and Farce', interview with Balasko in *Sight and Sound*, no. 6, issue 4, pp. 24–6, p. 25.
4. Strauss, 'L'empire des sens', p. 62.
5. Vincendeau, 'Twist and Farce', p. 25.
6. Ibid.
7. C. Straayer (1981), 'The Hypothetical Lesbian Heroine', *Jump Cut*, no. 35, pp. 50–7, p. 50.
8. Vincendeau, 'Twist and Farce', p. 25.
9. Straayer (1981), 'The Hypothetical Lesbian Heroine', p. 50.
10. Vincendeau, 'Twist and Farce', p. 25.
11. E. Benveniste (1971), *Problems in General Linguistics*, Miami.
12. It is not too difficult to see how this reasoning meshes with Lacan's concept of the divided subject, introduced in the early paper 'The Mirror Stage as Formative of the Function of the I'. See J. Lacan (1977), *Ecrits: a Selection*, London and New York. The Mirror Stage essay ('Le Stade du Miroir comme formateur de la fonction du Je') occupies pp. 1–7 in A. Sheridan's translation.
13. J. Butler (1990), *Gender Trouble*, London and New York, p. 103.
14. Ibid., pp. 22–3.
15. J. Butler (1993b), *Bodies that Matter*, London and New York, pp. 1–2, 10.
16. Ibid., p. 10.
17. Ibid.
18. Ibid.
19. Ibid., p. 3.
20. Vincendeau, 'Twist and Farce', p. 25.
21. In film culture, as in psychoanalysis, it has been traditionally thought that the male is the holder of the gaze. He looks, and looks upon, the woman and does not look for a returning/equal gaze; the desiring gaze, the agent of the look, is the male not the female. Debate around the theory of the gaze has developed significantly from this earliest equation, and has addressed the issue of what happens when the woman does look (usually this means trouble – for her). For an interesting essay on the cinematic agencing of desire in ways that differ from the traditional visual/scopic position accorded to women, which also contains some useful insights into play with the Oedipal triangle, see P. Benson (1990), 'Screening Desire', *Screen*, vol. 31, no. 4, pp. 377–89.
22. Butler, *Gender Trouble*, p. 29.
23. Ibid., p. 92.

24. T. Minh-ha (1989), 'Outside In, Inside Out', in J. Pines and P. Willemen (eds), *Questions of Third Cinema*, London, pp. 133–49, p. 133.
25. Vincendeau, 'Twist and Farce', p. 25.
26. Minh-ha, 'Outside In, Inside Out', p. 135.
27. Vincendeau, 'Twist and Farce', p. 26.
28. Ibid.
29. Space precludes my exploring this idea further, but it is worth noting that Trinh Minh-ha's discussion of the Inappropriate Other within every 'I' and the ethnographer–film-maker's unawareness of this particular Inside–Outside position ('Outside In Inside Out', p. 148) opens up another approach to the problems Balasko's film presents.
30. Trinh Minh-ha, 'Outside In, Inside Out', p. 145.
31. I am indebted to my friend and colleague Jean-François Diana of the University of Metz for his neologism '*livisibilité*', which he created to refer to the readability of live performance on TV. I freely adapt it here to refer to Marijo's visible and readable performance.
32. Butler, *Gender Trouble*, p. 136.
33. Ibid.
34. Ibid.
35. Ibid.
36. See A. Kuhn (1985), *The Power of the Image: Essays on Representation and Sexuality*, London and New York; and R. Dyer (1986), *Heavenly Bodies: Film Stars and Society*, London.
37. Butler, *Gender Trouble*, p. 137.
38. Ibid.
39. Ibid.

– 7 –

'A Walk along the side of the Motorway': AIDS and the Spectacular Body of Hervé Guibert

Murray Pratt

As Leo Bersani asserts in *Homos*, 'Nothing has made gay men more visible than AIDS';[1] the irony being that rather than heralding the equality and justice demanded by gay rights movements, the visibility bestowed upon gay male bodies by the epidemic has most often been contrived in the public eye in order to delimit, contain and stigmatize. In Western societies, the bodies of gay men are subjected daily to social critiques aimed at discerning their HIV status, assessing their risk factor and determining their value, while at the same time the symptoms of AIDS are persistently reinscribed as the caricatural signs of sexual difference on which homophobia feeds. Further, the straight mainstream in the USA uses AIDS to produce and police its fantasized boundaries. Bersani writes: 'Thanks largely to television and movies, the entire country has been able to take in (while of course distancing itself from) images of our wasted bodies. The normal fear of homosexuality has been promoted to a compelling terror as a secret fantasy becomes a public spectacle' (Bersani 1995: 19). My intention here is to argue that, in opposition to the demonizing logic of this kind of 'telespectacle', Hervé Guibert's writing offers an alternative representation of AIDS identity, thanks to which the body is produced as a different kind of spectacle, that touches, confronts and mobilizes its audience instead of confirming their prejudices across a safe distance. In so doing, I shall advance an assessment of the political potential of Guibert's AIDS narratives that works against that offered by Act Up-Paris, for whom Guibert's writing serves to collude with the scandal of AIDS by focusing on his individual destiny as 'expiatory victim' rather than on a critique of the socio-political factors sustaining the epidemic.[2] Drawing on theories of visuality and power from Michel Foucault's *Discipline and Punish* (1977), my aim is to show how Guibert's 'hospital diary', published as *Cytomégalovirus* (1992), offers up the body of the writer not as a sacrifice, but as a site of visions and visualizations of the trauma of his AIDS-related illness. A close reading of two adjacent extracts from *Cytomégalovirus* will permit me to address the ways in which Guibert's affirmative re-imagining of his identity with AIDS, like that offered by Derek Jarman's *Blue*, generates a spectacular disruption and reconfiguration of the disciplinary apparatus of homophobia.[3]

During his stay in hospital, Guibert uses his diary to rhythm the time of, and give meaning to, his experience. He notes events occurring around him and records his own thoughts and feelings as he undergoes one painful operation and awaits the possibility of another. The diary includes passages describing the disorganized treatment he receives, and, in particular, his own efforts to retain some human dignity in the face both of systematic institutional dehumanization and of his own illness. On 29 September 1991, after twelve days of hospitalization, he writes:

> This morning, a friendly woman house doctor came to tell me that my pneumothorax was not at all resorbed, the X-ray still showed a fair-sized air pocket beneath the detached pleura. After the initial examination of this X-ray I had been told that it was completely resorbed, only to be told a few days later, with some embarrassment, that there still remained an insignificant air pocket which would disappear in its own time. I am coughing. I must not cough. I take some syrup. I'm in a bit of pain. I'm very pessimistic about how things will turn out.[4]

Recording the narrator's reception of the prognosis of his pneumothorax, this paragraph positions the Guibertian body as an unremarkable object of medical attention. The scrutinized body is one that has been operated on, and whose progress is assessed, measured and generally controlled according to established, routine practices. These factors suggest that the purpose of the narrative of the body contained in the extract is simply to graft a 'human' dimension on to Guibert's story, provoking a response that enables readers to sympathize with his suffering. However, the paragraph also implies a fuller narrative scale, by referring to previous inaccurate assessments and to future possibilities, and ends by focusing on Guibert's despairing response to his revised prognosis. In so doing, it affords its readers a particularly privileged insight into the emotions of its narrator/protagonist; specifically, his discontent with the system in which he finds himself and his sense of foreboding about future events. In other words, the description it offers already strains to work against objectivizing images of 'an AIDS patient', by involving readers in Guibert's personality, his subjective evaluations and the physical process of his illness, as conveyed by the staccato sequence implicating us in the discomfort of his coughing. As with 'reality shows', which document medical 'emergencies' as they really happen, or fictional hospital dramas, a sense of pathos is created from the play between wider contexts and systems that treat illness and death in a matter-of-fact, routine way, and the shock – often potentially transformative – of the individual's encounter with his/her fragility and mortality.

Television dramas often ensure their viewers' emotional participation by providing them with a comfort zone between their securely sofa'ed world and on-screen events, whether by emphasizing the 'extraordinary' nature of accidents, or by establishing their protagonists as readily identifiable, socially sanctioned stereotypes (reluctant Asian daughters destined for pre-arranged marriages; long-suffering wives only too aware of their husband's 'secret' bisexuality and spared a positive HIV-test result). If viewers are encouraged to identify with characters' predicaments, it is most often so that they may participate more fully in the virtual thrill of the televisual ride, without becoming over-involved. As with such telespectacles, *Cytomégalovirus* privileges the narrative of the body as worth telling, as extraordinary. However, the diary genre to which Guibert's text belongs ensures a different kind of reader response, both by opening up new possibilities of voice and agency to the patient, and by providing a format that can record differences and variations of response.

Published in 1992, after Guibert's death in December 1991, *Cytomégalovirus*'s diary format also allows its author to breach one of the first laws of the television spectacular by allowing its public to get familiar with a character who does not survive. In fact, by writing his readers into the day-to-day fabric of his life, Guibert is bridging the comfortable distance used to frame the issue of AIDS for general consumption. In an essay entitled 'Délibération', Barthes records his uneasiness about the 'Journal' form, which he sees as elevating the humdrum to the status of the extraordinary. He defines diary extracts as '*infinitely suppressible*',[5] signalling the ephemeral qualities of the events transcribed, and doubts whether he would consider any part of his own life interesting enough to record. Situated in the context of these latter observations, it is hard to read the first passage cited from Guibert's 'Journal' as anything other than a banal medical bulletin, an anecdotal episode expressing 'essentially the inexpressible of the world, the world as inexpressible'.[6] Yet the best-kept diaries, as Barthes himself goes on to acknowledge, are characterized by that same 'suppleness' with which literature answers the double charge that what it conveys (i) cannot be proved and (ii) is not worth saying. Barthes further qualifies this quality as 'both a rhythm (fall and rise, elasticity) and an illusion (I can never attain my own image); in short, a form of writing which tells of the truth of the illusion, and which guarantees that truth by the most formal of operations, rhythm'.[7]

These remarks powerfully illuminate Guibert's achievement in *Cytomégalovirus*. As his diary progresses, his precarious sense of self and the various points of view brought to bear upon him by different staff in the hospital are constantly scrutinized under the sign of 'the illusion'. Moreover, *Cytomégalovirus*, even more than Guibert's later AIDS texts, corresponds to the natural rhythming of its author's strength and fatigue: extracts expand or contract according to how much or how little he is able to write. Likewise, the writing activity owes much to the rhythm of the day-to-day goings-on in the hospital, as Guibert notes when he explains: 'Writing is also a way of giving the time a certain rhythm, and of whiling it away.'[8] In other words, in common with Guibert's earlier writing, *Cytomégalovirus* is a text that edges towards the suspension of questions about truth and accuracy, answering instead to the necessity of its own writing in phrases such as: 'I thought I would no longer be able to write in this diary any more, from the trauma, but it's the only way of forgetting.'[9] Indeed, much of the diary's value as an emotive forcefield is guaranteed by the perilousness of its own existence. As with *To the Friend Who Did Not Save My Life*,[10] Guibert's own health and the completion of his text are mutually implicated: the game plan of *Cytomégalovirus* entails ensuring that Guibert remains well enough to continue recording his impressions, while being ill enough for the experiences he conveys to present danger and suspense. This is best illustrated when, after three hours of surgery, the diary entry contains only the message: 'Wrote nothing this evening. Too shocked. I'll try tomorrow.'[11] Guibert's paranoid desire to hide his notebooks under his pillows whenever he leaves his bedside also serves to enforce our perception, as readers, of the threats to the very survival of his writing.[12]

The paragraph outlined above, ending with Guibert's pessimistic prognosis on how events might unfold, is immediately followed by another, detailing a second 'event' of the same morning: 'This morning, the head of the clinic came to offer me a day-pass valid until eight o'clock in the evening, because of the good weather. A walk along the side of the motorway?'[13] This last enigmatic sentence is introduced elliptically, so that it is not immediately apparent how it relates to the offer of leave. However, Guibert's ironic portrayal throughout *Cytomégalovirus* of patient mismanagement makes it impossible for the reader not to interpret it as part of a broader, sarcastic commentary on the gulf between well-meaning intention and the reality he exposes in his journal. The hospital where Guibert is being treated is situated next to *le périphérique* surrounding Paris. Recovering from a serious operation, and with no advance notice, he is hardly likely to be able to make any arrangements. The only way he could benefit from his day-pass, he jokes, would be to go for a walk alongside the motorway. On one level, all we are being offered here is another sideswipe at the short-sightedness of the medical establishment. However, it seems to me that the image Guibert plays with can also be opened out to offer a new gloss on the body as spectacle, or perhaps spectacular, and can thus be used to initiate a commentary on Guibert's wider writing practice as a person with AIDS.

'A walk along the side of the motorway?' is clearly posited as a ludicrous, inappropriate proposition, yet it is also one that Guibert – however ironically – is prepared mentally to entertain. It is ludicrous, firstly, because walking alongside a major arterial road is unhealthy and dangerous, even for those whose lungs are intact, and, secondly, because motorway walking holds out the danger of being hit by fast-moving traffic. Why, then, does Guibert visualize the walk in question? His attachment to the possibility of suicide (notably the dose of digitalin evoked in his other texts on AIDS)[14] might suggest that the motorway walk he contemplates is motivated simply by some kind of death wish, or, perhaps, by a desire to choose his own means of dying and to gain thereby a degree of control over the process of his illness repeatedly refused him by the medical establishment. These hypotheses are convincing enough. However, I would like to suggest a further explanation for Guibert's ironic question, and for the motorway walk it foregrounds. Motorways are exclusively for vehicles, so that the sight of someone walking along the side of a busy motorway such as *le périphérique* is rare. It is difficult, moreover, to imagine the frail and emaciated figure of Guibert, wearing the blue fedora he sports in *Cytomégalovirus* and attached to a drip, taking step after careful step along the side of a busy road. What *is* certain is that were he to do so, he would undoubtedly become a spectacular centre of attention. And it is in such terms – that is, as spectacular, promenading body – that he elects to envision himself in his text. Why might this be the case?

The spectacle that Guibert evokes in the phrase 'A walk along the side of the motorway?' allows him to move beyond the hospital drama format and suggest, metaphorically, a less objectified image of someone with AIDS. Before teasing out the positive implications of Guibert's Zen-like phrase, though, we need to look at some of the questions of representation and visibility that AIDS raises. The history of the epidemic in the West has been marked by incomplete, partial and concealed information, as well as by an official resignation that those who test HIV-positive could be written off as beyond help, to the extent that the most potent slogan of resistance to date is the campaigning group Act-Up's castigation of attitudes that equate AIDS with death. To these, Act-Up replies simply: 'Silence=Death'. When

HIV and AIDS do get represented in the media, it is most often as part of a script that separates safe, healthy consumers from an abject and dangerous world of the other, against which the News aims to inoculate them. Procedures of classification limiting the HIV virus to minority and marginal groups, principally homosexuals and intravenous drug users, have allowed dominant representations of AIDS to position the epidemic as outside mainstream concern. Simon Watney describes this mechanism thus:

> [I]t is impossible not to relate the widespread denial of the imminent danger of an HIV epidemic among British heterosexuals to the grotesque homophobia of British society [. . .] It is a denial which not only regards the possible deaths of tens and hundreds of thousands of gay men with complete indifference, but places those who are themselves so shockingly indifferent to the fate of others at real risk.[15]

Certainly in North America, as Cindy Patton has observed,[16] it is in the interests of the conspiracy logic deployed by the Right to concede to (mis)representing its other, and to figuring AIDS actively *as* homosexuality, and vice versa, as part of its insistence on promoting monogamous heterosexuality as the only safe form of sexuality. This in turn helps to remould public concern about HIV infection as a fear of becoming visible as queer, and consequently of occupying an exposed position where visibility serves to stigmatize.

Less often noticed is a further 'permissible' representation of AIDS within dominant discourses, that which foregrounds the suffering of the disease's 'innocent' victims. Entirely consistent with the portrayal of the epidemic as the abject essence of homosexuality, these accounts have a secondary function in confirming myths of the HIV virus as something that infiltrates society from the outside, often from abroad, or that contaminates 'our' blood supplies, or is transmitted as a result of bisexuals impersonating heterosexuals. Douglas Crimp makes clear the double logic operating behind these forms of representation when he recalls how Kimberly Bergalis, when she engaged in debates about the possibility of the transmission of the HIV virus from dentists, 'spoke not as a person with AIDS ("I didn't do anything wrong", she protested), but as the "victim" of people with AIDS. ("My life has been taken away")'.[17]

In France, where homosexuality has perhaps been less visible, and consequently figured less hysterically than in Britain and the USA, the 'innocent victims' portrayal has become one form of representing *all* people with AIDS, as was witnessed during the 1994 AIDS telethon, *Tous contre le sida,* which achieved this representation by air-brushing over sexuality rather than by challenging the distinction itself.[18] Jean-Luc Maxence's *Les Écrivains sacrifiés des années sida* (1995) astonishingly sidesteps questions of sexual orientation almost entirely as it establishes a hagiographical tribute to the lost generation of French artists and intellectuals, including Guibert, Cyril Collard, Michel Foucault, and the gay writer and theorist Guy Hocquenghem. For Maxence, who never ceases to stress the youth of most of his subjects, their fate and their writings perform a function almost identical to the lives of saints:

> Obviously they provide us *post mortem* with a powerful lesson in life, indeed in hope, which often contrasts with the defeatist despair of other writers, themselves spared and yet infinitely more sorrowful! [. . .] And we firmly refuse to shed crocodile tears on our words. We shall not lament obligingly over the great new tombs beneath an AIDS moon where too too many victims, cut down in their prime by this virus, now rest for all eternity. Among the messages left behind, it seems more pressing that we should pick up their confrontation with death, the head-to-head with its seemingly almighty power, always a major turning-point in the life of a man who is destined to soon take his leave.[19]

Not only does the vocabulary of the epitaph used by Maxence figure AIDS as an edifying tragedy, but his emphasis on the immense treasures that his slaughtered lambs have left behind verges on a glorification of the battlefield of AIDS.[20] Modes of representation and visibility of AIDS are, then, politically charged. The body ill with AIDS, when it is not made to vanish from sanitized discourses, already appears therein as a mediatized spectacle. How then, as Paul Julian Smith asks in an article comparing the films of Guibert and Collard with Derek Jarman's *Blue*, can we find a positive way to 'represent an invisible virus whose transmission cannot be seen and whose carriers have been subject to hostile surveillance and revelation?'[21] Jarman's cinematic answer is to offer a vision rather than a representation. The blue screen and often incantatory soundtrack provoke meditation rather than stares, and lead the film's (non-)spectators towards other forms of identification with Jarman and his illness. Smith rightly notes that the triumph of *Blue* lies in the way it can escape the hostile looks with which people with AIDS are scrutinized, but he is less convinced of the ability of the self-representations of Collard and Guibert to do likewise. He writes: 'By refusing to image the body, by offering only the blue screen on which spectators project their own image, Jarman brilliantly eludes the double bind of representing Aids – bearing witness to illness, but avoiding both the narcissism of Collard and Guibert and the invasive intrusions of the documentary gaze' (Smith 1993: pp. 18–19).

Here, Smith is referring specifically to *La Pudeur ou l'impudeur* and Collard's film *Savage Nights*. The charges of narcissism that he brings against these films, however, have wider implications for Guibert's literary responses to AIDS. Texts such as *To the Friend* and *The Compassion Protocol*[22] proceed by insistently framing the author's body as the object of the reader's imaginary gaze. Each returns to moments when Guibert's image is discussed, glimpsed in mirrors, seen by others or produced in their imagination. Even Maxence is keen to qualify his accounts of Guibert's writing with the misgiving that 'there are some who confess with a degree of detail which could be accused, at times, of exhibitionism'.[23] Yet, as more nuanced accounts have shown, within the context of Guibert's writing, the accumulation of his own images, identities, impersonations, both literary and photographic, offers much more than the voguing of 'immaculate bodies' that Smith implies. Jean-Pierre Boulé points out in his analysis of *To the Friend* that Guibert's self-exposure is part of his project of 'saying everything' ('tout dire'); of delving beneath his skin to reveal even the vulnerability of his deteriorating blood.[24] And Derek Duncan's reading details how the stability of the writer's body and identity is shattered, rather than affirmed, in its encounter with the look of AIDS: 'This look becomes the place where the unspeakable returns, threatening the integrity of the self as it indelibly traces its effects on the body [. . .] The more the body is irrevocably eroded by the virus, the more the look itself constitutes the place where the self's loss of presence comes to be felt.'[25]

These accounts converge in locating Guibert's exposure to the look as an activity that takes him beyond the limits of identity as it is conventionally conveyed, whether it be towards 'the looming presence of Thanatos, which [. . .] the body has been ultimately trying to inscribe all along and from the very first text, *La Mort propagande*, but cannot', or 'that element of impossibility at the heart of the self and its inscriptions in writing'.[26] In either case, the contrast with Smith's focus on the striking looks of Guibert's body as evidence of its collusion with the voyeurism of dominant discourses is stark. Indeed, Lee Edelman,[27] in choosing to conclude his influential chapter on AIDS and representation by quoting Guibert's *To the Friend*, further confirms the resistant, transformative potential which the defiantly visual might offer. Drawing on a passage from the text where the mirror image of Guibert's emaciated body is viewed approvingly by his own self-affirming gaze, Edelman points to the ways in which images such as these can work in tandem with AIDS activism in confronting dominant ideologies, offering 'a strategic mode of resistance not to be slighted by the discourse of "politics" as our lives are rewritten by "AIDS"'.[28]

Returning to the spectacular image of Guibert walking alongside the motorway provided by *Cytomégalovirus*, the spectre produced by such an unusual act can be seen to assume the status of a strategic challenge to the representational and discursive restraints placed on the visibilization of AIDS. In order to explore the nature of this challenge, I want to turn to one of Guibert's *maîtres*, Michel Foucault. Foucault appears as the fictional philosopher in a short story by Guibert,[29] and again as Muzil, the friend whose AIDS-related hospitalization and death are described in the first half of *To the Friend* in such a way as to prefigure the narrator's own fate: '[I]t was less the agony of my friend which I found myself describing, than the agony which was awaiting me, and which would be identical. From now on it was a belief that over and above friendship, we were closely tied to each other by a shared thanatological destiny.'[30] Initial responses to the publication of *To The Friend* in France tended to view the inclusion of Muzil in tabloid terms, as a betrayal of the great man's secrets and as an outing of Foucault as gay, HIV-positive, and a practitioner of S/M. Ralph Sarkonak provides an antidote to these reactions in his account of how the text functions as a literary tribute to Foucault,[31] and of the intertextuality of the 'shared thanatological destiny' which links the descriptions of Muzil's death to *Cytomégalovirus*:

> It is perfectly clear that the scenes in *To the Friend Who Did Not Save My Life* giving detailed descriptions of the death of an author in an institutional hospital setting, with all the impersonality – and worse, absolute banality – of the situation, that these scenes ought in some way to be inserted between the pages of the diary.[32]

Sarkonak goes on to demonstrate how the scintillating, inter-implicating prose of Guibert's writing, his 'AIDS-text', opts for writing and life in defiance of the silence and death imposed by industrial and medical definitions of AIDS.[33] In addition to the literary and biographical bonds linking the two writers, I would like to suggest that to draw on aspects of Foucault's political and theoretical agenda in this context offers the possibility of considering the spectacle of Guibert's body as a resistant practice of the kind envisaged by Foucault: that is, one which is engaged in the promotion of 'new forms of subjectivity' in the face of disciplinary technologies bent on enforcing both totalization and state-defined modes of individualization.[34] James Miller's *The Passion of Michel Foucault* refers to an encounter between Foucault and a militant student group in 1971 as a way of describing the 'different thinking' implicit within a resistant practice. It entails, he writes: 'a kind of "'cultural' attack" that would threaten old institutions by experimenting with new practices: "the suppression of sexual taboos, limitations and divisions; the exploration of communal existence; the loosening of inhibitions with regard to drugs; the breaking of all the prohibitions that form and guide the development of the normal individual"'.[35]

Yet, as Miller's account of the meeting emphasizes, the aim of these new experimental forms of subjectivity, for Foucault, is as much to transform institutions as to change the self. And this transformation operates first and foremost by countering the omnipresent and intrusive gaze of the panopticon (the institution *par excellence*) with an affront to vision. Martin Jay pulls together several strands of Foucault's writing in order to demonstrate some of the ways in which this spectacular resistance might operate:

> Can Foucault himself be said to have offered a visual antidote to the disciplinary power of the gaze? How strong a weapon was that 'optic of astonishment' noted by de Certeau in Foucault's struggle against the policing of space? [. . .]
>
> At times, Foucault did explicitly call on the disruptive power of images [. . .] What in *The Order of Things* he called 'heterotopias' were disturbingly inconsistent spatial configurations which undermined the alleged coherence of linguistic systems.[36]

What else, if not an 'optic of astonishment', would the spectacle of Guibert's body present to the passing traffic? Guibert's suggested performance would mean taking AIDS and illness out of the hospital ward and confronting mile upon mile of bumper-to-bumper traffic with an image rich in resistant, transformative potential. The skeletal body that Guibert himself confronts in *To the Friend* and that he consents to film in *La Pudeur ou l'impudeur* (but that French television flinched from showing until after his death)[37] would present a representation of someone with AIDS, which, far from being constrained by the dominant and prurient discourses discussed earlier, breaks the bounds of the institution by insisting on its visibility, not as obscenity, nor as object of pity, but rather as sheer spectacle of difference. Rather than being subjected to the constant physical surveillance of the hospital, or to the normalized identity of the 'blood gruel pancake'[38] that its routine of dehumanization aims to impose, the image evoked would effectively turn the very practice of institutionalization inside out. Indeed the confrontation with marginality that this spectacle entails, both on the street and in the text, might be considered a kind of panopticism in reverse.

In the model that Foucault borrows from Jeremy Bentham, the disciplinary apparatus functions by subjecting the confined bodies of the sick, the imprisoned or the insane to the constant gaze of the supervisor. Shut away behind their car windscreens, in Guibert's version, it is the supervisors and regulators who occupy motorized cells, their consciousness and identity effectively triggered and controlled by the singular figure of the person with AIDS. For, just as the surveillance of the Foucauldian panopticon seeps into the 'internalized and self-regulating mechanism[s]' (M. Jay 1986: 192) of our subjective experience of everyday practices, so the spectacle of Guibert's body serves to shatter the normalized responses of his spectators. Rabinow includes an excerpt from *Discipline and Punish* where Foucault describes how resistance to the panopticon happens through the disruption of the consciousness of the day-to-day bounds of the possible:

> The minute disciplines, the panopticisms of everyday [. . .] have been [. . .] the political counterpart of the juridical norms according to which power was redistributed [. . .], hence the affirmation that they are at the very foundation of society, and an element in its equilibrium, whereas they are a series of mechanisms for unbalancing power relations definitively and everywhere; hence the persistence in regarding them as the humble but concrete form of every morality, whereas they are a set of physico-political techniques (Rabinow 1984: 212–13).

Cytomégalovirus produces textually the motorway walk that it proposes as metaphor, and in so doing poses a real challenge to the restraints on the visibility of AIDS imposed in France and the West. Its title alone audaciously displays, for public consumption, the scientifically privileged discourse of a medical condition, the unspoken name of an AIDS-related illness, and the private fear of blindness and death that its onset provokes in Guibert; in each case breaking down the defences of discursive convention. Guibert's writing further conforms to the logic of the anti-panopticon by 're-visioning' each of the 'physico-political techniques' to which he is subjected, in order to offer its readers a wider picture.

For Guibert, 'Hell is hospital',[39] and *Cytomégalovirus* details its author's confrontations with the medical gaze and the meaningless practices it imposes on patients. At times, the disciplinary apparatus of the hospital is experienced as presenting as much of a mortal threat to Guibert as the illnesses for which he is ostensibly being treated. He writes: 'If you don't resist, if you don't run, you get flattened.'[40] A key example of the dehumanizing mechanisms to which he is subjected is the insistence that he wear the regulatory uniform of the patient, to the extent that his decision to appear in the operating theatre in civvies rather than the transparent blue tunic leads to the auxiliaries asking him to justify his presence there. As Guibert remarks in a one-sentence paragraph: 'The transparent blue smock served no purpose other than humiliation.'[41] A key symbol of Guibert's defiance against the process of hospitalization is his blue hat. An entry towards the end of the diary bears witness to the disruptive potential of what should be an innocuous piece of headgear:

> The other morning, a porter who has just taken me to ophthalmology although I don't need his help since I can walk on my own is excessively annoyed by my blue hat, he wants to get me to take it off, and says, 'You don't need that to go to ophthalmology'. I say to him, 'What has my hat ever done to upset you?' He is still in a huff. I manage to placate him by giving him the wrong solution to the puzzle: 'My head's freezing.'[42]

On this occasion, Guibert backs down from confrontation. Perhaps this is because the real signification of Guibert's blue fedora does not translate into the codes of institutional transactions, precisely because it is worn, much as the green flowers of a bygone age,[43] as the defiant symbol of the excessively spectacular self wherever the right to enjoy a self is put in question. Guibert's confrontation with the institution, epitomized in a flourish that is beyond its ken but cries out for delightful recognition, is also a joke at its expense.

Like his hat, Guibert's humour (and this can just as easily be ill-humoured crotchetiness as sharing a joke) serves both to mark him out as an individual and to expose the rituals of the AIDS care institution as disciplinary (rather than uniquely therapeutic) practices. The sense of personality which *Cytomégalovirus* displays – via, for instance, its accounts of its author/narrator's *amourette* with a handsome auxiliary and his battles with nurses over non-functional equipment – constructs an oppositional identity for Guibert, challenging the disciplinary ethos of the institution. In addition, by aligning him, as a person with AIDS, with visibility and flamboyance rather than with invisibility, it contributes to a strategy of counter-representation that works against homophobic identifications. Guibert's spectacular strategy, rather than contrasting with Jarman's *Blue*, here seems to complement the latter's meditative approach, by offering, instead of a one-sided caricature, a mandala of intersecting but different identifications as writer, PWA, gay man, friend, son, reader. Likewise, in *Blue*, Jarman 'steps into a blue funk' (1993: 3), which entails a spectacular construction of science-fiction sexualities that are chanted as the film's refrain. The list of impossible new identities that Jarman provides conforms also to the kind of cultural attack envisaged by Foucault:

> I am a mannish
> Muff diving
> Size queen

With bad attitude
An arse licking
Psychofag
Molesting the flies of privacy
Balling lesbian boys
A perverted heterodemon
Crossing purpose with death (Jarman 1993: 21).

If the oppositional nature of this representation is not already clear, it becomes evident as the incantation tails off into the repeated affirmation/ refusal, 'I am a Not Gay' (Jarman 1993: 22). Patton's work on discourses of AIDS makes a plea for a proliferation of different kinds of identities as strategies (1993: 175), and this call seems to endorse the forms of social resistance to representations of AIDS that the texts of both Guibert and Jarman describe and practise. Resistant strategies of the spectacular would serve both to produce an affirmative site of aestheticized and sexualized (counter-)identity for those for whom this is proscribed by the AIDS panic and to celebrate and publicize the excessively different in order to show the gaps in the hegemonic logic of socio-sexual disciplines. A parallel to Guibert's unacceptable blue hat and Jarman's impossible 'psychofag' can be found in the feminist practice of resistance through performance. This practice is exemplified by Scheherazade, whose stories were spun to keep her alive. In the introduction to a collection of essays that includes her post-Foucauldian critique of the regulatory regime of the epidemic, Linda Singer describes the political import of 'S' in terms that also help to illustrate the contestatory impact of spectacular AIDS writing:

> S has produced the position from which she is no longer simply the object of the male gaze and its functional economy. Her stories, dances, performances also have the effect of dislocating or decentering power by capturing it in the shifting veils of its own misrecognitions [. . .] S's power is neither that of the rebellious slave nor that of the seductress. Her power is that of performing the spectacle of difference which cannot be mastered. This disruption works, at some level, by confounding the anticipatory structures of a masculinist scopophilia and voyeurism, in which the truth is seen, illuminated, optimally and in the most neutral medium. S shows that the antinomies of this economy can be exploited in a way that disappointment is recoded as pleasure and as a perpetual promise.[44]

Guibert's motorway walk, together with his fedora and Jarman's incantation, confound the masculinist, homophobic gaze in each of its bids to determine how, when and where AIDS is signified. In so doing, these entities bring into being a textual arena where readers encounter impossible, and impossibly bold, visions, spectacles in spaces where such things ought not to be. The hallmark, or quintessence, of this arena – the disruptively spectacular, visible presence; the 'too much' (as Guibert puts it) that generates both laughter and resistance – is powerfully evoked in Hector Bianchiotti's description of a chance meeting with Guibert in a hospital corridor:

> One day, early in the morning, I was sitting in one of the waiting rooms, blindingly sunny; I was wearing very dark sunglasses. Suddenly, in the corridor, the noise of a lift stopping, and Hervé's voice, as he steps out flanked by a drip apparatus which he is sliding along; he notices me and bursts out laughing, or rather stifles a laugh – with the same movement taking from his top jacket pocket some dark glasses, very dark glasses, which he hadn't dared put on, '*It was too much!*'[45]

One further aspect of the spectacle 'A walk along the side of the motorway?' remains to be explored. In addition to turning the institution of the hospital inside out and forging a representation of life with AIDS as life, Guibert's spectacle would also provoke astonishment at the risk he is taking. Deprived of the protective carapace of a Peugeot or a Renault, the vulnerability of the lunatic with the drip offers a figure for the weakness of Guibert's immune system, hammering home to the enraged drivers the realities of accident, of illness and death, of the cybernetic interdependencies of people and machines, which their counter-panoptical cells are designed to protect them from acknowledging. Likewise, texts like *Blue* and *Cytomégalovirus* consist of a writing which takes a risk. A phrase near the beginning of Jarman's film offers a very similar metaphor to 'A walk along the side of the motorway?': 'I step off the kerb and a cyclist nearly knocks me down. Flying in from the dark he nearly parted my hair' (1993: 3).

Stepping off the kerb also finds its counterpart in Foucault's work in the form of the 'limit-experience', a term used by James Miller to encapsulate each of the philosopher's most powerfully resistant strategies. The Foucault of the limit-experience is, for Miller, 'a discomfiting thinker', who 'issued a brave and basic challenge to nearly everything that passes for "right" in Western culture' by '[p]ushing his mind and body repeatedly to the breaking point' (Miller 1993: 384–5). Most controversially, Miller explores the vexed question of Foucault's changing attitudes and behaviour in relation to the information and disinformation disseminated during the early years of the AIDS epidemic. What becomes clear, however, from his *The Passion of Michel Foucault* is that following his discovery of the Californian s/m scene in the 1970s, Foucault's interest in the sexual theatres of control and mutilation provided him with a physical model for the 'limit-experience' that complemented his methodological curiosities. Not only did s/m present him with models of practice that justified his work in contesting and transfiguring relations of power, but, as Gayle Rubin points out, it also gave him the occasion to push his own life to the limits, which the hyper-disciplinary invention of 'a gay plague' in the early 1980s and the consequent instigation of 'safe sex' both confirmed and threatened to foreclose (Miller 1993: 382).[46]

In what way might the spectacular writing of Guibert's body also constitute a 'limit-experience'? Is there a sense in which his textual resistances to hospitalization and dominant representations of AIDS also conform to the anti-logic of the risk? Certainly, *Cytomégalovirus* follows Guibert's earlier AIDS texts in the hazardous betrayal of his closest friends. But, as if to parody the furore over his depiction of Foucault as Muzil and to point to the bourgeois sensibilities behind such reactions, the risk of betrayal is here reduced to a niggling story of personal preferences. Mocking the prurient responses to *To the Friend*, he includes an episode where his close friend, 'C', thinking she was doing him a favour, brought him a cup of expresso coffee from the canteen rather than the standard coffee-machine variety, which he much preferred. Guibert immediately swears that he will never reveal the disappointment he felt as a result. However, by sharing the episode in his text he is of course cancelling out his promise of secrecy. Yet if this extract functions as a comic rebuke of the popular depiction of Guibert as traitor on one level, it suggests the kind of risk with which Guibert's textual practices engage more dangerously on another. For the spectacle of the body that Guibert presents in his writing is one that is composed around a secret, or rather that is designed to make public the secret vulnerabilities of all our bodies, their realities as matter and decay, in a move not dissimilar to that detailed in Foucault's *The Birth of the Clinic*. And the risk that such a writing runs, as it struggles to represent all that is linguistically proscribed, is perhaps the most threatening for all writing – that of non-communication.

'Writing in the dark',[47] an idea that *Cytomégalovirus* ends by proposing as its own *mise-en-abyme*, would mean freeing language to spin off into the realms of madness, as indeed Guibert's *Le Paradis*, published posthumously in the same year as his hospital diary, proceeds to do. It is, in many ways, as futile an activity as 'A walk along the side of the motorway?', but it can be just as spectacular.[48] Writing, for Guibert, is already a spectacle of affirmation and contestation, and writing with AIDS, as Sarkonak reveals, is a form of writing that affirms his survival: 'That the writer was able to keep writing while his sight was threatened and in conditions where the treatment and even the hygiene with which he had to live were far from their best proves how much writing meant survival for him.'[49]

A writing that spectacularly affirms his survival, certainly, but one that is no less astonishing in its continuing contestation of the regulatory disciplines that aim to circumscribe the way in which our lives are experienced, and to impose limits on how much we are allowed to know about our deaths. In *La Mort propagande*, originally written as early as 1975, Guibert prefigures the spectacular writing of death that his later texts, including *Cytomégalovirus*, will come to enact. He describes his death, and, crucially, the effect of its spectacle, in the following terms:

> We gag it [death], censure it, try to drown it in disinfectant, smother death in ice. But I want to let death raise its powerful voice and sing, like a diva, through my body. Death will be my only partner, and I will be its interpreter. Never to let this source of immediate, visceral spectacle be lost. To kill myself on stage, before the cameras. To offer up in my death this extreme, excessive spectacle of my body [. . .]
>
> The public will be shaken with convulsions, contractions, repulsions, erections, vibrations, orgasms, all kinds of spewings. Its general body, in turn, will begin to speak.[50]

Reflecting on his own practice in *Cytomégalovirus*, Guibert wonders whether his is a writing that does any good.[51] In the light of Foucault's resistant practices and 'limit-experiences', the answer would seem to be yes, in that it proposes a remapping of the boundaries of self and other, death and life, illness and health that, like all revolutions, is probably both bloody and necessary. In the context of representations of AIDS, *Cytomégalovirus* and Guibert's other late texts do a great deal of political good in contesting the practices of concealment and division that have been used as a cover for institutional ignorance. In a writing that breaks the limits of what can and cannot be represented regarding AIDS, Guibert is confronting his readers, the French television-viewing public, the various disciplines of journalism, criticism and theory that his work has attracted, and, of course, the drivers on the *périphérique*. And the confrontation is one that reveals to each of these audiences that AIDS cannot be isolated from the rest of their world, but is produced by the societies in which HIV occurs. As Louis-Thomas Vincent puts it, AIDS 'discloses the particular characteristics of today's world',[52] and chief among these, I would argue, are the procedures of discipline and surveillance that aim to define and confine. A walk along the side of the motorway? The writing of Guibert's body is a practice that dares to be spectacular.

Notes

1. L. Bersani (1995), *Homos*, Cambridge, Mass. and London, p. 19.
2. Act Up-Paris (1994), *Le Sida, combien de divisions?*, Paris, pp. 171–80. My translation. The original reads 'victime expiatoire'. All translations here are my own unless indicated otherwise. Original versions of translated segments are given in the following Notes.
3. M. Foucault (1977), *Discipline and Punish*, New York; Hervé Guibert (1992a), *Cytomégalovirus*, Paris; Derek Jarman (1993), *Blue*, West Sussex. This last is the text of the film first shown on Channel 4 and broadcast simultaneously on Radio Three in September 1993.
4. 'Ce matin, une gentille interne est venue m'annoncer que mon pneumothorax n'était pas du tout résorbé, qu'il restait à la radio une bonne poche d'air sous la plèvre décollée. À la première lecture de cette radio on m'avait dit qu'il était complètement résorbé, quelques jours plus tard, avec une certaine gêne, qu'il restait une toute petite bulle d'air qui allait disparaître d'elle-même. Je tousse. Il ne faut pas que je tousse. Je prends du sirop. J'ai un peu mal. Je suis très pessimiste sur la suite des événements' (*Cytomégalovirus*, p. 77).
5. R. Barthes (1984), 'Délibération', in *Essais Critiques IV, Le Bruissement de la langue*, Paris, pp. 399–413, p. 410. The original reads: '*suppressibles à l'infini*'.
6. '. . . essentiellement l'inessentiel du monde, le monde comme inessentiel' (ibid., p. 411).
7. '. . . à la fois un rythme (chute et montée, élasticité) et un leurre (je ne puis atteindre mon image); un écrit, en somme, qui dit la vérité du leurre et garantit cette vérité par la plus formelle des opérations, le rythme' (ibid., p. 413).
8. 'Écrire est aussi une façon de rythmer le temps et de le passer' (*Cytomégalovirus*, p. 15).
9. 'J'ai cru que je ne pourrais plus du tout écrire dans ce journal, par traumatisme, mais c'est la seule façon d'oublier' (ibid., p. 64).
10. H. Guibert (1991a), *To the Friend Who Did Not Save My Life*, London. Originally published as *À l'ami qui ne m'a pas sauvé la vie* (Paris, 1990).
11. 'Rien écrit ce soir. Trop choqué. J'essaierai demain' (*Cytomégalovirus*, p. 59).
12. Guibert's writing is often concerned to convey a sense of its own vulnerability. In addition to writing against time in *To the Friend Who Did Not Save My Life*, *The Man in the Red Hat* (London, 1993a), originally published as *L'Homme au chapeau rouge* (Paris, 1992b) ends by referring to some fifty or so pages of Guibert's writing that were in his

luggage, lost on a flight from Ouagadougou to Roissy. Even earlier texts such as *Voyage avec deux enfants* (Paris, 1982) position his writing as implicated in scenarios of concealment and revelation.

13. 'Ce matin, le chef de clinique est venu me proposer une permission de sortie jusqu'à vingt heures, à cause du beau temps. Marcher au bord de l'autoroute?' (*Cytomégalovirus*, p. 77).
14. See especially Guibert's video-diary, '*La Pudeur ou l'impudeur*', originally shown on TF1, 30 January 1992.
15. S. Watney (1989), 'Psychoanalysis, Sexuality and AIDS', in S. Shepherd and M. Wallis (eds), *Coming on Strong: Gay Politics and Culture*, London, pp. 22–38, pp. 32–3.
16. C. Patton (1993), 'Tremble, Hetero Swine!', in M. Warner (ed.), *Fear of a Queer Planet*, Minneapolis and London, pp. 143–77.
17. D. Crimp (1993), 'Right On, Girlfriend?', in M. Warner (ed.), *Fear of a Queer Planet*, pp. 300–20, quoting from *The New York Times*, 27 September 1991, section A, p. 12.
18. Shown simultaneously on all French television channels on 9 April 1994. The letters page of *Le Figaro* (12 April 1994) contained several responses aimed at re-establishing the demarcation between 'innocent' victims and others (deemed responsible for spreading the virus) and restoring the dominant mythology. An example from Gérard Gachet of Paris reads:

> So as not to seem to 'exclude', must we now accept that everything gets mixed up, levelled out? Do we have to view all sexual practices in the same light [. . .]? [. . .] Must we [. . .] forget that alongside the innocent victims, children, blood transfusion patients for instance, certain groups – gays, bisexuals and drug users – have contributed to the existence and spread of the virus by their perverse behaviour.

The original reads: 'Pour ne pas sembler «exclure», faut-il donc accepter de tout mélanger, de tout égaliser? Faut-il mettre sur le même plan toutes les pratiques sexuelles [. . .]? [. . .] Doit-on [. . .] oublier qu'aux côtés des victimes innocentes que sont, par exemple, les enfants ou les transfusés, certains groupes – homosexuels, bisexuels et toxicomanes – ont favorisé par leurs pratiques déviantes l'apparition et la propagation du virus.'

19. J.-L. Maxence (1995), *Les Écrivains sacrifiés des années sida*, Paris, pp. 14–15. The original reads: 'D'évidence, ils nous offrent *post mortem* une formidable leçon de vie, voire d'espérance, qui fait souvent contraste avec le désenchantement défaitiste d'autres écrivains, épargnés et

pourtant infiniment plus tristes! [. . .] Et nous nous refusons avec fermeté à arroser nos mots de larmes de crocodile. Nous ne pleurerons pas complaisamment sur les nouveaux grands cimetières sous la lune sidéenne où reposent pour l'éternité tant et trop de victimes du virus broyeur de jeunesse. Ce qui nous semble plus urgent de capter parmi les messages donnés, c'est la confrontation avec la mort, le face à face avec son apparente toute puissance, qui est toujours un tournant capital dans la vie d'un homme promis à disparaître bientôt.'

20. Maxence begins his text by comparing the effects of AIDS to the loss of life incurred during the Great War. See ibid., p. 9.
21. P. J. Smith (1993), '*Blue* and the Outer Limits', in *Sight and Sound*, October 1993, pp. 18–19, p. 18.
22. H. Guibert (1993b), *The Compassion Protocol*, London, originally published as *Le Protocole compassionnel* (Paris, 1991c).
23. 'Certains se confessent avec une précision accusée parfois d'exhibitionnisme' (Maxence, *Les Écrivains*, p. 18).
24. See J.-P. Boulé (1995a), *Guibert: À l'ami qui ne m'a pas sauvé la vie and Other Writings*, Glasgow, pp. 19–25.
25. See D. Duncan (1995), 'Gestes autobiographiques: le sida et les formes d'expressions artistiques du moi', in J.-P. Boulé (ed.) (1995b), *Nottingham French Studies*, vol. 34, no. 1, Spring 1995, 'Special Issue: Hervé Guibert', pp. 100–11, 106–7. The original reads: 'Ce regard devient le lieu de retour de l'indicible, menaçant l'intégrité du moi en traçant de façon indélébile ses effets sur le corps [. . .] Plus le corps est irrévocablement rongé par le virus, plus le regard même constitue le lieu où la perte de la présence du moi se fait sentir.'
26. See Boulé 1995a, p. 25 and Duncan, 'Gestes autobiographiques', p. 110. The original of the latter reads: 'cet élément d'impossibilité au cœur du moi et de ses inscriptions graphiques'.
27. L. Edelman (1994), *Homographesis: Essays in Gay Literary and Cultural Theory*, New York and London: see the chapter, 'The Mirror and the Tank: "AIDS", Subjectivity, and the Rhetoric of Activism', pp. 93–117.
28. Ibid., p. 116. An article by Owen Heathcote builds on Edelman's reading of this passage by emphasizing the self-affirming potential of Guibert's gaze, and its ability to construct an identity 'which can draw strength from the co-existence of self and other, both in the self and in the other' (O. Heathcote (1995a), 'From Cold War to AIDS War: Narratives of Identity from Gide's *Retour de l'URSS* to Guibert's *Cytomégalovirus*', *Modern and Contemporary France*, vol. 3, no. 4, pp. 427–37, pp. 434–5). For a brief discussion of some of the ways in which

Guibert's autobiographical gaze might also be transformative for his onlookers, see M. Pratt (1995), '*Hôtel Old Cataract*: Image, texte', in J.-P. Boulé (ed.), *Nottingham French Studies*, vol. 34 no. 1, 'Special Issue: Hervé Guibert', pp. 5–7.

29. H. Guibert (1988), 'Les Secrets d'un homme' in *Mauve le vierge*, Paris, pp. 103–11.
30. '. . . ce n'était pas tant l'agonie de mon ami que j'étais en train de décrire que l'agonie qui m'attendait, et qui serait identique, c'était désormais une certitude qu'en plus de l'amitié nous étions étroitement liés par un sort thanatologique commun' (*A l'ami qui ne m'a pas sauvé la vie*, p. 107).
31. R. Sarkonak (1994), 'De la métastase au métatexte, Hervé Guibert', *Texte*, nos. 15–16, pp. 229–59, pp. 246–7.
32. Ibid., pp. 256–7. The original reads: '[I]l est clair et net que les scènes d'*À l'ami qui ne m'a pas sauvé la vie* qui décrivent en détail la mort d'un auteur dans le cadre d'une institution hospitalière, avec tout ce que cela implique d'impersonnel et, ce qui est pire, de parfaitement *banal*, ces scènes-là doivent s'insérer en quelque sorte entre les feuillets du journal'.
33. Sarkonak also includes a footnote (p. 256) exploring some of the links between Foucault and Guibert. Rather than simply looking for Foucault's influence on Guibert's work, he argues that 'what we are dealing with is a sequence of texts which call out to each other'. The original reads: 'ce à quoi nous avons affaire est une série de textes qui s'interpellent' (ibid., pp. 256–7).
34. P. Rabinow (1984), 'Introduction', in P. Rabinow (ed.), *The Foucault Reader*, New York, p. 22. Rabinow argues that if Foucault's work offers a challenge to increasing subjection, then it is best explored in those passages where he advocates a politics of refusing state-sponsored forms of individualization and identity. Significant in this context is M. Walzer's 1986 essay, 'The Politics of Michel Foucault', in D. Couzens Hoy (ed.), *Foucault: A Critical Reader*, Oxford, pp. 51–68, pp. 64–7. Walzer goes further than Rabinow by identifying possible sites of challenge in Foucault's work as local resistances geared at dismantling specific disciplines, such as protests led by unions of factory workers or groups of prisoners.
35. J. Miller (1993), *The Passion of Michel Foucault*, London, p. 200.
36. M. Jay (1986), 'In the Empire of the Gaze: Foucault and the Denigration of Vision in Twentieth-century French Thought', in D. Couzens Hoy (ed.), *Foucault: A Critical Reader*, Oxford, pp. 175–204, p. 194.
37. For a discussion of the controversy surrounding the screening of the

film see J.-P. Boulé (1992), 'The Postponing of "La Pudeur ou l'impudeur": Modesty or Hypocrisy on the Part of French Television?', *French Cultural Studies*, no. 9, pp. 229–304.

38. '. . . galette de bouillie de sang' (*Cytomégalovirus*, p. 24).
39. 'L'hôpital, c'est l'enfer' (ibid., p. 20).
40. 'Si on ne résiste pas, si on ne court pas, on se fait écraser' (ibid., p. 24).
41. 'La blouse bleue transparente n'avait aucune fonction, que l'humiliation' (ibid., p. 60).
42. 'L'autre matin, un brancardier qui vient m'emmener en opthalmo alors que je n' ai pas besoin de lui puisque je peux marcher seul est excessivement irrité par mon chapeau bleu, il veut me le faire retirer, il dit: «Vous n'avez pas besoin de ça pour aller en opthalmo.» Je lui dis: «Qu'est-ce qu'il a bien pu vous faire, mon chapeau?» Il rechigne toujours. J'arrive à le calmer en lui donnant la fausse clé de l'énigme: «Je caille du crâne»' (ibid., p. 86).
43. For a discussion of the gay symbol of the green flowers in the life and works of Oscar Wilde, see N. Bartlett (1988), *Who Was That Man?: A Present for Mr Oscar Wilde*, London.
44. L. Singer (1993), *Erotic Welfare, Sexual Theory and Politics in the Age of Epidemic*, edited and introduced by J. Butler and M. MacGrogan, New York, p. 20.
45. H. Bianciotti (1992), 'Postface', in H. G. Berger, *Dialogue d'Images*, Bordeaux, [p. ii of 'Postface']. The original reads: 'Un jour, de bon matin, j'étais assis dans l'une des salles d'attente, atrocement ensoleillée; je portais des lunettes de soleil très sombres. Soudain, dans le couloir, le bruit de l'ascenseur qui s'arrête, et la voix d'Hervé, qui en sort flanqué d'un appareil de perfusion qu'il fait glisser lui-même; il me découvre et pouffe en rire ou, plutôt, étouffe un rire – tout en prenant de sa main gauche, dans la petite poche de sa veste, des lunettes noires, très noires, qu'il n'avait pas osé mettre: «*Ça en faisait trop!*»'.
46. Miller draws on a letter to him from Gayle Rubin dated 24 January 1992.
47. My translation. The original reads 'Écrire dans le noir?' (*Cytomégalovirus*, p. 93).
48. Here Guibert echoes the precocious Poulou of Sartre's *Les Mots* (1964), who, revelling in a posthumous dream of his great-great-nephew's astonishment that Sartre could even write in the dark, provides an extreme indication of how the performance of a writing has an effect which goes beyond the bluntly semantic.
49. See Sarkonak, 'De la métastase', pp. 254–5. The original reads: 'Que l'écrivain ait pu continuer à écrire au moment où il était menacé de

cécité et où les conditions de traitement et même d'hygiène dans lesquelles il dut exister étaient loin d'être optimales, prouvent à quel point l'écriture pour lui représentait la survie.'

50. H. Guibert (1991b), *La Mort propagande*, Paris. 'On la bâillonne, on la censure, on tente de la noyer dans le désinfectant, de l'étouffer dans la glace. Moi je veux lui laisser élever sa voix puissante et qu'elle chante, diva, à travers mon corps. Ce sera ma seule partenaire, je serai son interprète. Ne pas laisser perdre cette source de spectaculaire immédiat, viscéral. Me donner la mort sur une scène, devant des caméras. Donner ce spectacle extrême, excessif de mon corps, dans ma mort [. . .] Le public sera pris de convulsions, contractions, répulsions, érections, vibrations, jouissances, dégueulis de toutes sortes. Son corps général, à son tour, se mettra à parler' (pp. 172–3).

    Madeleine Bunting discussed the public deaths and illnesses of Jarman, Guibert, Dennis Potter and other writers and media celebrities in 'Bowing out in front of the final curtain', *Guardian*, 7 April 1994. She writes: '[W]e need a vocabulary for the personal endurance demanded by the awful medical paraphernalia of tests, treatments and hospitals that attend most diseases' course [. . .] While our culture gorges itself on violent killing, it is ill at ease with death. We skirt it mawkishly and no longer mark it with the panoply of ceremony and ritual of our forbears [*sic*] [. . .] Now a collection of brave people have blazed a trail, revealing the messy, exhausting, terrifying and illuminating process of dying . . . We have reason to be grateful.'

51. Guibert, *Cytomégalovirus*, p. 35.

52. L.-V. Thomas (1991), *La Mort en question*, Paris, quoted in Maxence, *Les Écrivains*, p. 30. The original reads: 'révèle les traits spécifiques du monde d'aujourd'hui'.

– 8 –

Jobs for the Boys? Or: What's New About the Male Hunter in Duvert, Guibert and Jourdan?

Owen Heathcote

The self is a practical convenience; promoted to the status of an ethical ideal, it is a sanction for violence.[1]

Roman had nothing to say in reply, he could not say now that everything that was sexual violence came from a lack of love.[2]

I

The relations between sexual violence and representation are an increasingly important subject of study. From the films of Quentin Tarantino to the reporting of the trial of Rosemary West, sexual violence is being repeatedly emphasized, interrogated and judged. In the field of French literature, it is not therefore surprising that male authors such as the Marquis de Sade, Octave Mirbeau and Georges Bataille are currently being studied for their presentation of sexual violence,[3] or that women writers such as Rachilde, Alina Reyes, and Monique Wittig and homosexual writers such as Jean Genet and Pierre Guyotat should be being examined for possibly alternative perspectives.[4] One aspect of such literature, and of the criticism devoted to it, is, moreover, an interrogation of the very categories of male, female and homosexual writing and identifications. The sexual violence articulated in texts by the French authors cited above can, for example, be seen as symptomatic of stigmatization or marginalization; while the foregrounding of sexual violence is one of the ways of highlighting – to borrow Judith Butler's phrase – 'gender trouble'.[5]

As is evidenced by the terrifying sequestrations instigated by the *libertins* in *Cent Vingt Journées de Sodome* (*One Hundred and Twenty Days of Sodom*) through to Abel Tiffauges's 'photographic hunts' ('chasses photographiques') in Tournier's *Le Roi des Aulnes* (*The Erl-King*),[6] a favoured trope for the representation of human violence – and, notably, of male *sexual* violence – is that of the hunter or predator. In his fascinating survey *A View to a Death in the Morning: Hunting and Nature Throughout History*, Matt Cartmill demonstrates the intimate association that exists between hunting and a humankind seen as a discrete species, separate from the rest of nature. Commenting on Dart's hypothesis for 'the origin of the species', Cartmill writes: 'It was a taste for blood, not the rigors of life in the Transvaal, that made us human.'[7] Paradoxically, Cartmill reveals, human beings acquired human nature by separating from, and frequently destroying, the rest of nature, as is indicated by the widespread anthropological and popular belief that 'man' became 'man' when he began to hunt and kill. In the very process of becoming uniquely and preciously human, man acquired the bloodlust that would later be attributed to the 'Nature, red in tooth and claw' of the animals.[8] According to this prevalent but underexamined perception, by becoming distinctly and distinctively bestial, man became human and humanity became male. Whilst Cartmill cites few French examples to illustrate his thesis, it is incontestably the case that the literary and cultural references to the hunt and the chase contained in texts by Sade, Tournier *et al.* raise issues not only of sexual violence but of a sexual violence deeply embedded in notions of the human, nature, subjecthood and identity.

Social, cultural and anthropological references to the killer ape are also deeply embedded in concepts of masculinity. As Cartmill confirms: '[The] fundamental social pattern was the nuclear family, consisting of a male provider, a female nurturer, and a string of more or less incompetent, slow-maturing offspring'.[9] When the hunt is used as a metaphor for a lover's pursuit of the beloved, it is often also used as a metaphor for the male rape of woman and/or of nature. If not an actual woman or nymph, allegories of the erotic hunt or the amorous chase frequently have as their target the sobbing deer.[10] More recently, with the popularity of the Bambi myth, it is the innocent, vulnerable fawn that is the potential victim of wanton male aggression.[11]

In all such cases, the thematics of the hunt can be used either to criticize or to condone established hierarchies. Generally, however, the very recourse to the metaphor of the hunt tends to reinforce, if regretfully, the *naturalness* of such hierarchy. Since the victim – doe, fawn, forest or woman – is *naturally* vulnerable, and since the huntsman-sportsman is *naturally* aggressive, narratives of the hunt, whether pro-hunter or pro-hunted, tend to endorse – even if they mourn it – the status quo. Whether these various natures are deplored or celebrated, the bloodletting of the hunt narrative is a natural vehicle for what Leo Bersani terms 'the redemption of violence'.[12]

The aim of this chapter is to examine three texts or groups of texts that, in different but complementary ways, offer alternative perspectives on (sexual) violence. If notions of nature, subjecthood, identity and masculinity are embedded in narratives of the hunt, then stories with a gay signature, as well as a hunt theme, may unsettle some or all of these categories. Since, as Richard Dyer has argued, what is at stake in gay/lesbian authorship is a *decentring* of authorship and identity,[13] it will be interesting to see (i) whether the 'homotext' replaces the conventional heterosexual predator with a simple equivalent in a potentially homosexual relationship, and (ii) whether the potential or actual violence of the homosexual predator simply replicates that of his heterosexual counterpart, or whether the violence between single-sex male protagonists can be used to question not only stereotypical male violence but also stereotypical male homosexuality as an orientation and as an identification. In order to address these issues, a first section will examine *Journal d'un innocent* (1976) by Tony Duvert. Here, the apparent identification of author and main character as a self-proclaimed 'paedhomophile' makes it possible for Duvert to use his 'boy hunts' ('chasse aux garçons') to interrogate male-to-male identities.

A second section will turn to Hervé Guibert's *Vous m'avez fait former des fantômes* (You Made Me Create Ghosts) (1987), where the intertextual references to such as Sade, from whom the title is taken, self-consciously parody and possibly subvert male-to-male violence. A third and final section will study Eric Jourdan's three linked novels, *Charité* (1991a), *Révolte* (1991b) and *Sang* (1992), to assess the cumulative effect of three male hunt novels, showing male-to-male cruelty perverting and inspiring a whole society. The aim of the chapter is, therefore, to see whether the novels under discussion are simply gay novels with more than a hint of conventional homophobic violence, or, indeed, texts that use that violence in order to marginalize homosexuality as orientation or identification and thereby posit a much more generalized fusion of the homosocial and the homoerotic.

II

In one of his two recent books on homosexuality in French literature, Lawrence Schehr draws attention to the possible shared identity of Renaud Camus and Tony Duvert.[14] Whether Camus and Duvert are one, or two, writers, it is certainly tempting to associate works like Camus's *Tricks* and Duvert's *Journal d'un innocent*. Both volumes are highly personalized, self-consciously provocative accounts of a series of relatively short-lived male-to-male affairs. Although Duvert differs from Camus in choosing partners much younger than himself, they both describe essentially physical relationships with an intimacy and a passion that make it difficult to dissociate fiction and autobiography. Since, moreover, Duvert's reputation, indeed notoriety, derives largely from his defences of pederasty, in works such as *L'Enfant au masculin* (1980), it is easy to overlook the fact that *Journal d'un innocent* is a *récit*, and that author and narrator may not overlap and coincide. It is easy to forget, too, that Duvert's reputation as a writer of fiction was confirmed with a revealingly entitled work, *Paysage de fantaisie*, a private fantasy passing itself off in part as experience. What characterizes Duvert is a confusion of genres and narrative points of view: the first person is not a guarantee of 'authenticity' but one of a number of perspectives adopted by a highly self-conscious writer in what becomes a series of spatial, temporal and narrative loops, layerings or *reprises* – that is, a series of *mises en abyme* – where sexuality and textuality are provocatively intertwined.[15] As Duvert writes in *Journal d'un innocent*: 'I always write totally naked and I don't wash beforehand' ('J'écris toujours tout nu, et je ne me lave pas avant').[16] When this self-consciousness is combined with the adoption of literary names for his boys – 'I'd better find a name for some of the boys. I'll use names from a Quevedo novel, I've hardly any books here and that'll do' (p. 10) ('Il vaut mieux que je baptise certains garçons. Je vais prendre les noms dans un roman de Quevedo, je n'ai guère de livres ici et cela peut convenir') – another layer is added to the *mises en abyme*. Indeed, the series of conquests recounted by Duvert/narrator is itself a kind of horizontal layering throughout the *récit*, the amorous chase constituting a kind of sexual/textual *mise en abyme*.

What is, perhaps, most notable about this narrative self-consciousness and narrative uncertainty is that it also reflects and reinforces a sexual uncertainty, and, in particular, an uncertainty about maleness and masculinity. In *Tricks* and *Journal d'un innocent*, the narrator is, in many ways, a recluse who lives for *la drague*. As Duvert writes in the *Journal*: 'I need the cities for the boys. The only reason I get civilized is for them, I gear my days to seeking them out and taking them in [. . .] For puritans, the pleasure of love is a desiccated fruit [. . .] for me it's my social life and my sustenance'.[17] Thus, after a brief period in a *hôtel de passe* and a longer stay in a new apartment block, Duvert's narrator moves into spacious but cloistered maisonette in the old quarter of his city. For this is where the boys themselves live, where they can visit freely and yet where he can withdraw in Sadian seclusion: 'With its sturdy partitions, its solid luxury, its windows pierced high in the walls like those of a dungeon but offering plenty of light, this abode has a gentle, powerful atmosphere, which takes control, ensconces and encloses.'[18]

Although Duvert sees the double doors in his apartment as '[a] filter for children' ('[un] filtre à enfants') and his bed as its altar (p. 200), he is nonetheless particular about whom he invites. In accordance, no doubt, with his earlier habit – 'I prefer to go out to hunt rather than be picked up at home' (p. 174) ('[J]e préfère sortir chasser que d'être dragué à domicile') – he declines the persistent offers of boys who try to sell themselves at his door or who pursue him elsewhere on their bicycles. Indeed, although he has the reputation of being 'an unrepentant hunter' ('un dragueur impénitent'), he is, in fact, faithful to three or four boys, 'without playing the field and only taking a tiny proportion of those who offer, unwilling as I am' (p. 173) ('sans chercher aventure et en ne prenant qu'un nombre dérisoire de celles qui se présentent à mon corps défendant'). Even among the three or four boys he *is* faithful to, he rejects one, Diego, because, as Christopher Robinson has pointed out, he is 'readily assimilable to a picture, and therefore too readily objectifiable, as though he were no more than an image in a pornographic magazine'.[19] He also finally rejects the homosexual Francesco, because, with his 'look of a besotted star putting on the erotics' ('face de star gâteuse qui joue les érotiques'), he, too becomes objectified as 'a leftover from Hollywood' (p. 92) ('un débris d'Hollywood').

This unrepentant boy-hunter is, therefore, neither quite the hunter nor quite so unrepentant as he might appear – despite the uncompromising stance of other works such as *L'Enfant au masculin* and *Le Bon sexe illustré* (1974).[20] As he writes in the *Journal*: 'I will not take in children, any more than I could be a father, mother or teacher' (p. 203) ('Je ne serai donc pas hôte d'enfants – pas plus que je ne saurais être père, mère ou pédagogue'). If he 'adopts' a boy, it will be neither to love nor to sequester him, but to teach him a new kind of *normality*: 'I will encourage him to denigrate me, to spit on the tiniest thing that I touch or admire. And since I will be for him a living embodiment of the unpleasantness and the problems of indiscipline, I will turn him into a more normal, more average kind of man than any normal or average father can make of his children.'[21]

Clearly, then, the representation of masculinity, pederasty, and male-to-male relations in *Journal d'un innocent* is neither as monolithic nor as stereotypical as even Duvert himself seems at times to pretend. As Robinson has pointed out, there is 'no fixing of roles according to age – the narrator of *Journal d'un innocent* is as likely to be penetrated by his young partners as to penetrate them – and their tendency to construct a hierarchy among themselves based on machismo is a subject for critique, a set of pretensions to be dismantled within the privacy of the bedroom'.[22] Indeed, the pederastic hunter of the *Journal* seems to favour the passive role, perhaps because he is less well endowed than some of his younger partners and even, on at least one occasion, 'impotent' (p. 172) ('impuissant').[23] If, as Leo Bersani has pointed out in 'Is the Rectum a Grave?', *'[t]o be penetrated is to abdicate power'* (an idea also proposed by Michel Foucault in relation to ancient Athens),[24] then *Journal d'un innocent* is less a narrative of conquest than of increased withdrawal and isolation. Although the narrator exploits the uninhibited, polymorphous sexuality of the boys, who move effortlessly between homosex and heterosex and back again, it is the boys, rather than the narrator, who can luxuriate in this freedom, in the same way as it is they who profit from his money. Despite his claims for freedom and equality, the narrator realizes that, however dependent or disadvantaged, ultimately his boys neither need nor want him (p. 125). Nor, as has been seen, does he want them, whether they are homosexual, heterosexual, bisexual, or uninterested in these categories. The narrator is neither at home in France (p. 124) nor in the supposedly freer cities of, one supposes, North Africa. The narrator is finally alone, either with or without his male harem. Like a number of earlier sexual tourist narratives (for example, those of Flaubert and Gide), *Journal d'un innocent* does, therefore, recount what Joseph Boone has called 'the story of a crisis in male subjectivity – the crisis that by definition is occidental masculinity itself'.[25] In addition, what *Journal d'un innocent* perhaps more interestingly shows, is that even gender trouble, in the form of exchangeable sexual roles, permeable sexual categories, and fluid sexual identifications, seems to be a symptom of, rather than a solution to, that crisis in masculinity.

Given that *Journal d'un innocent* narrates a loss of sexual confidence, it is interesting that the narrator retreats into his flat not merely for sex but also to write: 'For it is also lack of money and the writing of this book which keep me indoors' (p. 51) ('Car c'est aussi le manque d'argent et la rédaction de ce livre qui m'enferment'). Indeed, the imperatives of writing can be even more irresistible than his other needs: 'I loathe going out when I'm involved in this book, I ate something cold and uncooked' (p. 271) ('Je déteste sortir quand je suis dans ce livre, j'ai mangé froid et cru'). Since, for the narrator, sex and writing both benefit from the same conditions – cloistered privacy and obsessive fascination – there is a sense in which writing already *imitates* sex, in which sex is the natural and inevitable subject of writing, and whereby, therefore, it is impossible for writing not to substitute for sex and for writing not to chart that substitution. In the same way that many of Renaud Camus's 'tricks' are intrigued by him as a writer, the *Journal* narrator's last partner is fascinated with his typewriter.

It is, therefore, wholly appropriate that the narrator should see his *Journal* as pornography – 'this is a pornographic book I'm writing, all it needs is cock' (p. 75) ('c'est un livre pornographique que j'écris, il n'y faut que des bites') – and as a pornography that exposes and deconstructs its own fascinations. As Duvert also writes: 'I'm a strange pornographer. The only ones I'll turn queer are old maids like myself. I need to revise the way I deprave and corrupt' (p. 234) ('Je suis un singulier pornographe. Je ne rendrai pédé que les vieilles demoiselles comme moi. Il faut que je revoie mes méthodes d'incitation à la débauche'). The final irony of *Journal d'un innocent* is that it is, in a sense, not a misnomer: the sexual hunter is also an ascetic. For, by the end of the *Journal*, the sexual hunter is excluded, or excludes himself, from the uninhibited sexual brotherhood he seemed to be unproblematically celebrating. Thus, the serial sodomy recounted in *L'Enfant au masculin* becomes 'mere' narrative *mise en abyme.*

III

When compared to *Journal d'un innocent*, Hervé Guibert's *Vous m'avez fait former des fantômes* (1987) offers a rather different kind of *mise en abyme* and a very different kind of hunt. Or, indeed, hunts, since the work, like so much of Guibert's writing, is double, and virtually comprises two novels.[26] In the first section, entitled 'Many night-games' ('Beaucoup de jeux de nuit'), a semi-mafia-style group of ruthless bounty-hunters, rejoicing under such nicknames as Lune, Loup, Tigre, Puma, Léopard and Pirate, abduct, sequester and torture a group of young boys in order to train them for combat against 'infanteros' who will slaughter them in crowded arenas. In a second section, entitled 'Surrendering to boys' games is, like a wolf, lying on a bed of dying flowers' ('S'abandonner au jeu des garçons, c'est, comme un loup, se coucher sur un lit de fleurs mourantes'), a young would-be infantero, Mickie, steals and cobbles together the necessary 'costume of light' ('habit de lumière'),[27] and contrives to fight alongside the declining but still charismatic Rudi. Mickie's infantero career is brief; but he is rescued from death by the head-hunter, Baleine, on condition he will betray the whole infantero mafia, led by Homard and Hombre. Mickie is now 'virgin of fantasies' (p. 203) ('vierge de fantasmes') and the game, we are led to believe, will soon be over.

As this summary indicates, one of the main preoccupations of the almost exclusively male world of *Vous m'avez fait former des fantômes* is, indeed, 'jobs for the boys'. If the gangsters' fiendish cruelty – removing teeth, branding, hanging the boys in jute sacks – is geared solely to increasing the boys' aggression, the boys seem to respond either with relish – 'the torture had become a game' (p. 41) ('la torture s'était transformée en jeu' – or with docility. Even of the escapee called 2 it can be said: 'Training had erased his memory. He recalled neither his parents' features nor the home which had sheltered his early years' (p. 46) ('Le dressage l'avait rendu amnésique. Il ne se souvenait plus du visage de ses parents ni des cloisons qui avaient abrité ses premières années'), and, at the moment of their capture, the twins follow Pirate 'comme deux somnambules' (p. 60).

One of the paradoxes of *Fantômes* is, therefore, that the boy is both naturally aggressive and naturally compliant: he is both malleable victim and, as Mickie shows, willing executor of other boys as prey. Guibert's boys are as naturally versatile in violence as Duvert's are in their sexual roles, and in fact, as a celebration of male-to-male violence, *Fantômes* is even more provocative than the *Journal*'s paean to pederasty: the violence in *Fantômes* is perpetrated by organized groups, not by a single individual, and is, it seems, sanctioned by society and applauded – literally – by some 25,000 spectators (p. 191). Although reprisals may be threatened by Baleine at the end of the narrative, this belated and unconvincing prospect offers little evidence of a crisis in masculinity and even less of an ethics of marginality: the animal appellations of the gangsters, the forests where they hunt, the human tauromachy for which they all prepare, the Aztec sacrifices invoked in the coda, all suggest a sempiternally natural and mythically validated association between hunting and mankind, one simply waiting to be added to Matt Cartmill's collection.

If the violence of *Fantômes* does indeed seem both natural and culturally endorsed, the same cannot, however, be said of male-to-male sexuality. Even though sex among the gangsters reminds one of the boys of dreamlike 'wondrous, coupling beasts' (p. 42) ('des bêtes fabuleuses qui s'accouplent'), sex with the boy-prisoners – who are not identified with animals but branded with numbers – is prohibited and punished with death. Lune's weakness for one of boys, 2, leads to 2's escape and to Lune's execution. Pirate, who falls for another 'two' in the form of the twins, is also condemned to be drowned. Jobs for the boys means no (blow)jobs with the boys, whether for the gangsters or for the infanteros: as Rudi tells Mickie: 'no infantero has carnal knowledge, of either man or woman; we remain virgin' (p. 184) ('aucun infantero n'a commis l'acte de chair, avec aucune femme, ni aucun homme; nous restons vierges'). On the relatively few occasions sex takes place, it is between partners who are unseen or unseeing – because the boy, 2, is blindfolded in his sack or because the twin that Pirate sodomizes is dead. Sex is invisible and/or hallucinatory. As Pirate at his trial remonstrates: 'vous m'avez fait former des fantômes' (p. 104). Sex in *Fantômes* is merely, if devastatingly, fantasmatic and phantomatic. It is both elevated and reduced to fantasy.

Given that the title of the novel, which Pirate has either wittingly or unwittingly quoted, is also a quotation from Sade, then the 'fantômes' to which he refers are doubly if not triply derealized. They are disavowed as shallow and derivative; even the visceral is ersatz.[28] While seeking to articulate, for the first time, his deepest urges and obsessions, Pirate encases himself in a web of intertextuality of which the whole book, with its echoes of the *bestiaires*, *Don Quixote*, Fellini, Rousseau, Genet, Wittig's *Les Guérillères*, Aztec myths and last, but not least, Sade, speaks. Hence the importance of the second part of the book, where the violence of the gangsters is replaced by the play-acting of the picaresque Mickie and where doubles, masks, fakes and shadows proliferate, from the stucco virgins to the 'trash' ('*pacotille*') with which Mickie dresses himself to become an infantero (p. 126). Another way of looking at all the boys is to see them not as unique, but, like the twins, as an imitation one of the other, and thus, as infinitely reproducible and expendable. Even the gangsters are only imitation animals and, possibly, like Guibert's other *Gangsters*,[29] also imitation gangsters. Thus while seeming to confirm the immutable naturalness and perennial appeal of male violence, and, more particularly, male erotic violence, *Fantômes* also undercuts this violence with a constant reminder of its constructedness, its facticity and its disposability. When juxtaposed, the spurious self-vindications of Pirate and Sade can be dismissed as so much sexual casuistry: beliefs in the mystical inevitability of male violence can be thrown, like the Aztec sacrifices, on the cultural scrap heap.

It follows that the ambivalences of the male hunt in *Journal d'un innocent* and *Fantômes* are reflected and conveyed through different forms of *mises en abyme*. In the *Journal* these were suggested by the ambivalences of a highly committed, highly passionate but at the same time self-distancing 'I', encapsulated in the ironic non-innocent 'innocent' of the title. In *Fantômes* a similar distancing effect is achieved through citation, self-citation, and self-recitation in this highly original but also stereotypical 'company of wolves'. Thus, in their very different but complementary ways, both *Journal d'un innocent* and *Fantômes* deconstruct, even as they feed on, the fascinations and the fornications of 'jobs for the boys'.

IV

In his 1990–1992 Journal, *L'Avenir n'est à personne* (1993), Julien Green refers to Eric Jourdan's *Charité* (1991a) as 'this narrative of unrelieved cruelty' ('ce récit d'une cruauté totale') and, in relation to *Charité* and *Révolte* (1991b), to the author's 'imperviousness in the suspense of horror'('insensibilité dans le suspense de l'horreur'). Of the third novel, *Sang* (1992), Green writes: 'Here cruelty attains, as it were, perfection' ('Ici la cruauté atteint, si l'on peut dire, la perfection').[30] Although, as Green also notes, the novels are separate and independent, 'with each having its own light like stars in a constellation' ('chacun [. . .] ayant sa propre lumière comme des étoiles dans une constellation'),[31] they are, in fact, linked by common themes and characters. *Charité* is the story of the arrest, sequestration, escape and hunting down of the apparently dissident student, Ian. At the end of this antithetically entitled novel, Ian is stoned to death by children, for no obvious reason other than that he is an outsider. In *Révolte* and *Sang*, Ian's place as human quarry is taken over by Roman, an ex-novice who tended Ian in his monastery-refuge. Roman is also pursued, interned in a death camp – Camp Zéro – and released, only to be beaten to death in his own flat by rampaging soldiers. He is replaced in his turn by a second Roman, the son of a friend of his long-time father-figure and military intelligence officer, Andréi. As he seeks to reunite with his former lover, Serge, this second Roman is also murdered by a group of local hunters, since he has 'the physique which lent itself to . . . Yes, to a sacrifice' ('le physique qui convenait à . . . Oui, à un sacrifice').[32] He is executed in the name of 'a purifying hunt' in the excitement of 'the sexual fury of murder'.

It is evident that the theme of the hunt is central to this trilogy of novels. Although, as with Duvert and Guibert, the quarry of the hunt is still the adolescent or post-adolescent boy, the originality of Jourdan is to make the hunted rather than the hunter the focus of the narrative and of all its characters' attention. In *Charité, Révolte* and *Sang*, it is Ian and Roman who exert a magnetic and almost mystical attraction over protectors and persecutors alike: 'the boy they were taking had a way of stealing into people's hearts' ('ce garçon qu'on emmenait vous prenait le cœur insensiblement').[33] Such is the charisma of Ian and Roman that their persecutors are infinitely more preoccupied with them than they are with their persecutors. Moreover, the roles of persecutor and protector are themselves confused: Adam, who betrayed Ian, becomes a protector and even dies in trying to save Roman; Andréi, who loves Ian, is being promoted within the secret police that is pursuing him.

The attraction of Ian and Roman is partly one of physical beauty, but since that beauty 'spoke to the boy's eyes, sex and heart' ('touchait chez le garçon les yeux, le sexe et le coeur'),[34] it is also an emotional, indeed spiritual beauty, a beauty that is both innocent and sexual, virginal, and, as Roman at one point becomes, meretricious. Both Ian and Roman appeal to all ages, sexes and sexual orientations – whether men or women, an old hairdresser or a blind monk, the heterosexual Andréi or the homosexual Serge. They even fascinate the guards at Camp Zéro and the Head of the Secret Police. A whole society and a whole country is mobilized in the pursuit of these boys,[35] and yet such is their indestructibility that once one is killed, another is born, even with the same name; and they bear uncanny resemblances to each other, as if they almost self-reproduced out of their own mythical power. This combination of potency, restraint, and self-regeneration – like that of the twins in *Fantômes* – ensures that all the characters they meet and all the environments they traverse are transfigured by their mix of highly sexualized and yet desexualized *maleness*. Their constant journeying and revisiting of the same sites and people ensures that the whole of the trilogy is bathed in post-adolescent male pansexuality.

This sexualization and, more specifically, masculinization, of characters and environments is reinforced by the very nature of the hunt novel. Whether the hunt is enclosed, as in the death camp, or spiritualized, as in the monastery where Ian and Roman take refuge, or whether it invades the ill-defined expanses of forests, beaches and open roads, the spaces of the novels are being constantly patrolled by different troops of men whose job it is to cover and control the territory. Here the distinctiveness of hunter and hunted is less important than the sexualized ciphering and deciphering of the environment, whether on foot, in patrol cars, or by helicopter. Here indeed, are jobs for the boys – and all the boys have the same job. Whether their trademark is sexual murder, a stolen ruby, a password – 'May the angels protect you!' ('Que les anges te protègent!')[36] – or a piece of jettisoned clothing, their job is to inscribe their environment with the passage of their animal traces, the evidence of their male trajectory.

At the same time, this constant reinscription and masculinization also shows the limitations of the hunt, and indeed of the hunt novel. As indicated above, it is not only the characters who are repeated – Ian, Roman and then a second Roman – but their visiting and revisiting of the same places, whether the hairdresser's, the monastery, or Camp Zéro. In constantly returning to the same sites, the characters consciously turn the hunt into a pilgrimage, just as they turn the urge for freedom from an oppressive present into a return to a past of which the violence, such as Ian's double murder, is conveniently overlooked. With their constant loopings of time and spaces in repeated hunts, retreats, and renewed hunts, the novels expose the circularity of their own structures and the claustrophobia of a maleness that seems to conquer territory, but, in fact, only turns in on itself. Man the adventurous or sexually liberated hunter is shown to be introverted and sterile, and man the hunted is shown to be isolationist and even vicious. It is no wonder, then, that there are parallels as well as differences between Camp Zéro and the Dormition monastery: both are characterized by their inwardness, their rituals and their rows of dead. Nor is it any wonder that Jourdan repeats in both *Révolte* and *Sang* the soldiers' assassination of Roman.[37] Jourdan's trilogy thus confirms both the association between the death drive and the compulsion to repeat, and the fact that, as Hal Foster neatly puts it, 'the death-drive may be the foundation rather than the exception to the pleasure principle'.[38] By means of its focus on the male hunt, the trilogy also confirms the fascination, and the danger, of associating the death drive with the compulsion to repeat and jobs for the boys.

It is also clear from the above that the ambivalences associated with the hunt are, as in *Journal d'un innocent* and *Fantômes*, conveyed formally through a kind of *mise en abyme*. In Jourdan the combined temporal, spatial and narrative loopings and layerings of *Charité*, *Révolte* and *Sang* give the sagas of Ian and the two Romans an allegorical, almost mythical status: the hunts become quests and pilgrimages; the protagonists become martyrs and their own reincarnations. Moreover, the *mises en abyme* in Jourdan create a distance and a detachment from the male hunt that, however different they may be from the self-ironizing of Duvert and Guibert, are at least equally critical of 'jobs for the boys'. For by showing the links between three separate murders in three separate narratives Jourdan not only uses *mise en abyme* to expose the imbrication of masculinity and violence, but also shows masculinity and violence themselves to be constructed like a *mise en abyme*. Male violence – whether the sadism of the prison commandants or the self-destructiveness of Ian and Roman – is, like the narratives themselves, represented and reconstructed through a mixture of repetition, imitation, and regeneration. By turning *Charité*, *Révolte* and *Sang* into myth via *mise en abyme*, Jourdan shows that it is precisely such myth itself that is complicit in the generation and regeneration of the sexual violences of 'jobs for the boys'.

V

It can be seen from the above remarks that the versions of the hunt novel offered by Duvert, Guibert and Jourdan confirm and yet also unsettle stereotypical representations of masculinity in different and yet complementary ways. However lyrical Duvert's defence of the 'paedhomophilic chase' might be, this lyricism is, like other examples of 'white man/brown boy' literature,[39] undercut by a sense of the writer's inadequacy and isolation from his companions, which is compounded by Duvert's espousal of the detachment and discipline of writing. In Guibert, too, the juxtaposition of the visceral and the vacuous in polymorphous male combats ensures that the naturalization of homoeroticism and paedophilia is also parodied and problematized. In Jourdan, textual repetitions and symmetries show male predation to be complicitous with mourning and death. Thus, in Duvert, Guibert and Jourdan, three different but equally self-conscious literary modes – lyric, pastiche and allegory – expose the ultimate moral, sexual, and, perhaps even more interestingly, *literary* bankruptcy of the male erotic chase. If representations of 'jobs for the boys' are either intertextual parodies or intratextual elegies, then it is time to move on to new and more fulfilling patterns of male-to-male relations.

There is, however, another dimension to these sexual stories that is surprisingly and yet revealingly easy to neglect: homosexuality. This neglect has been facilitated in *Journal d'un innocent* by the fact that the boys' sexual orientation has yet to be constructed (p. 78) ('The laws of the group [. . .] have to manufacture heterosexuality' ('Les lois du groupe [. . .] ont à fabriquer de l'hétérosexualité'), and, orientation notwithstanding, by the narrator's preference for the seemingly heterosexual over the homosexual partner.[40] In *Fantômes*, what is important is not the sexual *orientation* of the characters – the only identifiable homosexual is the provocatively named 'queer' ('*tapette*'), Sardine[41] – but whether or not gangsters and infanteros respect the taboo on all sexual *relations*. For the main characters in the Jourdan trilogy, sexual orientation is again not the issue: although the promiscuous and initially exploitative gymnast, Serge, can be identified as homosexual, the charisma of Ian and the two Romans is all the more powerful for being imbued with a sexuality above and beyond orientation. As Green writes of Jourdan: 'Sensuality cannot betray anything special [. . .] it is there because it is in man'('La sensualité ne peut rien trahir de particulier [. . .] elle est là parce qu'elle est dans l'homme').[42]

It can be seen, therefore, that all five of the books under consideration here marginalize homosexuality as an orientation or as an identification, while foregrounding a much more generalized fusion of the homosocial and the homoerotic. The importance of 'jobs for the boys' is that the boy can potentially do any sexual job: the boy combines sexual potency with sexual *indeterminacy*; he offers homoeroticism without, necessarily, a homosexual identity. In the hunt novel, jobs for the boys problematize certain forms of masculinity while, at the same time, positing the possibility of permanently *unproblematized* male-to-male *eroticism*. Paradoxically, this applies less to the sexual propagandist, Duvert, than to Guibert and Jourdan, where homosexuality can be ignored, and even occasionally stigmatized, because male-to-male desire is the ground on which the whole fabric of the novels is constructed.[43]

Homosexuality in the sense of orientation can be shown to be the exception to the rule here because homosexuality as a 'desiring machine' is the rule by which exceptions are to be defined.[44] In showing male gayness to be both 'off-centre' and all-pervasive, both supplement *and* norm, these novels offer a suggestive and challenging version of what John Champagne has called an 'ethics of marginality'.[45] For here is a view of the margin that is dependent on a centre that, by some standards, is itself decentred, and dependent on a homosexuality that is seen not from within the context of heterosexuality but from within a mixture of homoeroticism and homosociality – from what Leo Bersani might call 'homo-ness'.[46] There is, therefore, an interesting homology between the *mises en abyme* of the gay hunt novel and new and suggestive rewritings and re-envisionings of male-to-male relations. For the violent *mises en abyme* of the gay hunt novel enact, at the level of representation, the incorporation of homosexuality within a generalized homoeroticism, and the replacement of male-*to*-male by male-*within*-male relations. The *mises en abyme* of these novels can thus be seen as the narrative encapsulation of a generalized, serialized sodomy.

It follows from the above that the challenge of the novels under discussion is to be, and at the same time not to be, 'homosexual'. In the same way that the hunt was shown to naturalize and yet also denaturalize 'naturally' violent masculinity, these hunt novels denaturalize and yet also renaturalize 'homosexuality'. That is to say, they denaturalize myths of the homosexual, paedophile predator while at the same time renaturalizing myths of an empowered homophilia. At the same time as they critique stereotypical versions of 'jobs for the boys' and the male hunt, they lift that critique out of a vicious circle of ghettoization, guilt, recrimination, and redemption through catharsis. For it is in these celebratory, elegiac, parodic, and allegorical *reinscriptions* of essentially homophobic myths – as Guibert would say: 'Vous m'avez fait former des fantômes' – that the gay hunt novel can consciously, and corrosively, create space for a myth of its own: a space for compulsive, not to say ubiquitous, compulsory, homosexuality.

Notes

1. L. Bersani (1993), 'Is the Rectum a Grave?', in D. Crimp (ed.), *AIDS. Cultural Analysis. Cultural Activism*, Cambridge, Mass., p. 222.

2. See E. Jourdan (1991b), *Révolte*, Paris, p. 167. All the translations in this chapter are, unless otherwise indicated, my own.
3. See, for example, L. Frappier-Mazur (1991), *Sade et l'écriture de l'orgie*, Paris, and, on Bataille, K. Millett (1994), *The Politics of Cruelty*, London, pp. 155–62. For studies of the violence in other authors such as Breton, Char and Leiris, see J. Chénieux-Gendron and T. Mathews (eds) (1994), *Violence, Théorie, Surréalisme*, [Paris].
4. On Rachilde, see for example D. Kelly (1989), *Fictional Genders*, Lincoln, Nebraska, pp. 143–55; L. Frappier-Mazur (1994), 'Rachilde: allégories de la guerre', *Romantisme*, no. 85, 3e trimestre, pp. 5–18, and J. Beizer (1994), *Ventriloquized Bodies*, Ithaca and London, pp. 226–60. On Genet, see L. Bersani (1995), *Homos*, Cambridge, Mass., pp. 113–81.
5. On the indissociability of violence, gender and representation, see T. de Lauretis (1989), 'The Violence of Rhetoric. Considerations on Representation and Gender', in N. Armstrong and L. Tennenhouse (eds), *The Violence of Representation. Literature and the History of Violence*, London, pp. 239–58.
6. See M. Tournier (1970), *Le Roi des Aulnes*, Paris, p. 184 and also pp. 152, 180, 223.
7. M. Cartmill (1993), *A View to a Death in the Morning*, Cambridge, Mass., p. 5.
8. Quoted ibid., pp. 125–6.
9. Ibid., p. 9.
10. Ibid., pp. 76–91.
11. See 'The Bambi Syndrome', ibid., pp. 161–88.
12. L. Bersani (1990), in *The Culture of Redemption*, Cambridge, Mass., questions theories of 'the restitutive or redemptive power of cultural forms' as themselves 'symptomatic versions of the very process they purport to explain' (p. 22).
13. See R. Dyer (1991), 'Believing in Fairies: The Author and the Homosexual', in D. Fuss (ed.), *inside/out: Lesbian Theories, Gay Theories*, London, pp. 185–201. For homotextuality as homosexuality in performance, see O. Heathcote (1994), 'Masochism, Sadism and Homotextuality: The Examples of Yukio Mishima and Eric Jourdan', *Paragraph*, vol. 17, no. 2, pp. 174–89.
14. L. Schehr (1995b), *The Shock of Men*, Stanford, CA, p. 140.
15. For one of the most thorough studies of the narrative *mise en abyme*, attributed to Gide but developed by C. E. Magny and others, see L. Dällenbach (1977), *Le Récit spéculaire. Essai sur la mise en abyme*, Paris, who defines *mise en abyme* as 'any internal mirror which reflects the

whole of the narrative by either simple, repeated or specious reduplication' (p. 52) ('tout miroir interne réfléchissant l'ensemble du récit par réduplication simple, répétée ou spécieuse').

16. T. Duvert (1976), *Journal d'un innocent*, Paris, p. 114. Future references to this text will be given in parenthesis.
17. 'J'ai besoin des villes à cause des garçons. Je ne me civilise que pour eux, c'est pour les chercher, les accueillir que je discipline mes journées [. . .] Chez les puritains, le plaisir amoureux est une friandise desséchée [. . .] moi, il est ma vie sociale et ma nourriture' (p. 112). In Renaud Camus's *Tricks* (Paris, 1988) the hunting metaphor is less in evidence, partly no doubt because all the meetings described are, however brief, 'successful'. In the episode entitled 'A Perfect Fuck' Camus does, however, write: 'I have spoken of pleasure, but I do not see what economy would prevent me from calling such moments happiness, precisely because they are so precarious. When they are experienced, their perfection seems a culmination, as if there is nothing more to be sought [. . .] But they simply return one to the quest – for how can one not desire afterwards to live other similar moments, once more, just once more?' (p. 459) ('J'ai parlé de plaisir, mais je ne vois pas quelle économie m'empêcherait d'appeler bonheur, et justement parce qu'ils sont si précaires, de tels moments. On croit, à les vivre, que leur perfectionnement est un aboutissement, qu'il n'y a plus rien à chercher [. . .] Mais ils ne font que renvoyer à la quête, car comment ne pas désirer, ensuite, en rencontrer de semblables une fois encore, une seule fois?').
18. 'Avec ses fortes cloisons, son luxe rugueux, ses fenêtres haut percées dans les murs comme celles d'un cachot, mais généreuses en lumière, ce lieu a une atmosphère puissante, douce, qui saisit, accueille et renferme' (Duvert, *Journal*, p. 200). See also the more specific reference to Sade (ibid., p. 202) and *Paysage de fantaisie* (Paris, 1973) where the boys are also detained in a kind of *maison close*.
19. Quoted by C. Robinson (1995), *Scandal in the Ink: Male and Female Homosexuality in Twentieth-Century French Literature*, London, p. 243. See also Duvert, *Journal d'un innocent*, pp. 148–52.
20. It is in *L'Enfant au masculin* (p. 21) that Duvert invents the term 'pédhomophile'.
21. 'Je l'encouragerai à me persifler, à cracher sur la moindre des choses que je touche ou que j'admire. Et, en étant pour lui un exemple vivant des laideurs et des soucis de l'indiscipline, j'en ferai un homme plus normal, plus moyen qu'aucun père normal et moyen ne saurait faire de ses enfants' (pp. 204–5).

22. Robinson, *Scandal in the Ink*, p. 161.
23. For the narrator's consciousness of his own (small) penile size, see pp. 149, 184.
24. Bersani (1993), p. 212. According to Michel Foucault, the ancient Greek male-to-male relations were not even seen as 'homosexual' or 'feminizing' so long as the older partner was 'actif dans le rapport sexuel et actif dans la maîtrise morale sur lui-même' (*Histoire de la sexualité*, vol. 2, *L'Usage des plaisirs*, Paris, p. 98) ('active in the sexual relation and active in his moral self-mastery'). Such relations, however, became increasingly stigmatized when 'le rôle de l'éraste et celui de l'éromène ne peuvent plus être distingués, l'égalité étant parfaite ou la réversibilité totale' (*Histoire de la sexualité*, vol. 3, *Le Souci de soi*, Paris, p. 258) ('the role of the erastes and that of the eromenos can no longer be distinguished, the equality [of their bond] being perfect or their reversibility complete').
25. J. Boone (1995), 'Vacation Cruises; or, The Homoerotics of Orientalism', *PMLA*, vol. 110, no. 1, p. 104.
26. For comments on the double in Guibert, see O. Heathcote (1995b), '*Les Chiens* d'Hervé Guibert: analyse d'"une plaquette pornographique"', *Nottingham French Studies*, vol. 34, no. 1, pp. 61–9.
27. H. Guibert (1987), *Vous m'avez fait former des fantômes*, Paris, p. 150. Future quotations from this text will be given in parenthesis.
28. In July 1783 Sade wrote to his wife: 'For example, I would wager you thought you were achieving miracles, when you reduced me to hideous abstinence in *the sins of the flesh*. Well, you were deceived: you fired my brain, you made me create ghosts to which I will have to give life' ('Par exemple, vous avez imaginé faire merveille, je le parierais, en me réduisant à une abstinence atroce sur *le péché de la chair*. Eh bien, vous vous êtes trompés: vous avez échauffé ma tête, vous m'avez fait former des fantômes qu'il faudra que je réalise' (See G. Lely (ed.) (1967), *Œuvres complètes du marquis de Sade*, vol. 12, Paris, Letter CLXII, p. 397). I am grateful to Ralph Sarkonak for indicating this reference.
29. In *Les Gangsters*, too, writing takes over from 'reality': 'In the evening at T.'s, at C.'s request, I told my story once again. At each retelling, it grew more and more into a tale formed, and perhaps deformed, by writing' (p. 61) ('Le soir chez T., sollicité par C., une fois de plus je racontai mon histoire. A chaque récit de vive voix, elle se fortifiait davantage en récit formé par l'écriture, peut-être déformé'). It is also interesting to note that in Dennis Cooper's *Frisk* (London, 1992), the graphic descriptions of sexual murders are also revealed to be fantasy – whether those supposedly committed by 'Dennis' or those portrayed

in the supposed snuff movies. According to Gregory W. Bredbeck (1995), this anticipation of fantasy by (faked) representation shows that '[b]oth the hegemony of the social and the difference of the antisocial are revealed as *always already* constructs within the social construct of representation itself.' ('The New Queer Narrative: Intervention and Critique', *Textual Practice*, vol. 9, no. 3, p. 487).

30. J. Green (1993), *L'Avenir n'est à personne*, Paris, pp. 208, 216, 354.
31. Ibid., p. 354.
32. E. Jourdan (1992), *Sang*, Paris, p. 343.
33. E. Jourdan (1991a), *Charité*, Paris, p. 63.
34. Ibid., p. 176.
35. As with *Journal d'un innocent* and *Fantômes*, the geographical setting of the Jourdan trilogy is too imprecise to locate it in France or elsewhere. The student unrest may be a pointer to France, but the Eastern Orthodox Church – and the concentration camps – suggest a different location.
36. 'Que les anges te protègent!' is initially murmured by Andréi to Ian (*Charité*, p. 64) and then reprised at intervals, creating an increasing sense of mystical community between the male protagonists (pp. 167, 194, 318).
37. See *Révolte*, pp. 319–26 and *Sang*, pp. 227–35.
38. H. Foster (1993), *Compulsive Beauty*, Cambridge, Mass., p. 11.
39. See Boone, 'Vacation Cruises; or, The Homoerotics of Orientalism', p. 104.
40. See the narrator's objection to Francesco's 'tête de femme' (p. 97), his 'figure de star' (p. 104) and his status as 'un acteur consommé' (p. 108).
41. See Guibert, *Fantômes*, p. 189.
42. Green, *L'Avenir n'est à personne*, p. 216. It could be argued that the sexuality in Monique Wittig's *Les Guérillères* is also above and beyond both gender and sexual orientation. See M. Wittig (1992), 'The Mark of Gender', in *The Straight Mind and Other Essays*, New York and Hemel Hempstead.
43. However interesting in terms of 'gender trouble', all three authors under discussion here pay scant attention to women, and aspects of *Fantômes* could be seen as misogynistic. See O. Heathcote, 'L'Erotisme, la violence et le jeu dans *Vous m'avez fait former des fantômes*' (forthcoming). On the question of boys' changing sexual identities, see B. Gibson (1995), *Male Order: Life Stories from Boys Who Sell Sex*, London, p. x.
44. For 'Les Machines désirantes', see G. Deleuze and F. Guattari (1972), *L'Anti-Œdipe*, Paris, pp. 7–59.

45. See J. Champagne (1995), *The Ethics of Marginality*, Minneapolis, p. 32. See also in this regard B. Smith's review of *Critical Quarterly: Gay Lives?*, ed. by D. Trotter, (1995/6), Oxford, in *Perversions*, Issue 6, p. 170: 'I fail to see what self-esteem can be found in identifying with a sensibility which defines itself as a *sub*culture. A walk in the closet in still a closet.'
46. See Bersani, *Homos*, p. 10: 'If homosexuality is a privileged vehicle for homo-ness, the latter designates a mode of connectedness to the world that it would be absurd to reduce to sexual preference.'

– 9 –

Visions of Excess: Filming/Writing the Gay Self in Collard's *Savage Nights*

Brigitte Rollet and James S. Williams

> AIDS may be a sort of language that has something to tell us [. . .] It brings to light the dysfunctions and aberrations in our society. (C. Collard)

I

Savage Nights and the French Cultural Context

When the film *Savage Nights* (*Les Nuits fauves*) was released in France in October 1992, it took the country by storm. With his debut feature – an adaptation of his 1989 autobiographical novel of the same name – director Cyril Collard became an instant celebrity, a media phenomenon and icon, a status eventually sealed by his public burial at the Père Lachaise cemetery in Paris following his AIDS-related death in March 1993. This form of media hype was not new in French cinema. What was unusual was that never before had a director attracted such a degree of interest and enthusiasm across the entire media spectrum. From the front page of *Le Monde* on 21 October 1992, which announced a 'hymn to life', to countless articles in *Libération*, *Première*, *Cahiers du Cinéma* and other magazines, the film provoked a shower of critical praise. Collard was compared to not only Maurice Pialat but also John Cassavetes, Youssef Chahine and Pier Paolo Pasolini. Finally, just days after his death, *Savage Nights* won four Césars, including one for best film. Was this extraordinary response due to the film's main topic – rare in French cinema – of a bisexual man, Jean, who essentially betrays his female lover with whom he is having unprotected sex by not revealing that he is HIV-positive, all the while continuing to lead a full gay lifestyle? Or was it more the fact that the film was made by a bisexual, HIV-positive director who also played the leading role?

Collard was already known before *Savage Nights*, not least because of his

Cocteau-esque versatility. He was a scriptwriter, novelist and poet; a photographer, film-assistant and director of both dramas and documentaries; an actor, composer and singer. In addition to the novel *Savage Nights* ('for adult readers only' according to its back cover), and, before that, the autobiographical novel *Condamné amour* (1987) (a pun on *condamné à mort*, 'condemned to die'), Collard had made several short films (*Grand Huit* (1982) and *Alger la blanche* (1986)), the detective telefilm *Taggers* (1989–90), and various pop videos. He had also directed art documentaries for museums, including the visually stunning *Les Raboteurs* (1988) (commissioned by the Musée d'Orsay and the French television channel La Sept), and had worked as an assistant-director on Pialat's *To Our Loves* (1983) (*A nos amours*), in which he also played a minor role. *Alger la blanche*, about the impossible love of an adolescent (Jean) for a young *beur* (Farid), quickly established Collard's key concerns: the portrayal of French immigrant culture and the representation of gay male desire. However, *Savage Nights*, with its helter-skelter ride through different levels of the Parisian sexual landscape, carried the force of a thunderbolt. In *Cahiers du Cinéma*, Frédéric Strauss celebrated a 'new art' that entered into urgent, direct dialogue with the 'noise' of the contemporary world and assumed all the risks of contradiction, provocation and confusion that that entailed. By opening up new parameters in cinema and allowing passion, jealousy, rage and tenderness free rein, Collard, according to Strauss, liberated the beauty and emotion of film-making from aesthetic dogma.[1]

Strauss's appreciation of *Savage Nights* as form is to be contrasted with the film's rather lukewarm reception in the Anglo-Saxon world, where it was criticized mainly on political grounds. Writing in *Sight and Sound* Simon Watney attacked Collard for a lack of commitment, in particular for the way in which *Savage Nights* refused to engage with AIDS as a social issue and positively flouted the health campaign for safer sex.[2] Jean's individualism and narcissism, Watney argued, were symptomatic of the general inability in France to come to terms collectively with the highest rate of HIV infection in Europe. If *Savage Nights* disqualified itself as a 'gay film', it could not, however, according to Mark Nash, be regarded as 'queer' either, since '[q]ueer is an anglophone word and has developed a currency in countries where the oppression of gay people has a very different history than in France'.[3] For Jonathan Romney in the *New Statesman and Society*, the film had a depoliticizing effect because it indulged in Romantic fantasies as old as Dumas's *La Dame aux camélias* by presenting AIDS as yet another form of the malady of love. Romney adds – and this is a view shared by many – that the film is locked in the Surrealist logic of *amour fou*, typically at the expense of its young female protagonist, the seventeen-year old Laura

(Romane Bohringer), who is left paying the price for her older man's sentimental education.[4] Certainly, the final scene of the film, where Jean, having escaped to the most extreme tip of Europe (the Cape Saint-Vincent promontory in Portugal), finally utters on the phone to Laura the simple words 'je t'aime', does little to burst its apparent narcissistic bubble. All the while, according to Adrian Rifkin, the traditional position of gay sexuality in France as an urban space of abjection remains unchanged.[5]

The different reactions triggered by *Savage Nights* reflect the importance of the social and cultural context in which it was made. Unlike in other Western countries, especially the United States, which was the first to deal with the subject filmically in *Parting Glances* (1984) and, more recently, in *Longtime Companion* (1990) and *Philadelphia* (1993), French culture and society had still not in the early 1990s fully confronted the reality of the AIDS epidemic. A few film-directors had, admittedly, explored the symbolic dimension of the disease. In *The Night is Young* (1986) Léos Carax romantically associated love and death with the notion of a virus that only infects those who make love without feeling (the original French title is *Mauvais Sang* (Bad blood)). In 1987, with his film *Encore*, Paul Vecchiali became the first director to link AIDS with homosexuality, and, in the violent *Merci la vie* (1990), Bertrand Blier tied the theme of AIDS to other sexually transmitted diseases in order to demonstrate in highly misogynistic terms the 'impurity' of women. Finally, François Margolin's debut feature *Mensonge* (1991) marked a serious attempt to portray the impact and threat of the 'homosexual disease' on a 'normal', heterosexual family. *Savage Nights*, however, was the first French film to address the subject from all sides – homosexual, heterosexual, bisexual – and in so doing achieve a major impact on AIDS awareness in the country.

The paucity of filmic representations of AIDS in France can be attributed to many factors, including the fear shared by young French actors that playing in such films could damage their careers (Jean-Hugues Anglade was one of many who turned down the role of Jean).[6] In addition, there is the overriding conservatism of French cinema, one of the most telling signs of which is that it was not until 1994 that a gay and lesbian film festival took place in France at all. Although financially supported by the French Minister of Culture and several AIDS associations, this festival was held, almost inevitably, at the American Center in Paris. A programme editorial acknowledged that, as far as gay cinema was concerned, 'the spirit of community and activism in France [fell] far below what can be found in Anglo-Saxon countries and that French cinema [reflected] this tendency. It would be pointless to look for directors "specializing" in homosexual themes.'[7] Accordingly, only three French films relating to AIDS were screened during the entire festival, and it was noticeable that neither there, nor at a twin event held a year later in Lille, was Collard's film screened.[8]

Such facts, of course, raise the whole question of what it is to be a gay film director and gay film spectator in France, where the very notion of a 'gay film' still has very little currency. In his 1979 listing of films containing representations of gays and lesbians (not including those films where there are no gay characters as such but that still might be considered as offering a gay perspective), Richard Dyer mentioned only a handful of French films, and these were made almost exclusively by gay men.[9] Similarly, Frédéric Martel, in his recent chronology of the key gay events in French culture, society and politics between 1968 and 1996, identifies fourteen fiction films, but, as he warns his readers, '[t]he mention of a name in this book does not imply in any way a belonging to some unlikely [sic] "homosexual identity"'.[10] Indeed, the books, films and music he refers to are not to be viewed as 'homosexual works', but rather as belonging to the collective memory of 'homosexuals, whatever the initial intention of their authors'.[11] Such critical caution may seem surprising to an Anglo-Saxon reader, yet it is very frequent in France, where the reluctance to refer to anything as distinctively homosexual is common, even amongst the country's rare out-gay men and women. It would thus be very difficult to attempt a classification of post-war French gay film and film-makers, although among the latter Vecchiali, Jacques Demy and André Téchiné certainly stand out.[12] If we accept, however, Vito Russo's general idea that 'the key to gay films, whether they are made by heterosexuals or homosexuals, is that they do not view the existence of gay people as controversial',[13] then we can agree without too much difficulty that *Savage Nights* presents itself as a gay film. A key feature of its composite, all-inclusive nature is that various forms of gayness are manifested, from Jean's sexual cruising to an episode in a bar with a male transvestite to scenes in a male brothel.

In this chapter, we want to explore the particular gay status and significance of *Savage Nights* by focusing not on its real or perceived deficiencies, but rather on its very intertextual excess, both of content and style. By intertextual excess we are referring not simply to the multiple influences at play in Collard's work, whether filmic or literary, acknowledged or unconscious. These would include most obviously Jean Genet, to whom the narrator directly attributes the idea that only violence can put an end to male brutality (he even notes *en passant* that he and Genet were born on the same day of the year).[14] In addition, the film pays clear tribute to recent European cinema, notably Pasolini's *Teorema* (1968), with its tale of multi-sexual seduction in a bourgeois family, but also Michelangelo Antonioni's *The Passenger* (1975), with its ironic use of the bisexual actress Maria

Schneider as a real or imagined figure of prophecy ('Open yourself up to others [. . .] profit from the ordeal of your illness', she states at the beginning of *Savage Nights*). In fact, the signature of the intertextual excess of *Savage Nights* is inscribed most fundamentally on and around the very body of Collard: Collard/director adapts the novel of Collard/writer, and Collard/actor plays Jean/cameraman, thus creating multiple layers of truth and fiction. These layers increase still further if we consider that the film includes extracts from Collard's notebooks, a mixture of diary, poetry and correspondence published posthumously in 1993 under the title *L'Ange sauvage* (1993b). What, therefore, are the theoretical implications of this textual and (auto)biographical blurring? Can the marginalized gay/bisexual body support such a level of multiple inscription, and what does the process reveal of the ambiguities involved in filming the gay self? To begin our analysis we must first turn to *Savage Nights* the novel.

II

AIDS Narratives: Issues of Gender and Genre

In a discussion of AIDS and literature, Martel distinguishes those French authors who, before becoming so-called 'AIDS writers', were already labelled as 'homosexual writers'. Included in his list are Yves Navarre, Guy Hocquenghem, Dominique Fernandez and Renaud Camus.[15] No new novelists, he asserts, came into being as a direct result of AIDS, the one exception being Collard, who acquired the marginal status of a 'bisexual HIV-positive writer' within the field of AIDS writing. Let us place *Savage Nights* in the particular context of the most well-known and widely read exponent of this new genre, Hervé Guibert, whose *To The Friend Who Did Not Save My Life* (*A l'ami qui ne m'a pas sauvé la vie*) and *The Compassion Protocol* (*Le Protocole compassionnel*) were published shortly after, in 1990 and 1991 respectively.

For novelists writing on AIDS, a common method of approach is autobiographical, with textual play around identity, space and time functioning as a form of personal denial. Through the sometimes paradoxical structures of their work, Collard – and even more so Guibert – articulate various forms of refusal: the refusal of time as a marker in literature and life, the denial of fixed identities, and the dissolving of boundaries between the narrating and the diegetic 'I'. While in Collard's novel this process is evidenced by the shifting use of personal pronouns such as the diegetic 'I' and the third-person 'he', in Guibert's work it entails a rejection of chronology.[16] Nash has underlined the tragic elements of AIDS narratives, for instance, the fact that an unhappy ending is invariably guaranteed.[17] Similarly, Martel writes about the 'unity of space' in such novels, evidenced by the recurring names of Paris hospitals visited by the hero/narrator/author. Other unities stand out, however, notably that of time. The discovery that one is HIV-positive often provides the starting-point for narratives that adopt a version of the classical twenty-four-hour rule imposed on French seventeenth-century dramatists to create a sense of tension and urgency. Since writing constitutes an act of survival (Guibert: 'When I stop writing, then I'm dead';[18] Collard: 'I am compelled to write',[19]) it also achieves thereby a unity of action in the act of writing the self, however precarious the final outcome. As Murray Pratt has argued with reference to Guibert, because 'the writing of an autobiographical text always precedes death, authorial access to that determining event is always an anticipation. Writing autobiography is, ironically, an activity which bases the false promise of individual identity on the never yet experienced moment of its dissolution.'[20]

The flagrant lack of an obsession with death, together with a positive, linear sense of forward progression, is perhaps what most marks Collard out from AIDS novelists such as Guibert, a fact that Collard understood only too well. In *L'Ange sauvage*, he inveighs against the comparison made by the French magazine *Actuel* between himself and Guibert, according to which they both express 'French morbidity and narcissism'. Guibert, he proclaimed, 'is on the side of death while I am on the side of life'.[21] Far from offering a self-pitying portrait of his protagonist, Collard offers his French audience the first – and possibly only – optimistic HIV-positive character. The narrator of *Savage Nights* (film as well as novel) concludes with this stunning paean to life: 'I am alive [. . .] I shall probably die of AIDS, but it is not my life any more. I am "inside" life [*je suis dans la vie*].' Collard himself, in a notebook entry dated 9 July 1990, wrote the following: 'Seeing me in "good health", some people probably think that everything is invented and staged to sell books [. . .] I am not ill enough to have Guibert's success.'[22]

It is true that in the novel *Savage Nights*, the usual minimum condition of literary autobiography – i.e. that the name of the author and that of the narrator/protagonist be identified as the same – is not fulfilled, despite the fact that the narrating 'I' and diegetic 'I' share a similar date of birth. Yet in the film *Savage Nights*, the first-person voice-over in the opening sequence of Collard filming in Morocco with a camcorder immediately establishes Collard as the protagonist and narrative voice. Although there are just three voice-over sequences in the film – all that remain of the thirty or so in the original script – they help to generate its immediate autobiographical charge, as does the extensive use of the more verifiable televisual image of video, a form increasingly favoured by directors attempting a more subjective, intimate form of film-making (one thinks of Jean-Luc Godard's 1995 short, *JLG/JLG: autoportrait de décembre*). It is immediately clear that Collard had used his own life and work as his primary source material. The year of Jean's diagnosis as HIV-positive is, as for Collard, 1986, and the name Laura can be found in both the novel *Savage Nights* and Collard's own notebooks, where some of the film's scenes feature almost verbatim (although it is Laurence in *L'Ange sauvage* who most resembles the Laura of the film). This process is mirrored in reverse in the film, when Laura replays for real the lines about jealousy that she had initially acted for Jean during her video audition. The power of Jean's directorial gaze – evident in the way he video-records Laura and his male lover Samy (Carlos Lopez) prior to initiating a sexual relationship with each of them – is an exact reflection of Collard's absolute command of his material, which results in whole episodes, particularly descriptive scenes, being either streamlined or omitted. The link between possessing people physically and visually is reinforced biographically by the fact that two of the actresses – Corine Blue, who plays Laura's mother, and Laura Favelli, who plays Jean's ex-girlfriend – were former lovers of Collard. (A further parallel can be drawn with a statement Collard made after being accused of appropriating the memory of a young *beur*, killed by the police during the shooting of *Grand Huit* and to whom Collard later dedicated that film: that his desire to sleep with young hooligans (Arab or not) ultimately gave him the right to film them.)[23]

Samy and Laura represent extensions, or idealized mirror-images, of Jean's divided personality: Samy is physically handsome, sexy, independent and elusive; Laura is the girl-child capable of romance and deep emotions. As in Guibert's work,[24] Collard also frequently uses the mirror to 'double' Jean's reflection, which is already refracted and multiplied by his roving, intrusive camera, so producing a quasi-literal representation of narcissism. Jean is both in front of, and behind, the camera, and there are very few shots in which he is neither seen nor heard, his music and lyrics frequently invading the sound-track as his body swells the visual frame. Indeed, the formally inventive and erotic visual pleasure characteristic of much recent gay male film-making, especially of the so-called 'New Queer Cinema' (e.g. Todd Haynes's *Poison* (1991) and Tom Kalin's *Swoon* (1992)), reaches fascinating proportions in *Savage Nights*, where the degree of physical desire on display is matched by a breathless heterogeneity of form and style, ranging from passages of pure drama to face-on-camera monologues, from hand-held video sequences to split-screen editing.[25] As some critics have remarked, it is as though Collard were running one last time through every cinematic possibility in order to protect himself against imminent death.

Of course, much of Jean's seductive power derives precisely from his sexual indeterminacy, born of a seemingly limitless *disponibilité*. Just as his lovers present a crisis of racial and class identity – Laura comes from a well-to-do North-African colonial family, Samy from an immigrant family of Spanish gypsies – so, too, Jean, neither 'completely' straight nor 'totally' gay, confounds the traditional boundaries of gender and sexual difference and drives both sexes to a state of abandon. Laura descends into hysteria and is sent to a private clinic; Samy imitates – and attempts to disqualify – Jean's suffering by cutting into his body with a knife in front of a mirror. Yet by being open to everything, Jean/Collard aligns himself with no one, a position echoed in the following extract from Collard's autobiographical note-book:

> You queers, who have reproached me for sleeping with women, you find them disgusting and you don't believe I could have had pleasure with them. You think I am exactly like you. But I am not exactly like you. I can make love to women, and, unlike you, I can think of their sex without vomiting. Sometimes, however, but sometimes only, the idea of a woman's sex disgusts me [. . .] And you straights, and especially you women, and you Laura, you are no better than them. You want to convert me, cure me, make me happy, make me forget, make me love, make me love you. [. . .] According to you queers, I'm a coward, I try to avoid the truth [. . .] You would like me to be more of an activist, more of a preacher [. . .] I hate you as much as the others. Or rather, I despise you, since hate takes up too much time and requires too much energy (30 August 1987).[26]

Collard considered that the value of *Savage Nights* was that it made AIDS a universal issue, the bisexuality of its protagonist allowing it to escape the ghettoizing label of 'gay film' and thus to attract a general audience: 'I talk about AIDS in the first person [. . .] Once you step out of the ghetto of queers and junkies and consider AIDS in the context of other social problems, you're perhaps making progress.'[27] Yet although Collard never publicly identified himself as a gay/bisexual director or writer, and while no male character in the film chooses to identify himself as gay, the viewer receives Jean's sexual desire as predominantly gay in nature. This is partly because *Savage Nights* demands to be read through previous work by Collard such as *Alger la blanche*, where the character of Jean, played by an actor who looks like Collard, has a job and lifestyle similar to that of his namesake in

Savage Nights. The principal reason, however, is Jean's recurring sexual encounters with men, including the ritualized, nocturnal orgies of casual sex he experiences by the Seine at Bercy, and the dutiful manner in which the camera follows the consistently half-naked body of Samy (Laura's body, by contrast, is never shot with the same interest). If Collard had already made public both the nature of his sexual orientation and his HIV-positive status in his literary work, the film *Savage Nights* performs the highly staged 'coming out' of a gay artist living with the disease. In one scene, Jean/ Collard is pictured taking the drug AZT, which, in 1986, had only just become commercially available. In another, he attempts to burn off visibly real lesions caused by the AIDS-related illness, Kaposi's sarcoma. Thus, for all its bisexual focus, the viewer responds to *Savage Nights* as a preeminently gay artefact.

To determine, however, the full gay significance of *Savage Nights*, it is necessary to consider it in the light of one definition of gay film proposed by the American critic, Thomas Waugh. In his study of gay cinema since 1916, Waugh argues that it is 'gay male filmmakers, competing with photographers as prophets of the homosexual body, who most definitely take up the job of constructing the gay subject [. . .] In the new configuration of character types, the cinema provides two points of entry for the gay spectator: a site for identification with the narrative subject, and a site for specular erotic pleasure in his object.'[28] Waugh shows that the gay subject tends to take on 'one of, or a combination of, several recurring social roles, namely those of the artist, the intellectual, and/or the teacher [. . .] he looks at and desires the object within the narrative [. . .] he also bespeaks him, constructs him, projects him, fantasizes him, in short, *represents* him' (original emphasis).[29] Seen from this perspective, Collard's film would appear to offer a rather conventional construction of the gay subject: Jean is a video-maker and writer with an acute visual and linguistic sense, who teaches and moralizes as much as he learns (he even corrects Samy's use of grammar). The difference lies in the fact that the pleasure described by Waugh is effectively diverted or 'perverted' in *Savage Nights*, for the process of identification functions less in terms of a viewed object of desire than of the narrative subject's desire for yet further extensions of himself. Jean/ Collard – but also, by implication, the viewer – is a *voyeur* of the many different self-images projected on to others and then reappropriated narcissistically, the result being that the identity between the objectified, autobiographical body (Collard) and the subjective, fictional self (Jean) is sealed almost monumentally.

III

Autobiographical Film Narrative: The Ethics of Referentiality

We could continue in this vein by drawing out all the parallels between Jean and Collard, stopping only at the incontrovertible evidence of Collard's death, a manifestation of the Romantic trope of the artist who dies young. This trope goes hand in hand with the figure of the outsider (as Martel explains, AIDS marks for writers 'the return of an "early death", etched with the images of Rimbaud, Radiguet, Büchner, Huguenin, Crevel').[30] But we need to be clear about what it means exactly to say that *Savage Nights* (film) is autobiographical. In a discussion of the pioneering work of Elizabeth Bruss on film and autobiography, Philippe Lejeune has highlighted the problems inherent in transposing a literary term to a cinematic context.[31] It is a paradox that because of its inescapable, visible link with the referent, the cinematic image, unlike the linguistic signifier, never lets us completely forget its quotient of fiction. That is to say, however realistically a child is playing *my* childhood, from the film-maker's perspective it is never the reality the film claims it to be. In fact, the more a film-maker attempts to approach the autobiographical real, the greater, often, is the film's impression of fictionality. For this reason, *cinéma-vérité* is best conceived of as more appropriate for reportage and travelogue, where the camera is turned towards the other and the present, than for autobiography, where the focus is on the self and normally the past. *Savage Nights*, although set in the recent past of 1986, appears, however, to render such issues irrelevant through the sheer force of its presence and dynamism. For it is the very excess of Jean's selfhood and narcissism, coupled with the sensational quality of the images and their intensive editing, that suspend both our moral judgement and any doubts we may have regarding the referentiality or personal truth of Collard's autobiographical narrative. Jean's final statement in the film – his buoyant assertion that he is not so much facing life as 'inside' it – merely confirms that we have, as it were, been inside the very skin of Collard.

Yet the last moments of *Savage Nights* demand careful attention. They come immediately after an episode – absent from the novel – where Jean saves a hapless foreigner from being mutilated by a gang of fascist skinheads (among them the confused Samy) by threatening to infect the leader with his own contaminated blood. For the first time in *Savage Nights* Jean, instead of merely accepting circumstances, acts decisively to reverse them. According to Godfrey Cheshire, this one episode enables the film to subsume and transform the solipsistic drama it contains, revealing it after all to be dedicated to community and the life that exists beyond illusion.[32] Yet no sooner has this been achieved than we head with Jean directly to Cape Saint-Vincent to witness the final stage of his sentimental education, which began in the film's preamble in Morocco. Through his eyes, as the camera turns away from the bustling port towards the setting sun, we experience an abstract prism of shade and colour, a gentle, patterned flux sublimating the chaos of mismatched reflections that have characterized the film thus far. The smiling young boys filmed in the balmy glow of long-shot provide a sense of peace and well-being, confirmed by Jean's quiet statement of love for Laura on the phone ('je t'aime'), which he delivers as if for the sole benefit of the camera. This is another inversion of the original novel, which ended with Jean resigning himself to his inability to love, a point rammed home by the graphically described stench of urine evoking 'savage nights'. Hence, unlike the reader of the novel, the viewer of *Savage Nights* participates in a more elevated, cinematic solution: in the absence of any identifiable other, the barrier between viewer and Jean/Collard is dissolved. We are obliged to enter into total complicity with Jean and lift off with the camera towards a form of spiritual – and yet always erotic – transcendence. In other words, a spectacular gesture of concern for a foreign other has provoked the powerful inversion of one form of excess (self-image) into another (the beatific celebration of the cosmos). After Jean's turbulent experience with Samy, we have now arrived at a kind of Iberian catharsis born of romantic and redemptive beauty.

But the real cannot be so easily made a matter for abstraction, any more than the ethical can be presented simply as the aesthetic. Although *Savage Nights* succeeds in transcending the major dualities and divisions it puts into play, autobiographical reality, the driving force of the film's fascination and seduction, must eventually exact its price. A year after Collard's death, it came to light indirectly that he had committed an act similar to that of Jean: he had infected the granddaughter of the noted French novelist Suzanne Prou through an incident of careless sexual behaviour. Erika Prou subsequently died of the disease in November 1993, aged twenty-six. Suddenly, what had been originally taken as the very proof of the fictional status of *Savage Nights* and a courageous way of breaking a taboo – i.e. posing the question of whether it is necessary to inform your partner that you are HIV-positive – became instead a fatal sign of Collard's cynicism and indifference to social responsibility. The general malaise caused by the discovery that Jean's 'lie' was not completely fictional retroactively forced Collard into the familiar gay role of social pariah, and provoked what quickly became known as the 'Collard Affair'. After the scopophilic pleasure enjoyed by a voyeuristic public, there followed a period of moral reckoning, guilt and repression. Some of those who had contributed to Collard's success felt themselves exposed as indirect 'accomplices' to an 'unspeakable' act and, true to the film's logic of reversibility, began publicly to disown their interest in him. Dominique Jamet, for example, writing on 21 April in the current affairs magazine *L'Evénement du jeudi*, described Collard as an 'irresponsible criminal' who had committed murder through negligence. Writers and intellectuals such as Françoise Giroud and Bernard-Henri Lévy lashed out against the false hero-worshipping of Collard as the 'angel of death' and the romanticization of AIDS that went with it.[33]

By revealing himself to be all too human, Collard, who had always played dangerously with reality and fiction, appeared, therefore, to have 'infected' his audience with an unacceptable confusion. For while the film ended on a note of spiritual uplift and communion with the Other, the reality of Collard had returned to remind the audience in absolutely concrete terms that *Savage Nights* was fundamentally a film dealing with AIDS, marginal sexuality, and death. It is as though the whole moral question had finally resurfaced around Collard's autobiographical body, the radical, irreversible force of which had remained latent during its multiple inscription in Jean's first-person, self-idealizing discourse. One may, of course, seek to resolve the question by saying that *Savage Nights* – which, as we mentioned earlier, includes the statement: 'It is not my life any more' – reads in retrospect more as a public confession designed to provoke forgiveness: by endorsing the 'fault' and the 'sins' of his fellow men, Jean/Collard, as the final shot of himself in Christ-like isolation emphasizes, had granted himself personal absolution, aided and abetted by a willing, captive audience. Yet that would be to provide moral closure where none really exists. Indeed, the excessive glorification of Collard and his subsequent infamy say less, ultimately, about Cyril Collard and his private intentions than about the ambivalent response in France both to the phenomenon of AIDS and to any major public departure from the established heterosexual norm. Quite simply, if a film about bisexual desire but blessed with universalist ambitions and intimations of immortality is socially and even morally acceptable, the concrete instance of a queer film dealing with AIDS and death, and with ramifications in everyday reality, is not. It can only be hoped that the unhappy saga of *Savage Nights* will not deter future French film-makers from entering into commercial cinema and taking up this crucial challenge.

Notes

1. F. Strauss (1993), 'Un art neuf', *Cahiers du Cinéma*, no. 466 (April), pp. 5–6.
2. S. Watney (1993), 'French Connection', *Sight and Sound* (June), pp. 24–5.
3. M. Nash (1994), 'Chronicle(s) of a Death Foretold: Notes apropos of *Les Nuits fauves*', *Critical Quarterly*, vol. 36, no. 1, pp. 97–104 (p. 100).
4. J. Romney (1993), 'Sick with Desire', *New Statesman and Society*, 25 June, pp. 35–6. For a different account of the film's neo-romantic tendencies, see also C. Robinson (1995), *Scandal in the Ink: Male and Female Homosexuality in Twentieth-century French Literature* (London), pp. 83–91, 140–1.
5. See A. Rifkin (1996), 'From Renaud Camus to the Gay City Guide', in Michael Sheringham (ed.), *Parisian Fields*, London, pp. 133–49 (pp. 144–5).
6. Similarly, when the film had finally been approved by the Comité d'Avances sur Recettes following heated debates amongst its members, the producer was unable to find sponsors. Even the French condom industry refused to be involved with the project.
7. 'L'esprit de communauté et le militantisme sont en France bien en deçà de ce que connaît le monde anglo-saxon, et la production cinématographique en est le reflet. On cherchera vainement les cinéastes "spécialistes" des thématiques homosexuelles' (Festival programme, 15–18 December 1994, p. 5).
8. The 'twin' event in Lille entitled 'Question de Genre: 100 ans de cinéma gai et lesbien, 10 ans de prévention' was similar in style and content to the Paris festival, the aim of which, according to the organizers, was 'to stimulate reactions and initiate meetings between French and foreign film directors in the hope of sparking off future French productions'. Yet while both events proclaimed themselves engaged in the fight against AIDS, French-produced films, whether fictional or documentary, were scarce, not to say invisible. The exceptions were a documentary, *Sida: pour que cesse cette héctacombe* (1993), by two female directors from Act Up-Paris, Valérie Migeard and Brigitte Tijou; a 'video-testimony', *r.v.* (1994), made by Lionel Soukaz after the death of his partner; and Rémy Lange's *L'Omelette* (1993), the video diary of a 'coming out'. Also included in the Lille programme were Guibert's video *La Pudeur ou l'impudeur* and Jean-Paul Aron's *Mon sida après l'aveu*.
9. R. Dyer (1979), *Gays and Film*, London, pp. 58–71. The films are (in alphabetical order): *Les Amitiés particulières* (J. Delannoy) (1964), *Un chant*

d'amour (J. Genet) (1950), *L'Homme de désir* (D. Delouche) (1970), *La Meilleure façon de marcher* (C. Miller) (1976), and *Zéro de conduite* (J. Vigo) (1933).

10. F. Martel (1996a), *Le Rose et le noir. Les Homosexuels en France depuis 1968*, Paris, p. 6.
11. Ibid.
12. See, for example, Téchiné's *Les Innocents* (1987), *J'embrasse pas* (1993), *Les Roseaux sauvages* (1994), and *Les Voleurs* (1996). *J'embrasse pas* and *Les Roseaux sauvages* explore, respectively, the life of a male prostitute in Paris and a provincial boy's realization and acceptance of his homosexuality.
13. See V. Russo (1986), 'A State of Being', *Film Comment*, vol. 22, no. 2, p. 34.
14. To pursue a little further the connection with the *artiste maudit* tradition that Genet represents, it is worth noting that, like his character Jean, Collard was born into a wealthy family yet attempted to jettison his social origins. His self-styled rebellion against the middle class lent him in the eyes of many the air of the rebel figure played by James Dean in the 1955 film, *Rebel without a Cause*. Indeed, as Collard's autobiographer Philippe Delannoy points out, Collard's life lacked any real cause, a fact that once prompted Collard to ask himself: 'In which life will I be a mercenary or a bomb-layer? ('Dans quelle vie serai-je mercenaire ou poseur de bombes?') (P. Delannoy (1995), *Cyril Collard: L'Ange noir*, Paris, p. 99).
15. F. Martel (1994), 'Guibert, Koltès, Copi: littérature et sida', *Esprit*, no. 206 (November), pp. 165–73 (pp. 165–6).
16. This is one of the points made by Leslie Hill in his persuasive 1995 article, 'Ecrire la maladie', *Nottingham French Studies*, vol. 34, no. 1 (Special Issue: 'Hervé Guibert', ed. J.-P. Boulé), pp. 89–99.
17. Nash, 'Chronicle(s) of a Death Foretold', p. 100.
18. 'Quand je n'écris plus, je meurs' (H. Guibert (1992c), *Le Paradis*, Paris, p. 130).
19. 'Je suis condamné à écrire' (C. Collard (1993b), *L'Ange sauvage*, p. 31). This phrase recalls the conclusion of *Condamné amour*, where the narrator recognizes that the only way forward out of his life's erotic chaos is to write.
20. M. Pratt, 'Autobiography, Fiction, and Sexual Identity in Robbe-Grillet, Guibert, and Barthes' (Ph.D. thesis, University of Oxford, 1994), p. 215.
21. 'Guibert est du côté de la mort et moi de celui de la vie' (Collard, *L'Ange sauvage*, p. 192).

22. 'Me voyant en "bonne santé", certains doivent se dire que tout est inventé, mis en scène pour vendre des livres [. . .] je ne suis pas assez malade pour avoir le succès d'Hervé Guibert' (Collard, *L'Ange sauvage*, p. 156). In fact, the sales of *Savage Nights* rose almost tenfold after Collard's death, from 42,000 to 412,000. The same with the film: following Collard's death and the César award ceremony, the viewing audience increased from 900,000 at the end of March 1993 to 2.8 million by the end of the year. While it is difficult to establish whether there was any conscious rivalry between the two writers, Delannoy mentions Collard's anger at being made to feel 'the Poulidor of Hervé Guibert' (Delannoy, *L'Ange noir*, p. 124).
23. Cited by G. Médioni (1995) in *Cyril Collard*, Paris, p. 52.
24. For a fine discussion of this process in Guibert's work, see A.-C. Guilbard, 'De la pratique du narcissisme à la recherche de l'image vraie', *Nottingham French Studies* 34:1 (Special Issue: 'Hervé Guibert', ed. J.-P. Boulé), pp. 42–7.
25. The term 'New Queer Cinema' was first coined by B. Ruby Rich in 1992 when chairing a panel at the Sundance Film Festival on the sudden proliferation of British and American gay films in the early 1990s. See Ruby Rich (1993), 'Reflections on a Queer Screen', *GLQ* 1:1, pp. 83–91, and (1992) 'New Queer Cinema', *Sight and Sound* (September), pp. 30–9, where he characterizes these films as marked by 'appropriation and pastiche, irony, as well as a reworking of history with social constructionism very much in mind' (p. 32).
26. 'Vous les pédés qui m'avez reproché de coucher avec des filles. Elles vous dégoûtent, et vous ne pensez pas possible que j'aie pris du plaisir avec elles. Vous croyez que je suis exactement comme vous. Mais je ne suis pas exactement comme vous. J'aime faire l'amour à des femmes, et, au contraire de vous, je peux penser à leur sexe sans vomir. Quelquefois, c'est vrai, mais à certains moments seulement, l'idée d'un sexe de femme me dégoûte [. . .] Et vous, les hétéros, et surtout vous, les femmes, toi Laura, vous ne valez pas mieux qu'eux. Vous voulez me convertir, me guérir, me rendre heureux, me faire oublier, me faire aimer, me faire vous aimer [. . .] D'après vous, les pédés, je suis lâche. J'esquive la vérité [. . .] Vous aimeriez me voir plus militant, plus prosélyte [. . .] Je vous hais autant les uns que les autres. Je vous méprise, plutôt, car haïr prend trop de temps, exige trop d'énergie' (Collard, *L'ange sauvage*, pp. 90–2).
27. D. Heymann, 'Filmer la fureur de vivre': interview with C. Collard, *Le Monde*, 30 April 1992, p. 25.
28. T. Waugh (1993), 'The Third Body: Patterns in the Construction of

the Subject in Gay Male Narrative Film', in M. Gever, J. Greyson and P. Parmar (eds), *Queer Looks*, London, pp. 141–61 (p. 144).

29. Ibid., pp. 144–5.
30. 'Le sida est [. . .] pour les écrivains un retour de la mort "jeune", avec en filigrane les images de Rimbaud, Radiguet, Büchner, Huguenin, Crevel' (Martel, 'Guibert, Koltès, Copi: littérature et sida', p. 166).
31. P. Lejeune (1987), 'Cinéma et autobiographie: problèmes de vocabulaire', *Revue Belge du Cinéma*, vol. 19 (Special Issue – 'L'Ecriture du je au cinéma'), pp. 7–12. See also E. Bruss (1980), 'Eye for I: Making and Unmaking Autobiography in Film', in J. Olney (ed.), *Autobiography: Essays Theoretical and Critical*, Princeton, pp. 296–320.
32. See G. Cheshire (1994), 'Self Expressions: Cyril Collard's *Savage Nights*', *Film Comment*, vol. 30, no. 1, pp. 74–7 (p. 77). Cheshire continues: 'The drama insupportably offers a mere gesture as heroic; the film invites us to see the gesture as just that, the imaginary, unreal trace of an ideal that carries force only in the world beyond the movie theater.' Cheshire explains that this leap of poetic faith is proof of a 'temple of self-scrutiny' on Collard's part, one that holds a real challenge 'to find the thread that leads out of the narcissist's labyrinth into the world where every individual's fate hinges on collective self-recognition and will' (p. 77).
33. It was Giroud, in fact, who broke the news about Erika Prou, following both Suzanne Prou's appearance on the televised *Sidaction* on 7 April 1994, and the publication of her own book *Journal d'une Parisienne* by Editions du Seuil a few days later. Although aware that Erika had sworn her grandmother to secrecy over her relations with Collard, on 8 April Giroud went on the television programme *Bouillon de Culture* to explain Collard's role in the young woman's death. For a comprehensive overview of the Collard affair, one that questions the whole process of mythmaking in France, see the section in *Le Monde*, 17–18 April 1994, entitled 'Cyril Collard et les exorcistes', pp. 1–15, which includes articles by Thomas Sotinel, Josyane Savigneau and Frank Nouchi. For Nouchi, the outbreak of hysteria reflected badly on French society and in particular the Paris media. He draws attention to the strange conjuncture of events: several days before Giroud's revelation, the French Academy of Medicine had voted to reduce the necessity of medical confidentiality in order to favour the partner of a person infected with the HIV virus. In Nouchi's view, this amounts to a criminalization of the sexual act.

Chronology

	Political and historical events concerning gay men and lesbians	Writings and films of interest to gay men and lesbians
1945–1970	Launch of 'homophile' magazine, *Arcadie*, by André Baudry and others (1954)	Simone de Beauvoir: *Le Deuxième Sexe* (1949)
	Le Sept club opens in the rue Sainte-Anne (1968)	Jean Genet: *Les Bonnes* (1946); *Notre-Dame des Fleurs* (1946); *Un chant d'amour* (1951)
	Stonewall riots, New York (1969)	Marguerite Yourcenar: *Mémoires d'Hadrien* (1951)
	Arcadie club opens in the rue du Château-d'Eau (1969)	'Pauline Réage': *Histoire d'O* (1954)
	MLF (*Mouvement de libération des femmes)* established (1970)	Violette Leduc: *La Bâtarde* (1964)
	Yukio Mishima commits hara-kiri (1970)	Monique Wittig: *L'Opoponax* (1964); *Les Guérillères* (1969)
1970–1980	FHAR (*Front homosexuel d'action révolutionnaire*) founded (1971)	Pierre Guyotat: *Eden, Eden, Eden* (1970)

Les Gouines rouges established (1971/1972) with Marie-Jo Bonnet, Christine Delphy, Monique Wittig and others	Michel Tournier: *Le Roi des Aulnes* (1970); *Les Météores* (1975)
Interview with Guy Hocquenghem in *Le Nouvel Observateur* (January 1972)	Guy Hocquenghem: *Le Désir homosexuel* (1972); *La Dérive homosexuelle* (1977)
Henri de Montherlant takes his life (1972)	Monique Wittig: *Le Corps lesbien* (1973)
Editions des femmes founded (1974) under the leadership of Antoinette Fouque of the *Psychanalyse et Politique* (*Psychépo*) wing of the MLF	Julien Green: *Jeunesse* (1974) Tony Duvert: *Le Bon sexe illustré* (1974); *Journal d'un innocent* (1976)
FHAR folds up (1974)	Hélène Cixous: 'Le rire de la Méduse' and (with Catherine Clément) *La Jeune Née* (1975)
Valéry Giscard d'Estaing elected President (1974)	Michel Foucault: *Histoire de la sexualité* 1: *La Volonté de savoir* (1976)
Jean-Louis Bory comes out on Antenne 2 (1975)	Luce Irigaray: *Speculum de l'autre femme* (1974); *Ce sexe qui n'en est pas un* (1977)
Questions féministes co-founded by Christine Delphy and others (1977)	Roger Peyrefitte: *Roy* (1979); [*Les Amitiés particulières* (1943)]
First French Gay Pride (1977)	Yves Navarre: *Le Temps voulu* (1979)

	Gai Pied begins as a monthly magazine (1979)	Guy Hocquenghem and Lionel Soukaz: *Race d'Ep! Un siècle d'images de l'homosexualité masculine* (1979) (film)
	CUARH (*Comité d'urgence anti-répression homosexuelle*) founded in Marseilles (1979)	Renaud Camus: *Tricks* (1979)
	Bid by *Psychépo* group for the name of MLF (1979)	
1980–1990	François Mitterrand elected President (1981)	Yves Navarre: *Le Jardin d'acclimatation* (1980)
	Nouvelles Questions féministes founded by Christine Delphy and others (1981)	Hervé Guibert: *L'Image fantôme* (1981); *Des Aveugles* (1985)
	Front des lesbiennes radicales (1981–1982)	Conrad Detrez: *Le Dragueur de Dieu* (1981)
	First references to the 'gay cancer' (1981)	Hugo Marsan: *Un homme, un homme* (1983)
	Arcadie folds up (1982)	Eric Jourdan: *Les Mauvais Anges* (1984) (interdit depuis 1956)
	Homosexuality fully depenalized; equality of the age of consent (1982)	Roland Barthes: *Incidents* (1987)
	Death of Michel Foucault (1984)	Alain-Emmanuel Dreuilhe: *Corps à Corps. Journal de sida* (1987)

	Foundation of *Aides* by Daniel Defert and others (1984)	Dominique Fernandez: *La Gloire du paria* (1987)
	Death of Jean Genet (1986)	Guy Hocqenghem: *Ève* (1987)
	Jean-Paul Aron's 'Mon Sida' published in *Le Nouvel Observateur* (1987)	Michael Pollak, *Les Homosexuels et le sida* (1988)
	Deaths of Aron and Hocquenghem (1988)	
	Agence française de lutte contre le sida (AFLS) (1988)	Hervé Guibert: *Fou de Vincent* (1989)
	Foundation of *Act Up-Paris (Aids Coalition to Unleash Power)* (1989)	Cyril Collard: *Les Nuits fauves* (novel) (1989)
1990–1996	Death of Hervé Guibert (1991)	Hervé Guibert: *A l'ami qui ne m'a pas sauvé la vie* (1990); *Le Protocole compassionnel* (1991); *Cytomégalovirus* (1992)
	First trial in the affair of '*le sang contaminé*' (1992)	Jean-Noël Pancrazi: *Les Quartiers d'hiver* (1990)
	Gai Pied Hebdo ceases publication (1992)	Yves Navarre: *Ces amis que vent emporte* (1991)
	Death of Cyril Collard (1993)	Cyril Collard: *Les Nuits fauves* (film) (1993)
	First nationally televised '*Sidaction*' (1994)	Guillaume Le Touze: *Comme ton père* (1994)

Yves Navarre takes his life (1994)	Roger Vrigny: *Le Garçon d'orage* (1994)
Estimated total number of AIDS cases in France: over 36,000 (1995)	Hélène Cixous: *La Ville parjure ou le réveil des Érinyes* (text) (1995)
NGO Forum on Women, Beijing (1995)	Josiane Balasko: *Gazon Maudit* (1995)
Manifesto published in May 1996 by *Le Nouvel Observateur*, signed by 234 public figures, demanding an end to all anti-gay discrimination	Vincent Borel, *Un ruban noir* (1995)
By June 1996, 280 town halls have agreed to give upon request official gay partner status (*certificat de vie commune*)	Guillaume Dustan, *Dans ma chambre* (1996)
Brighton conference on violence, abuse and women's citizenship (1996): a new international radicalism in feminism?	

Select Bibliography

1. Primary Texts (Literature)

Barthes, R. (1975a), *Roland Barthes par Roland Barthes*, Paris: Seuil.

Barthes, R. (1977), *Roland Barthes by Roland Barthes*, London: Macmillan.

Barthes, R. (1987), *Incidents*, Paris: Seuil.

Barthes, R. (1992), *Incidents*, Berkeley, Los Angeles and London: University of California Press.

Camus, R. (1988), *Tricks*, Paris: P.O.L.

Camus, R. (1996) *Tricks*, New York and London: Serpent's Tail.

Chotard, L. (1994), *Tiers Monde*, Paris: Stock.

Collard, C. (1987), *Condamné amour*, Paris: Flammarion.

Collard, C. (1989), *Les Nuits fauves*, Paris: Flammarion.

Collard, C. (1993a), *Savage Nights*, London: Quartet Books.

Collard, C. (1993b), *L'Ange sauvage*, Paris: Flammarion.

Duvert, T. (1976), *Journal d'un innocent*, Paris: Minuit.

Guibert, H. (1987), *Vous m'avez fait former des fantômes*, Paris: Gallimard.

Guibert, H. (1988a), 'Les Secrets d'un homme', in *Mauve le vierge*, Paris: Gallimard.

Guibert, H. (1988b), *Les Gangsters*, Paris: Minuit.

Guibert, H. (1991), *The Gangsters*, London: Serpent's Tail.

Guibert, H. (1990), *A l'ami qui ne m'a pas sauvé la vie*, Paris: Gallimard.

Guibert, H. (1991a), *To the Friend Who Did Not Save My Life*, London: Quartet Books.

Guibert, H. (1991b), *La Mort Propagande*, Paris: Livre de poche.

Guibert, H. (1991c), *Le Protocole compassionnel*, Paris: Gallimard.

Guibert, H. (1992a), *Cytomégalovirus*, Paris: Seuil.

Guibert, H. (1992b), *L'Homme au chapeau rouge*, Paris: Gallimard.

Guibert, H. (1993a), *The Man in the Red Hat*, London: Quartet.

Guibert, H. (1993b), *The Compassion Protocol*, London: Quartet Books.

Jourdan, E. (1991a), *Charité*, Paris: Seuil.

Jourdan, E. (1991b), *Révolte*, Paris: Seuil.

Jourdan, E. (1992), *Sang*, Paris: Seuil.

Leduc, V. (1960), *Trésors à prendre*, Paris: Gallimard.

Leduc, V. (1964), *La Bâtarde*, Paris: Gallimard.

Leduc, V. (1965), *La Bâtarde*, London: Peter Owen.

Leduc, V. (1973), *La Chasse à l'amour*, Paris: Gallimard.
Malvande, E. (1985), *Déballage*, Gourdon: Dominique Bedou.

2. Primary Texts (Film/Video)

Balasko, J. (1995), *Gazon Maudit* (*French Twist*)
Collard, C. (1992), *Les Nuits fauves* (*Savage Nights*)
Guibert, H. *La Pudeur ou l'impudeur* (video, first shown on French television on 20 January 1992).

3. Primary Texts (Theory)

Barthes, R. (1973), *Le Plaisir du texte*, Paris: Seuil.
Barthes, R, (1976), *The Pleasure of the Text*, London: Jonathan Cape.
Barthes, R. (1977), *Fragments d'un discours amoureux*, Paris: Seuil.
Barthes, R. (1990), *A Lover's Discourse: Fragments*, Harmondsworth: Penguin.
Barthes, R. (1995), *Œeuvres complètes*, vol. 3 (1974–1980), ed. E. Marty, Paris: Seuil.
Bersani, L. (1995), *Homos*, Cambridge, Mass. and London: Harvard University Press.
Hocquenghem, G. (1972), *Le Désir homosexuel*, Paris: Editions universitaires.
Hocquenghem, G. (1977), *La Dérive homosexuelle*, Paris: Jean-Pierre Delarge.
Hocquenghem, G. (1980), *Le Gay Voyage. Guide et regard homosexuels sur les grandes métropoles*, Paris: Albin Michel.
Hocquenghem, G. (1987), 'L'Homosexualité est-elle un vice guérissable?', *Gai Pied Hebdo*, no. 278/9, pp. 64–5.
Hocquenghem, G. (1993), *Homosexual Desire*, Durham NH and London: Duke University Press.
Hocquenghem, G. and Bory, J.-L. (1977), *Comment nous appelez-vous déjà? Ces hommes qu'on dit homosexuels*, Paris: Calmann-Lévy.
Hocquenhem, G. and Schérer, R. (1986), *L'Ame atomique: pour une estéthique de l'ère nucléaire*, Paris: Albin Michel.
Irigaray, L. (1974), *Speculum, de l'autre femme*, Paris: Minuit.
Irigaray, L. (1977), *Ce sexe qui n'en est pas un*, Paris: Minuit.
Irigaray, L. (1981), *Le Corps-à-corps avec la mère*, Montreal: Editions de la pleine lune.
Irigaray, L. (1985a), *Speculum of the Other Woman*, Ithaca and London: Cornell University Press.
Irigaray, L. (1985b), *This Sex Which Is Not One*, Ithaca and London: Cornell University Press.
Wittig, M. (1992), *The Straight Mind and Other Essays*, Hemel Hempstead: Harvester Wheatsheaf.

4. Selected Secondary and Critical Reading on specific authors/directors/texts/films

Balasko

Strauss, F. (1995), 'L'Empire des sens', interview, *Cahiers du cinéma*, no. 489, pp. 60–3.

Vincendeau, G. (1996), 'Twist and Farce', interview, *Sight and Sound*, no.6, issue 4, pp. 24–6.

Bersani

Dean, T. (1996), 'Sex and Syncope', *Raritan*, vol. 15, no. 3, pp. 64–86.

Halperin, D. (1996), 'More or Less Gay-Specific', *London Review of Books*, 23 May, pp. 24–7.

Collard

Cheshire, G. (1994), 'Self Expressions: Cyril Collard's *Savage Nights*', *Film Comment*, vol. 30, no. 1, pp. 74–7.

Delannoy, P. (1995), *Cyril Collard: L'Ange noir*, Paris: Editions du Rocher.

Médioni, G. (1995), *Cyril Collard*, Paris: Flammarion.

Nash, M. (1994), 'Chronicle(s) of a Death Foretold: Notes apropos of *Les Nuits fauves*', *Critical Quarterly*, vol. 36, no. 1, pp. 97–104.

Romney, J. (1993), 'Sick with Desire', *New Statesman and Society*, 25 June, pp. 35–6.

Chotard

Worton, M. (1995), 'Labyrinths of Desire and Loitering (into) Literature: On Reading Theory – and Loïc Chotard's *Tiers Monde*', *Canadian Review of Comparative Literature/Revue Canadienne de Littérature Comparée*, vol. 22, no. 2, pp. 223–39.

Guibert

Apter, E. (1993), 'Fantom Images: Hervé Guibert and the Writing of "sida" in France', in T. F. Murphy and S. Poirier (eds), *Writing Aids: Gay Literature, Language and Analysis*, New York: Columbia University Press.

Boulé, J.-P. (1995a), *A l'ami qui ne m'a pas sauvé la vie and Other Writings*, Glasgow: University of Glasgow French and German Publications.

Boulé, J.-P. (ed.) (1995b), *Hervé Guibert*, *Nottingham French Studies* (special issue), vol. 34, no. 1.

Heathcote, O. (1995a) 'From Cold War to AIDS war', *Modern and Contemporary*

France, vol. 3, no. 4, pp. 427–37.

Heathcote, O. (1995b), '*Les Chiens* d'Hervé Guibert: analyse d'une "plaquette pornographique"', *Nottingham French Studies*, vol. 34, no. 1, pp. 61–9.

Sarkonak, R. (1994), 'De la métastase au métatexte, Hervé Guibert', *Texte*, nos. 15–16, pp. 229–59.

Sarkonak, R. (1996), 'Traces and Shadows: Fragments of Hervé Guibert', *Yale French Studies*, no. 90, pp. 172–202.

Hocquenghem

Marshall, B. (1996), *Guy Hocquenghem*, London: Pluto Press.

Irigaray

Grosz, E. (1988), 'The Hetero and the Homo: The Sexual Ethics of Luce Irigaray', *Gay Information*, nos. 17–18, pp. 37–44.

Holmlund, C. (1991), 'The Lesbian, the Mother, the Heterosexual Lover: Irigaray's Recodings of Difference', *Feminist Studies*, vol. 17, no. 2, pp. 283–308.

Whitford, M. (1991), *Luce Irigaray: Philosophy in the Feminine*, London and New York: Routledge.

Jourdan

Heathcote, O. (1994), 'Masochism, Sadism and Homotextuality: The Examples of Yukio Mishima and Eric Jourdan', *Paragraph*, vol. 17, no. 2, pp. 174–89.

Leduc

de Ceccatty, R. (1994), *Violette Leduc: Eloge de la bâtarde*, Paris: Stock.

Hughes, A. (1994), *Violette Leduc: Mothers, Lovers and Language*, London: MHRA.

Neuman, S. (1989), '"An appearance walking in a forest the sexes burn": Autobiography and the Construction of the Feminine Body', *Signature*, vol. 2, pp. 1–26.

Rule, J. (1975), *Lesbian Images*, Garden City, New York: Doubleday.

Wittig

Birkett, J. (1995), 'Sophie Ménade: The Writings of Monique Wittig', in A. Hughes and K. Ince (eds), *French Erotic Fiction*, Oxford: Berg, pp. 93–119.

Evans, M. N. (1987), 'The Lesbian', in *Masks of Tradition: Women and the Politics of Writing in Twentieth-Century France*, Ithaca and London: Cornell University Press, pp. 185–219.

Griffin-Crowder, D. (1983), 'Amazons and Mothers? Monique Wittig, Hélène Cixous and Theories of Women's Writing', *Contemporary Literature*, vol. 24, no. 2, pp. 117–44.

Shaktini, N. (1982), 'Displacing the Phallic Subject: Wittig's Lesbian Writing', *Signs*, vol. 8, pp. 46–55.

Vlasta, 1985, no. 4. Wittig special issue.

5. General Secondary and Critical Reading

Aron, J.-P. (1988), *Mon Sida*, Paris: Christian Bourgois.

Barthes, R. (1974), *S/Z*, New York: Farrar, Straus and Giroux/Hill and Wang/ Noonday (originally *S/Z*, Paris: Éditions du Seuil).

Barthes, R. (1975b), 'Twenty Key Words', in *The Grain of the Voice: Interviews 1962–80* (1985), London: Jonathan Cape, pp. 205–32.

Barthes, R. (1985), *The Grain of the Voice: Interviews 1962–80*, London: Jonathan Cape.

Barthes, R. (1989), *The Rustle of Language*, Berkeley, Los Angeles and London: University of California Press.

Baruch, E. and Serrano, L. (1996), *She Speaks/He Listens: Women on the French Analyst's Couch*, New York and London: Routledge.

Bazin, G. (1964), *Baroque and Rococo*, London: Thames and Hudson.

Berlant, L. and Warner, M. (1995), 'What does Queer Theory Teach Us about X?', *PMLA*, vol. 110, no. 3, pp. 343–9.

Bersani, L. (1987), 'Is the Rectum a Grave?', *October*, vol. 43, pp. 197–222.

Bersani, L. (1976), *A Future for Astyanax: Character and Desire in Literature*, Boston and Toronto: Little, Brown and Company.

Bersani, L. (1990), *The Culture of Redemption*, Cambridge, Mass: Harvard University Press.

Bersani, L. (1994), 'The Gay Outlaw', *Diacritics*, vol. 24, no. 2/3, pp. 5–18.

Boone, J. A. (1995), 'Vacation Cruises; or, The Homoerotics of Orientalism', *PMLA*, vol. 110, no. 1, pp. 95–107.

Bredbeck, G. W. (1995), 'The New Queer Narrative: Intervention and Critique', *Textual Practice*, vol. 9, no. 3, pp. 477–502.

Bristow, J. and Wilson, A. R. (eds) (1993), *Activating Theory: Lesbian, Gay, Bisexual Politics*, London: Lawrence and Wishart.

Buci-Glucksmann, C. (1994), *Baroque Reason: The Aesthetics of Modernity*, London: Sage (originally *La Raison baroque*, Paris: Galilée, 1984).

Butler, J. (1986), 'Sex and Gender in Simone de Beauvoir's *Second Sex*', *Yale French Studies*, no. 72, pp. 35–49.

Butler, J. (1990), *Gender Trouble: Feminism and the Subversion of Identity*, London and New York: Routledge.

Butler, J. (1993a), 'Critically Queer', *GLQ: Journal of Gay and Lesbian Studies*, vol. 1, pp. 17–32.

Butler, J. (1993b), *Bodies that Matter: On the Discursive Limits of Sex*, London and New York: Routledge.

Butler, J. (1994), 'Against Proper Objects', *Differences*, vol. 6, no. 2/3, pp. 1–25.

Cairns, L. (1996a), 'Gide's *Corydon*: The Politics of Sexuality and Sexual Politics', *Modern Language Review*, vol. 91, no. 3, pp. 582–96.

Cairns, L. (1996b), *Privileged Pariahdom: Homosexuality in the Novels of Dominique Fernandez*, Berne: Peter Lang.

Cairns, L. (1997), 'Homosexuality and Lesbianism in Proust's *Sodome et Gomorrhe*', *French Studies*, vol. 51, no. 1, pp. 43–57.

Camus, R. (1976), *Echange*, Paris: Éditions Flammarion.

Camus, R. (1978), *Travers*, Paris: Éditions Hachette/P.O.L.

Camus, R. (1982), *Eté (Travers II)*, Paris: Éditions Hachette/P.O.L.

Camus, R. (1988), *Elég ies pour quelques-uns*, Paris: Éditions P.O.L.

Canning, R. (1995), 'Faulty Constructions', *New Statesman and Society*, 21 April, p. 39.

Chambers, R. (1993), 'Messing Around: Gayness and Loiterature in Alan Hollinghurst's *The Swimming-Pool Library*', in J. Still and M. Worton (eds), *Texuality and Sexuality: Reading Theories and Practices*, Manchester: Manchester University Press, pp. 207–17.

Champagne, J. (1995), *The Ethics of Marginality: A New Approach to Gay Studies*, Minneapolis: University of Minnesota Press.

Collard, C. (1994), *L'Animal*, Paris: Flammarion.

Copley, A. (1989), *Sexual Moralities in France, 1780–1980*, London and New York: Routledge.

Creech, James (1993), *Closet Writing/Gay Reading: The Case of Melville's 'Pierre'*, Chicago and London: University of Chicago Press.

Dean, T. (1993), 'The Psychoanalysis of AIDS', *October*, vol. 63, pp. 83–116.

Dejean, J. (1989), *Fictions of Sappho 1546–1937*, Chicago and London: Chicago University Press.

de Lauretis, T. (1989), 'The Violence of Rhetoric: Considerations on Representation and Gender', in N. Armstrong and L. Tennenhouse (eds), *The Violence of Representation: Literature and the History of Violence*, London: Routledge, pp. 239–58.

Deleuze, G. (1993), *The Fold: Leibniz and the Baroque*, London: Athlone Press (originally *Le Pli*, Paris: Minuit, 1988).

Deleuze, G. and Guattari, F. (1984), *Anti-Oedipus*, London: The Athlone Press (originally *L'Anti-Oedipe: Capitalisme et schizophrénie*, Paris: Minuit, 1972).

Deleuze, G. and Parnet, C. (1996), *Dialogues*, Paris: Flammarion.

Dollimore, J. (1991), *Sexual Dissidence: Augustine to Wilde, Freud to Foucault*, Oxford: Clarendon Press.

Dollimore, J. (1995), 'Sex and Death', *Textual Practice*, vol. 9, no. 1, pp. 27–53.

Duvert, T. (1973), *Paysage de fantaisie*, Paris: Minuit.

Duvert, T. (1974), *Le Bon sexe illustré*, Paris: Minuit.

Duvert, T. (1980), *Essais, Livre premier. L'Enfant au masculin*, Paris: Minuit.

Dyer, R. (1979), *Gays and Film*, London: British Film Institute.

Dyer, R. (1991), 'Believing in Fairies: The Author and the Homosexual', in D. Fuss (ed.), *inside/out: Lesbian Theories, Gay Theories*, London: Routledge, pp. 185–201.

Edelman, L. (1994), *Homographesis: Essays in Gay Literary and Cultural Theory*, New York and London: Routledge.

Evans, M. N. (1987), *Masks of Tradition: Women and the Politics of Writing in Twentieth-century France,* Ithaca and London: Cornell University Press.

Foucault, M. (1976–84), *Histoire de la sexualité*, 3 vols, Paris: Gallimard (vol. 1 (1976): *La Volonté de savoir* (*The History of Sexuality: An introduction*); vol. 2 (1984): *L'Usage des plaisirs* (*The Use of Pleasure*); vol. 3 (1984) *Le Souci de soi* (*The Care of the Self*).

Foucault, M. (1977), *Discipline and Punish: The Birth of the Prison*, New York: Pantheon Books (originally *Surveiller et punir*, Paris: Gallimard, 1975).

Foucault, M. (1994), *Dits et écrits: 1954–88*, vol. 4 (1980–8), Paris: Gallimard.

Frappier-Mazur, L. (1991), *Sade et l'écriture de l'orgie*, Paris: Nathan.

Frosh, S. (1994), *Sexual Difference: Masculinity and Psychoanalysis*, London and New York: Routledge.

Fuss, D. (1990), *Essentially Speaking: Feminism, Nature and Difference*, London and New York: Routledge.

Fuss, D. (ed.) (1991), *inside/out: Lesbian Theories, Gay Theories*, London and New York: Routledge.

Green, J. (1993), *L'Avenir n'est à personne: Journal 1990–1992*, Paris: Fayard.

Guibert, H. (1982), *Voyage avec deux enfants*, Paris: Minuit.

Guibert, H. (1992c), *Le Paradis*, Paris: Gallimard.

Hammer, L. (1995), 'Art and Aids: or, How Will Culture Cure You?', *Raritan*, vol. 14, no. 3, pp. 103–18.

Harvey, R. (1992), 'Sidaïques/Sidéens: French Discourses on AIDS', *Contemporary French Civilisation*, vol. 16, no. 2, pp. 308–35.

Hocquenghem, G. (1979), *Race d'Ep! Un siècle d'images de l'homosexualité*, Paris: Albin Michel.

Howard, R. (1989), 'From Exoticism to Homosexuality', in D. Hollier (ed.), *A New History of French Literature*, Cambridge, Mass.: Harvard University Press, pp. 836–42.

Jay, K. and Glasgow, J. (eds) (1990), *Lesbian Texts and Contexts: Radical Revisions*, New York and London: New York University Press.

Jay, M. (1986), 'In the Empire of the Gaze: Foucault and the Denigration of Vision in Twentieth-century French Thought', in D. Couzens Hoy (ed.), *Foucault: A Critical Reader*, Oxford: Blackwell, pp. 175–204.

Kopelson, K. (1994), *Love's Litany: The Writing of Modern Homoerotics*, Stanford, CA: Stanford University Press.

Kristeva, J. (1987), *Tales of Love*, New York: Columbia University Press (originally *Histoires d'amour*, Paris: Denoël).

Lilly, M. (1993), *Gay Men's Literature in the Twentieth Century*, London: Macmillan.

Maclean, M. (1987), 'Gender and Identity in Modern France: Normality and Reality', in J. Bridgford (ed.), *France: Image and Identity*, London: Macmillan.

Marsan, H. (1983), *Un homme, un homme*, Paris: Éditions Autrement.

Martel, F. (1994), 'Guibert, Koltès, Copi: littérature et sida', *Esprit* (November), pp. 165–73.

Martel, F. (1996a), *Le Rose et le noir: les homosexuels en France depuis 1968*, Paris: Seuil.

Martel, F. (1996b), *Matériaux pour servir à l'histoire des homosexuels en France: chronologie, bibliographie, 1968–1996*, Paris: Question de Genre/Gay-Kitsch-Camp 35.

Martin, R. K. (1993), 'Roland Barthes: Toward an "Écriture Gaie"', in D. Bergman (ed.), *Camp Grounds. Style and Homosexuality*, Amherst: University of Massachussets Press, pp. 282–98.

Merrick, J. and Ragan, B. T. (1996), *Homosexuality in Modern France*, New York and Oxford: Oxford University Press.

Miller, D. A. (1992), *Bringing Out Roland Barthes*, Berkeley, Los Angeles and London: University of California Press.

Miller, J. (ed.) (1992), *Fluid Exchanges: Artists and Critics in the AIDS Crisis*, Toronto: Toronto University Press.

Miller, J. (1993), *The Passion of Michel Foucault*, London: Simon and Schuster.

Mohr, R. D. (1992), *Gay Ideas: Outing and Other Controversies*, Boston: Beacon Press.

Moi, T. (1994), *Simone de Beauvoir: The Making of an Intellectual Woman*, Oxford and Cambridge, Mass.: Blackwell.

Mossuz-Lavau, J. (1991), *Les Lois de l'amour: les politiques de la sexualité en France 1950–1990*, Paris: Payot.

Mulvey, L. (1996), *Fetishism and Curiosity*, London: British Film Institute.

Munt, S. (ed.) (1992), *New Lesbian Criticism*, Hemel Hempstead: Harvester Wheatsheaf.

Patton, C. (1993), 'Tremble, Hetero Swine!' in M. Warner (ed.), *Fear of a Queer Planet*, Minneapolis and London: Minnesota University Press, pp. 143–77.

Pérez-Torres, R. (1994), 'The Ambiguous Outlaw: John Rechy and Complicitous Homotextuality', in P. F. Murphy (ed.), *Fictions of Masculinity: Crossing Cultures, Crossing Sexualities*, New York and London: New York University Press.

Povert, L. (1994), *Dictionnaire Gay*, Paris: Jacques Grandier.

Preston, J. (1984), *I Once Had a Master and Other Tales of Erotic Love*, Boston: Alyson Publications Inc..

Preston, J. (1992), 'The Importance of Telling Our Stories', in B. Bergon (ed.), *Positively Gay: New Approaches to Gay and Lesbian Life*, Berkeley: Celestial Arts, pp. 21–5.

Rabinow, P. (1984), 'Introduction', in idem (ed.), *The Foucault Reader*, New York: Pantheon.

Rechy, J. (1978), *The Sexual Outlaw*, London: W. H. Allen.

Rifkin, A. (1996), 'From Renaud Camus to the Gay City Guide', in M. Sheringham (ed.), *Parisian Fields*, London: Reaktion Books, pp. 133–49.

Robinson, C. (1995), *Scandal in the Ink: Male and Female Homosexuality in Twentieth-century French Literature*, London: Cassell.

Ruby Rich, B. (1992), 'New Queer Cinema', *Sight and Sound* (September), pp. 30–9.

Ruby Rich, B. (1993), 'Reflections on a Queer Screen', *GLQ*, vol. 1, no. 1, pp. 83–91.

Schehr, L. (1995a), *Alcibiades at the Door*, Stanford CA: Stanford University Press.

Schehr, L. (1995b), *The Shock of Men: Homosexual Hermeneutics in French Writing*, Stanford CA: Stanford University Press.

Schehr, L. (1996), 'Body/Antibody', *Studies in 20th Century Literature*, vol. 20, no. 2, pp. 405–30.

Sedgwick, E. K. (1990), *The Epistemology of the Closet*, Berkeley, Los Angeles and London: University of California Press.

Sedgwick, E. K. (1995), *Tendencies*, Raleigh NC: Duke University Press.

Sellers, S. (1991), *Language and Sexual Difference: Feminist Writing in France*, Basingstoke and London: Macmillan.

Shepherd, S. and Wallis, M. (eds) (1989), *Coming On Strong: Gay Politics and Culture*, London: Unwin Hyman.

Smith, P. J. (1992), *Laws of Desire: Questions of Homosexuality in Spanish Writing and Film 1960–1990*, Oxford: Clarendon Press.

Smith, P. J. (1993), '*Blue* and the Outer Limits', *Sight and Sound*, October, pp. 18–19.

Stambolian, G. and Marks, E. (eds), (1979), *Homosexualities and French Literature*, Ithaca and London: Cornell University Press.

Stokes, A. (1967), *Reflections on the Nude*, London: Tavistock Publications.

Storzer, G. (1979), 'The Homosexual Paradigm in Balzac, Gide, and Genet', in G. Stambolian and E. Marks (eds), *Homosexualities and French Literature*, Ithaca and London: Cornell University Press, pp. 186–209.

Straayer, C. (1981), 'The Hypothetical Lesbian Heroine', *Jump Cut*, no. 35, pp. 50–7.

Warner, M. (ed.) (1993), *Fear of a Queer Planet*, Minneapolis and London: Minnesota University Press.

Waugh, T. (1993), 'The Third Body: Patterns in the Construction of the Subject in Gay Male Narrative Film', in M. Gever, J. Greyson and P. Parmar (eds), *Queer Looks*, London and New York: Routledge, pp. 141–61.

West, M. J. (1996), 'Homm(e)age' (review of D. A. Miller's *Bringing Out Roland Barthes*), *GLQ*, vol. 3, nos. 2–3, pp. 317–26.

Wetsel, D. (1992), 'The Best of Times, the Worst of Times: The Emerging Literature of AIDS in France', in E. S. Nelson (ed.), *AIDS: The Literary Response*, New York: Twayne, pp. 95–113.

Williams, J. S. (1995), 'The Moment of Truth: Roland Barthes, "Soirées de Paris" and the Real', *Neophilologus*, vol. 79, pp. 33–51.

Wilson, E. (1996), *Sexuality and the Reading Encounter: Identity and Desire in Proust, Duras, Tournier, and Cixous*, Oxford: Clarendon Press.

Wilton, T. (1995), *Lesbian Studies*, London and New York: Routledge.

Winterson, J. (1995), *Art Objects: Essays on Ecstasy and Effrontery*, London: Jonathan Cape.

Wittig, M. (1975), *The Lesbian Body*, London: Peter Owen.

Wolfe, S. J. and Penelope, J. (eds) (1993), *Sexual Practice/Textual Theory: Lesbian Cultural Criticism*, Oxford: Blackwell.

Worton, M. (1994a), 'You Know What I Mean? The Operability of Codes in Gay Men's Writing', *Paragraph*, vol. 17, no. 1, pp. 49–59.

Worton, M. (1994b), '(Re)Writing Gay Identity: Fiction as Theory', *Canadian Review of Comparative Literature*, vol. 21, nos. 1–2, pp. 9–16.

Yale French Studies (1996), no. 90, special issue: *Same Sex/Different Text? Gay and Lesbian Writing in French*, ed. B. Mahuzier, K. Mcpherson, C. A. Porter and R. Sarkonak.

Index

Index

Index